Nutshell Series

of

WEST PUBLISHING COMPANY

P.O. Box 3526

St. Paul, Minnesota 55165

December, 1978

———

I

Constitutional Analysis, December 1978, approximately 395 pages, by Jerre S. Williams, Professor of Law, University of Texas.

Constitutional Power—Federal and State, 1974, 411 pages, by David E. Engdahl, Professor of Law, University of Denver.

Consumer Protection, 1976, 322 pages, by David G. Epstein, Professor of Law, University of Texas.

Contracts, 1975, 307 pages, by Gordon D. Schaber, Dean and Professor of Law, McGeorge School of Law and Claude D. Rohwer, Professor of Law, McGeorge School of Law.

Corrections and Prisoners' Rights—Law of, 1976, 353 pages, by Sheldon Krantz, Professor of Law, Boston University.

Criminal Law, 1975, 302 pages, by Arnold H. Loewy, Professor of Law, University of North Carolina.

Criminal Procedure—Constitutional Limitations, 2nd Ed., 1975, 404 pages, by Jerold H. Israel, Professor of Law, University of Michigan and Wayne LaFave, Professor of Law, University of Illinois.

Debtor-Creditor Relations, 1973, 309 pages, by David G. Epstein, Professor of Law, University of Texas.

Employment Discrimination—Federal Law of, 1976, 336 pages, by Mack A. Player, Professor of Law, University of Georgia.

Estate Planning—Introduction to, 2nd Ed., 1978, 378 pages, by Robert J. Lynn, Professor of Law, Ohio State University.

Evidence, 1970, 406 pages, by Paul F. Rothstein, Professor of Law, Georgetown University.

Family Law, 1977, 400 pages, by Harry D. Krause, Professor of Law, University of Illinois.

Federal Estate and Gift Taxation, 1973, 343 pages, by John K. McNulty, Professor of Law, University of California, Berkeley.

Federal Income Taxation of Individuals, 2nd Ed., 1978, 422 pages, by John K. McNulty, Professor of Law, University of California, Berkeley.

Federal Income Taxation of Corporations and Stockholders, 1978, 374 pages, by Jonathan Sobeloff, Professor of Law, Georgetown University.

Federal Jurisdiction, 1976, 228 pages, by David P. Currie, Professor of Law, University of Chicago.

Historical Introduction to Anglo-American Law, 2nd Ed., 1973, 280 pages, by Frederick G. Kempin, Jr., Professor of Business Law, Wharton School of Finance and Commerce, University of Pennsylvania.

Injunctions, 1974, 264 pages, by John F. Dobbyn, Professor of Law, Villanova University.

Jurisdiction, 3rd Ed., 1973, 291 pages, by Albert A. Ehrenzweig, Late Professor of Law, University of California, Berkeley and David W. Louisell, Late Professor of Law, University of California, Berkeley.

NUTSHELL SERIES

Juvenile Courts, 2nd Ed., 1977, 275 pages, by Sanford J. Fox, Professor of Law, Boston College.

Land Use, 1978, 316 pages, by Robert R. Wright, Professor of Law, University of Arkansas, Little Rock and Susan Webber, Professor of Law, University of Arkansas, Little Rock.

Law Study and Law Examinations—Introduction to, 1971, 389 pages, by Stanley V. Kinyon, Late Professor of Law University of Minnesota.

Legal Interviewing and Counseling, 1976, 353 pages, by Thomas L. Shaffer, Professor of Law, University of Notre Dame.

Legal Research, 3rd Ed., 1978, 415 pages, by Morris L. Cohen, Professor of Law and Law Librarian, Harvard University.

Legislative Law and Process, 1975, 279 pages, by Jack Davies, Professor of Law, William Mitchell College of Law.

Local Government Law, 1975, 386 pages, by David J. McCarthy, Jr., Dean and Professor of Law, Georgetown University.

Mass Communications Law, 1977, 431 pages, by Harvey L. Zuckman, Professor of Law, Catholic University and Martin J. Gaynes, of the Washington, D.C. Bar.

Medical Malpractice—The Law of, 1977, 340 pages, by Joseph H. King, Professor of Law, University of Tennessee.

Post-Conviction Remedies, 1978, 360 pages, by Robert Popper, Professor of Law, University of Missouri, Kansas City.

NUTSHELL SERIES

Presidential Power, 1977, 328 pages, by Arthur Selwyn Miller, Professor of Law, George Washington University.

Procedure Before Trial, 1972, 258 pages, by Delmar Karlen, Professor of Law Emeritus, New York University.

Products Liability, 1974, 365 pages, by Dix W. Noel, Professor of Law Emeritus, University of Tennessee and Jerry J. Phillips, Professor of Law, University of Tennessee.

Real Estate Finance, April 1979, approximately 300 pages, by Jon W. Bruce, Professor of Law, Stetson University.

Real Property, 1975, 425 pages, by Roger H. Bernhardt, Professor of Law, Golden Gate University.

Remedies, 1977, 364 pages, by John F. O'Connell, Professor of Law, Western State University College of Law.

Res Judicata, 1976, 310 pages, by Robert C. Casad, Professor of Law, University of Kansas.

Secured Transactions, 1976, 377 pages, by Henry J. Bailey, Professor of Law, Willamette University.

Securities Regulation, 1978, 300 pages, by David L. Ratner, Professor of Law, Cornell University.

Titles—The Calculus of Interests, 1968, 277 pages, by Oval A. Phipps, Late Professor of Law, St. Louis University.

*

Hornbook Series
and
Basic Legal Texts
of
WEST PUBLISHING COMPANY

P.O. Box 3526

St. Paul, Minnesota 55165

December, 1978

———

Administrative Law, Davis' Text on, 3rd Ed., 1972, 617 pages, by Kenneth Culp Davis, Professor of Law, University of San Diego.

Agency, Seavey's Hornbook on, 1964, 329 pages, by Warren Seavey, Late Professor of Law, Harvard University.

Agency and Partnership, Reuschlein & Gregory's Hornbook on the Law of, 1978, 625 pages, by Harold Gill Reuschlein, Professor of Law, St. Mary's University and William A. Gregory, Professor of Law, Southern Illinois University.

Antitrust, Sullivan's Handbook of the Law of, 1977, 886 pages, by Lawrence A. Sullivan, Professor of Law, University of California, Berkeley.

Common Law Pleading, Koffler and Reppy's Hornbook on, 1969, 663 pages, by Joseph H. Koffler, Professor of Law, New York Law School and Alison Reppy, Late Dean and Professor of Law, New York Law School.

Common Law Pleading, Shipman's Hornbook on, 3rd Ed., 1923, 644 pages, by Henry W. Ballantine, Late Professor of Law, University of California, Berkeley.

Conflict of Laws, Goodrich and Scoles' Hornbook on, 4th Ed., 1964, 483 pages, by Eugene F. Scoles, Professor of Law, University of Oregon.

Conflict of Laws, Ehrenzweig's Treatise on, 1962, 824 pages, by Albert A. Ehrenzweig, Late Professor of Law, University of California, Berkeley.

Constitutional Law, Nowak, Rotunda and Young's Hornbook on, 1978 with 1978 Pocket Part, 974 pages, by John E. Nowak, Professor of Law, University of Illinois, Ronald D. Rotunda, Professor of Law, University of Illinois, and J. Nelson Young, Professor of Law, University of Illinois.

Contracts, Calamari and Perillo's Hornbook on, 2nd Ed., 1977, 878 pages, by John D. Calamari, Professor of Law, Fordham University and Joseph M. Perillo, Professor of Law, Fordham University.

Contracts, Corbin's One Volume Student Ed., 1952, 1224 pages, by Arthur L. Corbin, Late Professor of Law, Yale University.

Contracts, Simpson's Hornbook on, 2nd Ed., 1965, 510 pages, by Laurence P. Simpson, Professor of Law Emeritus, New York University.

Corporations, Henn's Hornbook on, 2nd Ed., 1970, 956 pages, by Harry G. Henn, Professor of Law, Cornell University.

Criminal Law, LaFave and Scott's Hornbook on, 1972, 763 pages, by Wayne R. LaFave, Professor of Law, University of Illinois, and Austin Scott, Jr., Late Professor of Law, University of Colorado.

Damages, McCormick's Hornbook on, 1935, 811 pages, by Charles T. McCormick, Late Dean and Professor of Law, University of Texas.

Domestic Relations, Clark's Hornbook on, 1968, 754 pages, by Homer H. Clark, Jr., Professor of Law, University of Colorado.

Environmental Law, Rodger's Hornbook on, 1977, 956 pages, by William H. Rodgers, Jr., Professor of Law, Georgetown University.

Equity, McClintock's Hornbook on, 2nd Ed., 1948, 643 pages, by Henry L. McClintock, Late Professor of Law, University of Minnesota.

Estate and Gift Taxes, Lowndes, Kramer and McCord's Hornbook on, 3rd Ed., 1974, 1099 pages, by Charles L. B. Lowndes, Late Professor of Law, Duke University, Robert Kramer, Dean and Professor of Law, George Washington University, and John H. McCord, Professor of Law, University of Illinois.

Evidence, Lilly's Introduction to, 1978, 486 pages, by Graham C. Lilly, Professor of Law, University of Virginia.

Evidence, McCormick's Hornbook on, 2nd Ed., 1972 with 1978 Pocket Part, 938 pages, General Editor, Edward W. Cleary, Professor of Law Emeritus, Arizona State University.

Federal Courts, Wright's Hornbook on, 3rd Ed., 1976, 818 pages, including Federal Rules appendix, by Charles Alan Wright, Professor of Law, University of Texas.

Future Interests, Simes' Hornbook on, 2nd Ed., 1966, 355 pages, by Lewis M. Simes, Late Professor of Law, University of Michigan.

Income Taxation, Chommie's Hornbook on, 2nd Ed., 1973, 1051 pages, by John C. Chommie, Late Professor of Law, University of Miami.

Insurance, Keeton's Basic Text on, 1971, 712 pages, by Robert E. Keeton, Professor of Law, Harvard University.

Insurance, Vance's Hornbook on, 3rd Ed., 1951, 1290 pages, by Buist M. Anderson, Counsel, Connecticut General Life Insurance Co.

Labor Law, Gorman's Basic Text on, 1976, 914 pages, by Robert A. Gorman, Professor of Law, University of Pennsylvania.

Law of the Poor, LaFrance, Schroeder, Bennett and Boyd's Hornbook on, 1973, 558 pages, by Arthur B. LaFrance, Professor of Law, University of Maine, Milton R. Schroeder, Professor of Law, Arizona State University, Robert W. Bennett, Professor of Law, Northwestern University and William E. Boyd, Professor of Law, University of Arizona.

Law Problems, Ballentine's 5th Ed., 1975, 767 pages, General Editor, William E. Burby, Professor of Law, California Western School of Law.

Legal Writing Style, Weihofen's, 1961, 323 pages, by Henry Weihofen, Professor of Law Emeritus, University of New Mexico.

New York Practice, Siegel's Hornbook on, 1978, 1011 pages, by David D. Siegel, Professor of Law, Albany Law School of Union University.

Oil and Gas, Hemingway's Hornbook on, 1971 with 1979 Pocket Part, 486 pages, by Richard W. Hemingway, Professor of Law, Texas Tech University.

Partnership, Crane and Bromberg's Hornbook on, 1968, 695 pages, by Alan R. Bromberg, Professor of Law, Southern Methodist University.

Property, Smith and Boyer's Survey of, 2nd Ed., 1971, 510 pages, by Chester H. Smith, Late Professor of Law, University of Arizona and Ralph E. Boyer, Professor of Law, University of Miami.

Real Estate Finance Law, Osborne, Nelson and Whitman's Hornbook on, (3rd Ed. of Hornbook on Mortgages), March 1979, approximately 850 pages, by George E. Osborne, Late Professor of Law, Stanford University, Grant S. Nelson, Professor of Law, University of Missouri, Columbia and Dale A. Whitman, Professor of Law, University of Washington.

Real Property, Burby's Hornbook on, 3rd Ed., 1965, 490 pages, by William E. Burby, Professor of Law, California Western School of Law.

Real Property, Moynihan's Introduction to, 1962, 254 pages, by Cornelius J. Moynihan, Professor of Law, Suffolk University.

Remedies, Dobbs' Hornbook on, 1973, 1067 pages, by Dan B. Dobbs, Professor of Law, University of Arizona.

Sales, Nordstrom's Hornbook on, 1970, 600 pages, by Robert J. Nordstrom, Professor of Law, Ohio State University.

Secured Transactions under the U.C.C., Henson's Hornbook on, 2nd Ed., January, 1979, approximately 500 pages, by Ray D. Henson, Professor of Law, University of California, Hastings College of the Law.

Suretyship, Simpson's Hornbook on, 1950, 569 pages, by Laurence P. Simpson, Professor of Law Emeritus, New York University.

Torts, Prosser's Hornbook on, 4th Ed., 1971, 1208 pages, by William L. Prosser, Late Dean and Professor of Law, University of California, Berkeley.

Trusts, Bogert's Hornbook on, 5th Ed., 1973, 726 pages, by George G. Bogert, Late Professor of Law, University of Chicago and George T. Bogert, Attorney, Chicago, Illinois.

Urban Planning and Land Development Control, Hagman's Hornbook on, 1971, 706 pages, by Donald G. Hagman, Professor of Law, University of California, Los Angeles.

Uniform Commercial Code, White and Summers' Hornbook on, 1972, 1054 pages, by James J. White, Professor of Law, University of Michigan and Robert S. Summers, Professor of Law, Cornell University.

Wills, Atkinson's Hornbook on, 2nd Ed., 1953, 975 pages, by Thomas E. Atkinson, Late Professor of Law, New York University.

Advisory Board

WELFARE LAW:

STRUCTURE AND ENTITLEMENT

IN A NUTSHELL

By

ARTHUR B. LaFRANCE

Professor of Law
University of Maine

ST. PAUL, MINN.

WEST PUBLISHING CO.

1979

COPYRIGHT © 1979 By WEST PUBLISHING CO.

All rights reserved

Printed in the United States of America

Library of Congress Cataloging in Publication Data

LaFrance, Arthur B
    Welfare law.
    (Nutshell series)
    Includes index.
    1. Public welfare—United States—Law. I. Title.
KF3720.Z9L33   344'.73'03   78–23544

ISBN 0–8299–2020–X

LaFrance Welfare Law

For

Jacobius tenBroek
whose scholarship
gave sight to the blind

*

PREFACE

This Nutshell is an effort to present in concise form the history of welfare in America, with its structure, programs and procedures. This task is made profoundly difficult by the conflicting policies implemented through a complex federal and state structure involving a myriad of agencies and programs which have developed piecemeal over two centuries. Any result is unfortunately superficial. Yet a comprehensive survey seems essential precisely because the bewildering complexity of the subject is overwhelming without an overview. This Nutshell attempts just such a perspective.

The discussion begins with the Elizabethan Poor Laws and traces their pervasive influence on American welfare. In the 1930s, through the Social Security Act, the federal government first entered the welfare scene in a comprehensive way through creation of "cooperative" programs with the states, which were to administer federal funds. The difficult issues raised concerning state/federal relations are therefore treated by this text, followed by the development of governing constitutional principles, such as due process and equal protection of the laws. The text then moves to examining the content of various programs, including in-kind programs, cash grant programs and, briefly, social insurance. The discussion concludes with a review of the common elements of such programs: eligibility, benefits and procedures.

The chief focus of this book is on the programs commonly referred to as "welfare": Cash grant programs for those whose eligibility is determined by need and whose benefits or eligibility are not determined by prior contributions. The paradigm of such programs is AFDC, Aid to Families with Dependent Children. Programs of social insurance, such as OASDI (Old Age, Survivors and Disability Insurance or "Social Security") and workmen's compensation or unemployment compensation, receive only limited treatment. Similarly, the provisions of in-kind programs such as housing, Food Stamps and Medicaid are reviewed only briefly. However, the major elements and characteristics of the cash grant programs, which are treated extensively in this work, apply to most programs of public assistance. Thus, the sections on constitutional considerations, eligibility, computation of benefits, rulemaking and administrative hearings, as well as others, have considerable relevance to social insurance and in-kind programs.

Necessarily, this text is highly selective. All relevant Supreme Court decisions are discussed. In addition most major programs, statutes and regulations are reviewed. But scholars will note that the intensive citation and development of authority characteristic of legal writing is omitted. So also, lengthy quotations and detailed references are avoided. All of this is done consciously to assure a balance between accuracy and coverage in a perspective which the author can only hope seems valuable. Through that perspective it is possible to perceive the dimensions of this nation's commitment to the poor.

It may be useful to survey briefly the development and enormity of that commitment both in financial and human terms. Welfare benefits vary from program to program, but family benefits usually are in the $200 to $500 range per month, roughly—when coupled with in-kind services such as Medicaid—approximating the poverty level. In 1929, public assistance totalled some $71,000,000; by 1940, it was $2,000,000,000; and by 1970 it had increased ten-fold, to $20,000,000,-000. See the 1975 Annual Statistical Supplement, *Social Security Bulletin*, Table 6. These figures do not include medical services which grew from $500,000,000 in 1960 to $14,000,000,000 in 1975. Id., Table 176. And in addition to these figures are payments for social insurance (OASDHI), which went from $1,000,000,000 in 1950 to over $15,000,000,000 in 1975, at which time the Trust Fund equalled $60,000,000,000. Id., Table 30.

The categorical assistance programs funded by the federal government have involved increasing numbers of children and adult recipients. In

1960, there were some 3,000,000 AFDC recipients, of whom 2,300,000 were children; by 1975 there were over 11,000,000 recipients, of whom 8,000,-000 were children. Aid to the Disabled involved 369,000 recipients in 1960; by 1973 this figure had increased four fold, to 1,200,000. In contrast, the total number of recipients of Aid to the Blind had decreased consistently from 100,000 in 1960 to fewer than 80,000 by 1975. Old Age Assistance reflected a similar pattern, decreasing from 2,-300,000 recipients in 1960 to 1,800,000 recipients in 1973. General Assistance through the states reaches nearly 1,000,000 people with $1,000,000,-000 in funding. See generally the 1975 Annual Statistical Supplement.

These figures present in skeletal form the growth and scope of welfare in America since the entry of the federal government through the Social Security Act during the Great Depression. Since that time there has been an equally dramatic increase in the statutory and regulatory complexity of these programs, raising serious questions about the effectiveness of these efforts. Yet they also evidence the progress of this nation in assuring economic justice to its poor. That assurance is now commonly accepted and protected by our legislatures and our courts as well as by the administrative agencies directly involved in providing welfare to the poor.

Perhaps it should be noted, in closing, that this text differs from many concerning welfare in its emphasis on court decisions. The subject is, after all structure *and* entitlement. Entitlement is a concept which implies not only a statutory or constitutional status but also a remedy for denial of benefits attached to the status. Within the last two decades, courts have come increasingly to the aid of welfare recipients, and that process is a primary theme of this text. To that extent, then, this text is not only about welfare but also social justice.

The author owes a considerable debt to many who have shared their thoughts concerning welfare and their comments concerning this manuscript. Susan Calkins, of Pine Tree Legal Assistance, gave freely of her extensive expertise in the field of welfare. Janet Gilligan, Steve Kottler and Margaret Ryan provided many hours of invaluable student assistance. Beyond these individuals are many who have, over the years, educated the author in this most complex of fields; of these, special acknowledgement is due to my students, who continuously challenge and enrich my teaching and without whom this volume would not have been possible.

ARTHUR B. LaFRANCE

Portland, Maine
November, 1978

*

OUTLINE

I. FEDERAL–STATE STRUCTURE

II. CONSTITUTIONAL ·ENTITLEMENT

III. WELFARE PROGRAMS

IV. ELIGIBILITY

V. BENEFITS

OUTLINE

VI. PROCEDURES

*

TABLE OF CASES

(References are to Pages)

TABLE OF CASES

TABLE OF CASES

TABLE OF CASES

TABLE OF CASES

TABLE OF CASES

TABLE OF CASES

†

WELFARE LAW:
STRUCTURE AND ENTITLEMENT
IN A NUTSHELL

I. FEDERAL–STATE STRUCTURE

§ 1. The Early American Experience

Any history of the American welfare system must begin with the Elizabethan Poor Laws adopted in the early 1600's in England. These statutes were a response to the Industrial Revolution and its disruptive impact on rural, feudal English life. Artisans could not find employment; families were displaced; private charities were unable to support the poor; communities often found themselves harassed, or so it seemed, by "valiant beggars." A shifting, rootless class of the permanently poor wandered across the countryside.

Until the 1600's, provision for the poor had been a matter of private charity. This had involved church programs and the largesse of feudal lords. But the breakdown of the feudal system, challenges to church authority and the increasing mobility of the citizenry all rendered inadequate the pre-existing systems of supporting the poor. Local solutions on a voluntary basis continued—indeed, remain active today in America—but could not remain the primary means of addressing poverty.

The Poor Laws constituted a radically different response to this problem. They represented for the first time a national acknowledgement of governmental responsibility for the poor, although reaffirming the primacy of the local vicinage or place of settlement as the governmental unit for administering governmental programs. The unemployed were required—indeed, could be compelled—to return to their place of abode if they could not find employment elsewhere. Localities were authorized to establish custodial facilities for the infirm or incompetent—the "worthy" poor—and work programs for those able to work, who were subject to criminal penalties if they persisted in idleness. Reimbursement could be sought from the families of those receiving assistance. The children of the poor could be taken from them and put out to work.

The Elizabethan Poor Laws traveled to America with the colonists. A localized, agrarian society was created. In many parts of the emerging nation the poor were directly indentured to and supported by the wealthy. In New England, communities of religious Protestants cared for the poor as part of their church responsibilities. But of necessity, survival was the primary concern. This meant that all must labor and there was little capital or concern available for the poor. The Protestant Ethic merged with the Poor Laws heritage to emphasize the importance of work as the primary means of subsistence for even the "worthy poor."

Governmental responsibilities and attitudes concerning the poor were shaped accordingly. Programs of assistance were usually in the form of public works or labor for private interests. The most significant form of public assistance was settlement and farming of new land. Alms houses were available for the very young and the very old. Otherwise, assistance was sparsely and begrudgingly available. And even then, assistance was available principally through one's place of settlement. Localities sought to protect their limited resources from the poor of other towns or villages.

An early case in the Supreme Court reflecting governmental attitudes towards the poor, as well as the inter-relationship of governmental responsibilities, is City of New York v. Miln, 36 U.S. 102 (1837). The State of New York had a statute which required the master of any ship to report within 24 hours to the mayor on the origins of passengers. The mayor was empowered to require the master to be bound with sureties to protect the City and the Overseers of the Poor from "all expenses of the maintenance of such persons, or of the child or children" of such persons if they should become "chargeable to the City within two years." The third section to the statute provided that whenever any person was deemed "liable to become chargeable on the City," the master could be required to remove such person "to the place of his last settlement."

The City brought action against the master of the ship "Emily" which arrived in New York in 1829 with 100 passengers, none of whom was reported. The defendant maintained that the legislation was unconstitutional because it regulated interstate commerce. The City maintained that, to the contrary, the statute simply advanced local concerns under the inherent "police powers" of the state.

The Supreme Court sustained the statute and upheld the argument of the City. It found that the statute was not in conflict with Congressional powers, but instead was a police power exercise within the prerogatives of the State of New York. The Court said, more particularly:

> ". . . the act immediately before us is obviously passed with a view to prevent her citizens from being oppressed by the support of multitudes of poor persons, who come from foreign countries without possessing the means of supporting themselves. There

can be no mode in which the power to regulate internal police could be more appropriately exercised. New York, from her particular situation, is, perhaps more than any other city in the union, exposed to the evil of thousands of foreign immigrants arriving there, and the consequent danger of her citizens being subjected to a heavy charge in the maintenance of those who are poor. It is the duty of the state to protect its citizens from this evil . . ." 36 U.S. at 141.

And further:

"We think it as competent and as necessary for a state to provide precautionary measures against the moral pestilence of paupers, vagabonds, and possibly convicts, as it is to guard against the physical pestilence, which may arise from unsound and infectious articles imported from a ship, the crew of which may be laboring under an infectious disease." 36 U.S. at 142–143.

The views expressed in City of New York v. Miln were of a piece with the Elizabethan Poor Laws. And they continued to underlie the development of American welfare during the 1800's. Departures from the Elizabethan approach did, however, emerge. The poor in the Colonies were encouraged to move West; indeed, by the 1860's 160 acres of land was available for anyone who would homestead it. This emphasis upon mobility and upon distribution of capital assets was in sharp contrast to the English approach. Similarly, apprentices and indentured slaves were tied to their masters for only limited terms, following which they could travel to seek employment. The poor were directly affected by several more general legislative developments including the Morrill Act creating federal land grant colleges, state mandates of compulsory education, the ending of criminal treatment of trade unions as common law conspiracies and the passage of broad bankruptcy legislation dealing with cyclical economic crises.

While these developments created opportunities for the poor, at the same time they relieved pressure to re-examine the welfare system which supported those who were poor. In the main, therefore, the Elizabethan pattern remained until the 1930's. By that time, there was no more land to settle. Agrarian America had become urban and industrialized. A national economy had emerged prior to the First World War and experienced disaster ten years later. The great Depression generated the same pressures for American welfare reform as experienced by the English following the advent of the Industrial Revolution. This led, in the 1930's, to the first comprehensive federal programs of welfare pursuant to the Social Security Act. As a result of these developments, the Supreme Court was forced to re-examine the assumptions which underlay its earlier decision in

City of New York v. Miln. Before turning to the Social Security Act itself, it may be worthwhile to review two decisions of the Supreme Court which, independently of the Act, reflected the changing national attitudes toward the poor: Massachusetts v. Mellon and Edwards v. California.

In Massachusetts v. Mellon, 262 U.S. 447 (1923), the Supreme Court entertained constitutional challenges to the 1921 Congressional legislation known as the Maternity Act. The Maternity Act was one of the first examples of cooperative federal and state welfare legislation. Federal funding would be available to states who chose to abide by the terms of the funding "to reduce maternal and infant mortality and protect the health of mothers and infants." A federal bureau was created to administer the funding and to assure state compliance.

The states argued that the statute was unconstitutional because there were no limits to the purposes for which the monies might be spent. The states further argued that the freedom of the states would be largely controlled by the requirement that they must submit detailed plans to the Children's Bureau. As to the argument that the program was voluntary with the states, who chould choose not to cooperate, Massachusetts maintained:

"The act is not made valid by the circumstance that federal powers are to be exercised only with respect to those states which accept the act, for Congress cannot assume, and state legislators cannot yield, the powers reserved to the states by the constitution [citations omitted]. The act is invalid because it imposes on each state an illegal option either to yield a part of its powers reserved by the Tenth Amendment or to give up its share of appropriations under the act.

"A statute attempting, by imposing conditions upon a general privilege, to exact a waiver of a constitutional right is null and void. [citations omitted] The act is invalid because it sets up a system of government by cooperation between the federal government and certain of the states, not provided by the Constitution." 262 U.S. at 468.

The Supreme Court rejected the arguments of the states in Massachusetts v. Mellon. The Court held that the powers of the states were not invaded, since the Maternity Act "imposes no obligation but simply extends an option which the State is free to accept or reject." 262 U.S. at 480. Further, the Court wrote:

"But what burden is imposed upon the states, unequally or otherwise? Certainly there is none, unless it be the burden of taxation, and that falls upon their inhabitants, who are within the taxing power of Congress as well as the states where they reside. Nor does the statute require the states to do or to yield anything. If Congress enacted it with the ulterior purpose of tempting them to yield, that purpose may be effectively frustrated by the simple expedient of not yielding." 262 U.S. at 482.

The Court therefore concluded that the question posed was "political and not judicial in character." After concluding that the state of Massachusetts could not assert any injury to itself, the Court also held that Massachusetts could not sue on behalf of its citizens. The Court said that:

"The citizens of Massachusetts are also citizens of the United States. It cannot be conceded that a state as *parens patriae*, may institute judicial proceedings to protect citizens of the United States from the operation of the statutes thereof." 262 U.S. at 485.

The Supreme Court's holding in Massachusetts v. Mellon thus reflected a constitutional holding that alleviating poverty was a permissible *national* objective. That case did not limit *local* legislation, however. The limits on local legislation, which had been the subject of City of New York v. Miln were squarely raised by Edwards v. California, 314 U.S. 160 (1941). That case involved the right of a state—as in *Miln*—to exclude the poor. Unlike *Miln*, however, the cause of concern in *Edwards* was not foreign immigration but domestic migrations generated by the Depression Era Dust

Bowl of the 1930's. A number of states, tapping the tradition of the Elizabethan Poor Laws, sought to zone out the poor and force them to remain in their places of settlement.

In Edwards v. California, the State of California sought to prosecute one of its citizens for bringing his wife's brother into California from the State of Texas. The defendant learned that his brother-in-law had no employment. Bringing him into the State of Califorinia therefore violated section 2615 of the California Welfare Code which made it a misdemeanor to bring or assist in bringing into the state "any indigent person who is not a resident of the state, knowing him to be an indigent person." California argued that the statute was constitutional, citing City of New York v. Miln. The defendant argued that the passage of persons from state to state constituted commerce, beyond the legislative competence of the states. Further:

> ". . . [T]he right to migrate in pursuit of livelihood, freedom of opportunity, freedom of passage from state to state, are not merely local, internal affairs and matters on which the state may have some power to affect interstate commerce." 314 U.S. at 162.

The defendant argued that the California legislation denied equal protection of the laws and due process, since "the right to remove from place to place according to inclination is an attribute of personal liberty secured by the Fourteenth Amendment." Id.

The Supreme Court rejected California's position. It accepted the California argument that the "huge influx of migrants into California in recent years has resulted in problems of health, morals, and especially finance, the proportions of which are staggering." It observed that a state could legitimately respond to these problems. But the Court held there are limits:

> "And none is more certain than the prohibition against attempts on the part of any single state to isolate itself from difficulties common to all of them by restraining the transportation of persons and property across its borders. It is frequently the case that a state might gain a momentary respite from the pressure of events by the simple expedient of shutting its gates to the outside world. But, in the words of Mr. Justice Cardozo, the Constitution was framed . . . upon the theory that the peoples of the several states must sink or swim together, and that in the long run prosperity and salvation are in union and not division." 314 U.S. at 173–4.

As to California's attempt to justify its statute on the traditions of the English Poor Laws, the Court commented:

> "We do, however, suggest that the theory of the Elizabethan Poor Laws no longer fits

the facts.   Recent years, and particularly the past decade, have been marked by a growing recognition that in an industrial society the task of providing assistance to the needy has ceased to be local in character. The duty to share the burden, if not wholly to assume it, has been recognized not only by state governments, but by the federal government as well. The changed attitude is reflected in the Social Security Laws under which the federal and state governments cooperate for the care of the aged, the blind, and dependent children. [citations omitted] It is reflected in the works programs under which work is furnished the unemployed, with the state supplying approximately 25 percent and the federal government approximately 75 percent of the cost .   .   . "   314 U.S. at 174–175.

Finally, in Edwards v. California, the Court turned to the state's argument that there was an exception to the Interstate Commerce Clause which enabled a state to deal specifically with transportation of "paupers". For these purposes, the State of California relied upon City of New York v. Miln. The Court rejected the contention, saying:

" .   .   . we do not consider ourselves bound by the language referred to. New York v. Miln was decided in 1837. Whatever may have been the notion then prevailing, we do not think that it would now be seriously contended that because a person is without employment and without funds he constitutes a 'moral pestilence'. Poverty and immorality are not synonymous." 314 U.S. at 177.

The Supreme Court's conclusions in Massachusetts v. Mellon and Edwards v. California laid to rest the Elizabethan concept that welfare was purely a local concern. The federal government was thus free to act. But neither case established the permissible bounds of federal legislation. Comprehensive federal legislation posed the danger of displacing local welfare programs. To that extent, it would be vulnerable to constitutional challenge under the Tenth Amendment, reserving traditional powers to the states. The outer bounds and permissible limits of comprehensive federal legislation were not explored by the Supreme Court until passage of the Social Security Act, with the resulting litigation challenging its constitutionality.

§ 2. The Social Security Act

The Depression made poverty a national problem requiring a national response: the Social Security Act. That legislation, born of the New Deal, was a curious blend of the old and the new. It constituted a new federal commitment of funds toward relieving poverty. But it chose to channel welfare funds through local units of government, the states, for administration: an approach consistent with the Elizabethan Poor Laws. And, as with those Laws, only the "worthy" poor—the aged, blind, disabled, or dependent children— would receive federal aid. All others would be left to state or local welfare programs of general assistance. In creating only these four programs of categorical assistance within a framework of "cooperative federalism", the federal government was thus preserving time-honored traditions of welfare.

There were some revolutionary aspects to the Social Security Act, however. It required that states submit plans for federal approval and any such plan was required to apply throughout the state. Thus, minimal uniformity and federal scrutiny were imposed. Further, assistance was to be in the form of cash grants, a fundamental policy choice which left considerable freedom of choice in the control of the recipient. Vendor payments and in-kind services were consciously rejected. Thirdly, any person whose benefits were terminated was entitled to a fair hearing. This provision was later supplemented by the requirement that applications receive prompt action. The sum effect was an acknowledgement that welfare beneficiaries were not mere recipients of charity but had an entitlement—if not a right—to benefits.

This cooperative system was similar to that sustained in Massachusetts v. Mellon, discussed in

§ 1. But it was considerably broader in scope and funding. Further, it created specific taxes in order to fund the benefits created with substantial impact on the taxing powers of states. It was therefore not long before the Social Security Act was challenged as being unconstitutional.

In Steward Machine Co. v. Davis, 301 U.S. 548 (1936), the Supreme Court entertained a challenge to the tax, measured by wages paid to employees, imposed on employers by the Social Security Act. The tax was payable into the general treasury of the United States and not earmarked for any specific purposes. However, if an employer had made contributions to an unemployment compensation fund under state law, a credit would be allowed. The effect was to encourage and induce states to adopt unemployment compensation statutes by returning taxes which would otherwise be retained by the federal treasury.

The impact of the tax and credit system challenged in Steward Machine Co. v. Davis was most vividly illustrated by the argument of the State of Alabama. The tax would generate 10,000,000 dollars in funds flowing to the federal government, with 9,000,000 being returned to the State of Alabama if it undertook a program of unemployment compensation. Alabama argued that:

"   .   .   now, in 1929, a period of high return in Alabama, the total revenues of the state were something under 40,000,000 dollars, so that the degree and the weight of the compulsion may be evaluated when it is seen that an amount equal to one-fourth of the total revenue of the state of Alabama is taken out of the state and can be returned to the state not merely for spending, but to the employees if and only if, certain state functions are abandoned or placed within the control of the federal government. And that in the face of repeated adjudications of this court that in no way can the federal government acquire, by treaty, consent, submission, petition, or what not, any function of the state." 301 U.S. at 568–569.

The Court rejected the challenges to the Social Security Act in Steward Machine Co. v. Davis. It held that the tax involved was not void as involving coercion of the states in contravention of the Tenth Amendment "or of restrictions implicit in our federal form of government." 301 U.S. at 585. The Court noted that the economic stresses of the Great Depression had led to widespread unemployment and that this condition was beyond the capacity or willingness of states to address individually. The legislation being challenged was a means of obtaining funds to address the problem, primarily through the cooperation of states who—absent the federal legislation— might not be able to provide unemployment compensation. The Court then observed "the difficulty with the petitioner's contention is that it confuses motive with coercion," and that "to hold that motive or temptation is equivalent to coercion is to plunge the law into endless difficulties":

> "The outcome of such a doctrine is the acceptance of a philosophical determinism by which choice becomes impossible. Until now the law has been guided by a robust common sense which assumes the freedom of the will as a working hypothesis in the solution of its problems. The wisdom of the hypothesis has illustration in this case. Nothing in the case suggests the exertion of a power akin to undue influence, if we assume that such a concept can ever be applied with fitness to the relation between state and nation. Even on that assumption, the location of the point at which pressure turns into compulsion, and ceases to be inducement, would be a question of degree,—at times, perhaps, of fact." 301 U.S. at 589–590.

In a companion case to *Steward Machine,* Helvering v. Davis, 301 U.S. 619 (1937), the United States Supreme Court upheld the portion of the Social Security Act which provided for retirement benefits through a system of taxation involving employers and employees. The taxes were to be held in an investment account and monthly pension payments were to be paid to a person after age 65. The suit was brought by a shareholder of a company who maintained that the taxes were generating a spiral of labor unrest and inflationary wage demands. The Court held that the scheme of benefits created was "not in contravention of the limitations of the Tenth Amendment." 301 U.S. at 640.

The holdings in *Steward Machine* and Helvering v. Davis established the constitutionality of the Social Security Act. The state arguments and fears were not groundless, however. The expansion of programs and taxes under the Act soon precluded any state from choosing not to participate. And the center of gravity in welfare shifted permanently to federally-subsidized programs.

The four decades following adoption of the Social Security Act were a period of mixed developments. Federal funding increased markedly. Federal assertion of controls also expanded, slowly curbing state efforts to impose additional criteria of eligibility. These chiefly concerned local attempts to terminate benefits to mothers receiving AFDC benefits while living with a man who was not making financial contributions. In a series of decisions, the United States Supreme Court held that states could not impose such eligibility requirements, since they conflicted with the essentially financial eligibility criteria of the Social Security Act.

The leading decision in this area, King v. Smith, 392 U.S. 309 (1968), illustrates how far the Social Security Act had departed from the early traditions of American welfare. In that case, Alabama had terminated AFDC to a mother who had occasional sexual relations with a neighbor. The Supreme Court held that the Alabama rule was invalid, since it conflicted with the Social Security Act's provisions concerning eligibility.

In King v. Smith, the Supreme Court noted that a significant characteristic of public welfare programs during the last half of the nineteenth century in this country was their preference for the "worthy poor". It was not surprising then, the Court said, that the Congressional Committee reports concerning the Social Security Act in 1935 acknowledged that the states were free to impose eligibility requirements relating to the "moral character" of applicants. Many states did, through "suitable home" requirements. However, the Court noted that during the 1940's these came under increasing attack because they "senselessly punished impoverished children on the basis of their mother's behavior, while inconsistently permitting them to remain in the allegedly unsuitable homes." 392 U.S. at 320–322.

In 1945 the predecessor of HEW produced a "state letter" arguing against suitable home provisions. Fifteen states abolished such provisions during the following decades. During the 1950's some 18 states considered whether to adopt such provisions; only one did. In 1960, Louisiana adopted a suitable home provision and eliminated some 23,000 children from its AFDC roles.   In 1961, the Secretary of HEW, Arthur Flemming, ruled that this was improper while the child continued to reside in the home.   The Flemming ruling was adopted by Congress at 42 U.S.C. § 604(b), with the result that AFDC could be denied to an "immoral" home only if the child were placed elsewhere and continued to receive assistance.

The Court in King v. Smith, after summarizing this history, concluded that:

> "In sum, Congress has determined that immorality and illegitimacy should be dealt with through rehabilitative measures rather than measures that punish dependent children and that protection of such children is the paramount goal of AFDC . . . it is simply inconceivable, as HEW has recognized, that Alabama is free to discourage immorality and illegitimacy by the device of absolute disqualification of needy children." 392 U.S. at 325–326.

King v. Smith thus established the primacy of the Social Security Act in defining eligibility for federally funded welfare programs.   The other innovations of the Social Security Act, calling for state-wide uniformity, cash assistance and prompt action on applications, were also held binding upon the states.   The primary latitude left to the states was in determining the level of benefits.   See Dandridge v. Williams, 397 U.S. 471 (1970).   Beyond that, states were prevented from imposing their judgments in opposition to those of Congress under the Social Security Act. And that Act by the 1960's had come to represent a set of values radically different from those of the Elizabethan Poor Laws.

However, recent legislation has eroded certain of the basic policy choices in the Social Security Act.   Approval of state plans has been largely *pro forma* and proceedings have been relatively infrequent by the Department of Health, Education and Welfare to force conformity by the states to federal legislation.   States have been allowed to depart from the state-wide uniformity requirements, in a few instances, for demonstration purposes.   The cash grant system has been eroded by expanded authorization of vendor payments; in-kind programs, such as housing, Medicaid, School Lunch and Food Stamps, have proliferated.   And criteria in addition to need have been added, including work requirements for the able-bodied and reporting requirements to assist prosecution of non-supporting fathers.

This confusing system of "cooperative federalism" was somewhat simplified in 1972 when Congress passed the Supplemental Security Income legislation (SSI), 42 U.S.C. § 1381 et seq., which "federalized" the adult programs, effective 1974.

Through SSI, Congress provided that administration and funding for the aged, blind and disabled would be solely through HEW. Of the original programs created by the Social Security Act in the 1930's, only Aid to Dependent Children remains on a joint federal-state framework. The goal was to remove the problems generated by several layers of bureaucracy and to assure a uniform level of support for the aged, blind and disabled in every state. The latter objective has been largely achieved.

The problems generated by SSI will be discussed infra, § 20. Although they are substantial, the fact remains that SSI has created a national guaranteed annual income for the aged, blind and disabled. This is a concept far removed from the Elizabethan Poor Laws and the assumptions underlying the state arguments in Massachusetts v. Mellon, *Steward Machine* and Helvering v. Davis. It remains true, of course, that AFDC is state-administered and that other forms of assistance which are not federally-funded are within the compass of state General Assistance or Home Relief programs. Yet the exclusionary arguments of the state in City of New York v. Miln seem incongruous today. Indeed, the irony now is that states are heard to argue that welfare is a *national,* not a *state,* concern.

In City of New York v. Richardson, 473 F.2d 923 (2d Cir. 1973), the City of New York and its mayor sued the Secretaries of Health, Education and Welfare and of the Treasury, as well as the state commissioner of social services. They invoked the Fifth, Ninth, Tenth and Fourteenth Amendments, as well as the general welfare clause of Article 1, Section 8, Clause 1 of the Constitution. The plaintiffs challenged the procedure under the Social Security Act which caused relatively poorer states to be reimbursed at a higher percentage than richer states, such as New York.

In City of New York v. Richardson the court noted that "it becomes more than a matter of legal curiosity that appellants revive a debate, albeit in somewhat altered form, that was current in the early days of the Social Security Act." At that time, the local units of government had challenged the Social Security Act on the basis that it infringed local prerogatives by intruding upon welfare, a matter of peculiarly local concern. In City of New York v. Richardson, the City was arguing the opposite: that welfare was a matter of purely national concern. The Court quoted from the district court's earlier opinion as follows:

> "It does not follow that because the federal government may validly pay part of the cost, it must therefore pay it all. Granted that the welfare problem is 'national' in the sense that it is widespread throughout the

country, it is still a problem of caring for people who live in each of the states. The cases cited uphold the scheme of the Act which provides for meeting that problem by cooperation between the nation and the states with each carrying a part of the load . . . ." 473 F.2d at 928.

Similar arguments were rejected in Lindsay v. Wyman, 372 F.Supp. 1360 (S.D.N.Y.1974). There, the Mayor of New York challenged the State's plan of distributing the cost of welfare upon localities in proportion to the number of recipients. The City argued that it had an unfair burden because it had a disproportionate percentage of the poor. The Court held that the state could properly treat welfare as a matter of uniquely local concern, in the Elizabethan tradition, and therefore shift costs accordingly.

In the latter part of the twentieth century, the welfare system in the United States thus presents a complex mixture of state, local and federal relations. Many of the legal issues posed by this system have dealt with adjusting these relations. The next five sections of this text will therefore address the questions thereby posed: how and when is federal law supreme, how may states be compelled to conform to that law, and to what extent are local programs pre-empted by federal legislation?

§ 3. Federal Law: Supremacy

The development of public assistance in the United States has been built upon the federal system of government. The Social Security Act in the 1930's represented the federal government's first major investment in public assistance. It created federal funding for four categories of welfare, assisting the aged, blind, disabled and dependent children. Federal funding was to be distributed to states which chose to cooperate in the program. Administration and matching funds were to be provided by the states. The states were thereby not free to determine who would be eligible for the programs of assistance, only *how much* would be paid to them. The advent of SSI in the 1970's has "federalized" the adult categories concerning the aged, blind and disabled, but AFDC remains a program of "cooperative federalism," as do Food Stamps and Medicaid.

The basic constitutional doctrine is that federal legislation may circumscribe state action, where Congress has acted within its authority, under the Supremacy Clause of the Constitution. Art. VI, cl. 2. Where states deny benefits which Congress conferred under the Social Security Act, the denial is void because the federal law is "supreme." Stating the principle is easier than applying it. Often Congress is not clear when it speaks and states may argue that a federal requirement was not intended to be binding, or that it relates only to structure and not expenditure of funds. Thus courts have been required to address complex questions in determining when or whether states have violated federal requirements.

An early example was reflected in the Supreme Court's decision in King v. Smith, 392 U.S. 309 (1968). There, Alabama had terminated the AFDC benefits to Mrs. Smith. It did so under a state rule which denied assistance to a woman cohabiting with a man. The Supreme Court found that the Alabama rule was in conflict with the Social Security Act, which has no such limit on aid to needy children. The Alabama rule was not consistent with the Social Security Act because there was no finding that the "man in the house" was contributing financially in such a way as to relieve the need of the children. Indeed, the facts in King v. Smith revealed that the man visiting the home did so infrequently and was not only incapable of contributing financially but was also incapable of supporting his own household.

A similar case was Townsend v. Swank, 404 U. S. 282 (1971). There, Congress had provided that AFDC would be available to dependent children until age 20 if they were enrolled in college or vocational school. But Illinois limited AFDC to those enrolled in vocational schools. Illinois maintained, as had Alabama in King v. Smith, that the state-imposed limitation furthered legitimate state concerns. In King v. Smith, these related to immorality. In *Townsend,* the state policy related to encouraging vocational education and conserving limited welfare funds.

The Supreme Court invalidated the Illinois policy. It found a clear conflict with 42 U.S.C. § 602(a)(10) of the Social Security Act, which requires prompt aid to all eligible individuals. Congress had defined eligibility to include children who were in college; hence, the state provision was in conflict. The Supremacy Clause, the Supreme Court reasoned, required that the state comply with the federal requirements. Any state, of course, remains free not to participate in the AFDC program. But if it chooses to participate, it must do so on the terms Congress dictated. Chief Justice Burger concurred separately to the opinion of the Court. He held that ". . . adherence to the provisions of Title IV is in no way mandatory upon the states under the Supremacy Clause." His view was that the only question in the case was whether the state had adhered to federal law and that the Supremacy Clause did not require adherence to federal law independently of the provisions of Social Security Act.

Under either view, the state must comply with Congressional requirements. It is not clear what, if anything, invoking the Supremacy Clause adds to this requirement. In a strictly technical and traditional sense, the Social Security Act is *not* "supreme," since the states remain free to provide welfare on any terms they choose so long as they are not using federal funds. Moreover, it would seem that the use of federal funds must be consistent with Congressionally imposed requirements quite apart from the existence of the Supremacy Clause.

Conceivably, the court in Townsend v. Swank invoked the Supremacy Clause as a means of limiting judicial review. In a number of cases, a state might well argue that deviation from Congressional requirements is justified by peculiarly local concerns. Or a state might argue that a deviation is so minor that it would be unreasonable to terminate all federal funding because of an insignificant departure. A third possibility might involve a state's arguing that its public treasury was so restricted that it could not fulfill all Congressional requirements for participation in AFDC.

Such arguments have force and merit. Indeed, all of them were advanced in Townsend v. Swank, which involved a relatively minor departure from federal policy and which involved a policy decision—that support should only go to students in vocational schools—of peculiarly local cognizance. The problem is that a court, in considering such arguments, has no guidelines. If it were to permit even one exception, such as that involved in

Townsend v. Swank, a multiplicity of departures would then be tolerated. The judiciary, in consequence, would be travelling on uncharted seas. Congress would have no way of assuring uniformity, however minimal, in federally-funded programs from state to state.

Consequently, Townsend v. Swank can be viewed as a decision withdrawing the judiciary from the task of reconciling disputes between Congress and the states. By using the Supremacy Clause as a touchstone, the Supreme Court has left Congress free to legislate as it chooses in making federal funds available to the states. It has also left the states free to reject those funds. But if the funds are accepted, the states are required to comply with *all* federal requirements, no matter how minor.

Supremacy of federal law, as in *King* and *Townsend,* may be based on Congressional legislation, binding the states only if they choose to participate. Or supremacy may be based on the Constitution, which governs both federal and state programs of welfare. Shapiro v. Thompson, 394 U.S. 618 (1969) involved both: AFDC recipients challenged state durational residency requirements which the states defended as being expressly authorized by the Social Security Act and the Constitution. The Court found no such authorization and held that such requirements denied equal protection of the laws under the Constitution. Chief Justice Warren dissented on the ground that Congress had sought to encourage state participation by permitting them to protect their budgets:

> "Faced with the competing claims of states which feared that abolition of residence requirements would result in an influx of persons seeking higher welfare payments and of organizations who stress the unfairness of such requirements to transient workers forced by the economic dislocation of the depression to seek work far from their homes, Congress chose a middle course. It required those states seeking federal grants for categorical assistance to reduce their existing residence requirements to what Congress viewed as an acceptable maximum. However, Congress accommodated state fears by allowing the states to retain minimal residence requirements." 394 U.S. at 646.

The debate in Shapiro v. Thompson between the majority and the dissent illustrates the importance of Supremacy Clause analysis in joint federal-state welfare programs. Where Congressional intent is clear, it overrides state concerns without involving the courts in balancing the importance of those concerns. Residency requirements were important to the states and such requirements, in the form of "settlement" laws, have been a part of Anglo-American welfare thinking since the time of the Elizabethan Poor Laws. Yet the price of participation in a federally-funded welfare program is abandonment of state prerogatives when Congress so prescribes.

Supremacy in federal-state relations obviously turns, in specific cases, upon Congressional intent. In some contexts, as with levels of benefits, Congress has chosen explicitly to leave states free to act. More often, Congressional intent, as in *Shapiro,* is unclear. In Burns v. Alcala, 420 U.S. 575 (1976), the Supreme Court upheld state legislation denying AFDC benefits to unborn children. The Court found no intent by Congress to require such benefits; indeed, the use of the word "child" was found to imply birth as a condition of eligibility. The Court looked to the meaning of the word "child" in common parlance, in medical terminology, and in the other provisions of the Social Security Act, such as those concerning caretaker relatives other than the mother or those relating to residence of children, as implicitly excluding a fetus as a "child." Although lower courts had held otherwise, the Supreme Court therefore found that Congress had not *required* that AFDC *must* be paid on behalf of unborn children. The states remained free to grant or deny such benefits.

Burns and Shapiro v. Thompson both illustrate that interpreting Congressional intent is often an obscure art. A third case illustrates this further. In Maher v. Roe, 432 U.S. 464 (1977), AFDC recipients maintained that Pennsylvania was required by federal law to provide Medicaid funding for abortion. Several lower courts had so held, on the ground that Medicaid funds reached all "necessary" services. The Supreme Court rejected this reading, finding no clear intent that Congress so intended and weighing in the balance the legitimate state interests in funding only live births as a means of encouraging life. It may well be that *Burns* and *Maher* indicate that Supremacy Clause analysis is more deferential to the states where the issue arguably involves the range of *benefits,* in contrast to *eligibility,* the issue involved in *Townsend* and King v. Smith.

Supremacy analysis is most often involved where a welfare beneficiary argues that the state has imposed a condition of eligibility *in addition* to those authorized by the Social Security Act. King v. Smith, Shapiro v. Thompson, and Townsend v. Swank illustrate this. But this raises the question of what constitutes a "condition of eligibility." Denial on state procedural grounds, such as failing to fill out an AFDC form does not constitute an "additional condition of eligibility." But other seemingly "procedural" requirements may, and the issues those posed are difficult to resolve. Often states have sought to deny benefits on grounds that they claimed were "procedural" or that they simply "interpreted" existing eligibility conditions prescribed by the Social Security Act.

In King v. Smith, the state sought to avoid the operation of Townsend v. Swank by arguing that its regulations simply interpreted existing conditions of eligibility in the Social Security Act rather than imposing new conditions. However, the Supreme Court rejected the regulation denying AFDC to a family where the mother "cohabited" with a man who was not her spouse. The Court held that Congress had intended to bar AFDC only if "a breadwinner" were in the home. By this Congress meant a man who was supporting the family or legally obligated to do so. Since the Alabama regulation went far beyond this narrow reading, the Supreme Court held that it was invalid.

Some state provisions have been defended on the grounds that they are not additional conditions of eligibility, although they do represent policies which supplement or deviate from those declared by Congress in the Social Security Act. For example, in Stoddard v. Fisher, 330 F.Supp. 566 (D.Me.1971), the State of Maine denied AFDC to families where the "continued absence" of the spouse was due to voluntary choice, in that case because of enlistment in the armed services. The court held that this was impermissible. The state argued that Townsend v. Swank should be distinguished because the state was not imposing an *additional* condition of eligibility but simply interpreting one which had been mandated by Congress. This argument was rejected.

While the Supremacy Clause precludes *additional* conditions of eligibility, it leaves states free to *compute* financial eligibility as they choose, since financial eligibility is an expressly authorized condition under the Social Security Act. In Jefferson v. Hackney, 406 U.S. 535 (1971), the plaintiffs challenged a Texas system which computed the monetary needs of individuals and then applied a percentage reduction factor. At that time, Texas was paying 100% of need for the aged, 95% of need for the blind, 95% of need for the disabled and 75% of need for dependent children. The plaintiffs challenged this method in two respects: First, that the percentage reduction should not be applied until *after* outside income had been deducted, and, secondly, that the discrimination in percentages of need was unconstitutional. The Supreme Court rejected both challenges.

The plaintiffs relied particularly on 42 U.S.C. § 602(a) 10, which provides that AFDC benefits must "be furnished with reasonable promptness to all eligible individuals." The Supreme Court had emphasized this section in Townsend v. Swank. However, in Jefferson v. Hackney the Court gave the section a narrower reading:

> "That section was enacted at a time when persons whom the state had determined to be eligible for the payment of benefits were placed on waiting lists, because of the short-

age of state funds. The statute was intended to prevent the states from denying benefits, even temporarily, to a person who has been found fully qualified for aid . . . § 402(a) 10 also forbids a state from creating certain exceptions to standards specifically enunciated in the federal act. See, e. g., Townsend v. Swank . . . It does not, however, enact by implication a generalized federal criterion to which states must adhere in their computation of standards of need, income, and benefits. Such an interpretation would be an intrusion into an area in which Congress has given the states broad discretion . . ." 406 U.S. at 545.

While the states remain free to define financial need for eligibility under the Social Security Act, that Act does, however, require that states consider only *available* assets and only to the extent that they are currently available. The emphasis upon *current* availability is a limitation on state latitude. In Buckner v. Maher, 424 F.Supp. 366 (D.Conn.1976), the court invalidated a Connecticut provision which made any property transfer within seven years of application without reasonable compensation a basis for denying AFDC eligibility. The court held that this was an additional condition of eligibility contrary to the Social Security Act. Similarly, in Owens v. Roberts, 377 F.Supp. 45 (D.Fla.1974), the court invalidated a rebuttable presumption that any transfer within two years of property for less than fair market value would constitute fraud. Although the presumption was only rebuttable, the court held that it was unlikely that a poor person would be able to maintain the burden of persuasion thereby imposed. Thus the presumption was viewed as an additional condition of eligibility.

In contrast, in Charleston v. Wohlgemuth, 332 F.Supp. 1175 (E.D.Pa.1971), aff'd 405 U.S. 970 (1972), Pennsylvania provisions were upheld which required an applicant to assign rights in property prior to receiving public assistance. The assignment as to personalty would operate immediately; the assignment as to realty would not be executed during the lifetime of the applicant. The court held that this was not a condition of eligibility contrary to the Social Security Act. The court noted that these regulations had been approved as part of the state plan by HEW for 25 years. Moreover, it was arguable that the condition of eligibility had itself been mandated by the Social Security Act, which requires considering assets. This was, the state maintained, simply a procedure for implementing the condition of eligibility imposed by federal law, in a manner consistent with federal law.

Computing financial eligibility thus leaves states broad latitude to deny benefits without creating invalid additional conditions of eligibility.

This becomes particularly significant where states seek to prevent fraud. Procedures for discovering fraud have been upheld, even where refusal to comply meant denial of benefits. Thus, in Wyman v. James, 400 U.S. 309 (1971), the Supreme Court upheld New York's requirement that an AFDC recipient submit to a home visit in establishing eligibility. Denial of benefits was permitted even though the Social Security Act and federal regulations did not expressly authorize home visits.

Dealing with fraud is a long established concern. At a minimum, welfare agencies are entitled to recoup benefits. Whether they may terminate benefits is a separate question. In J. A. v. Riti, 377 F.Supp. 1046 (D.N.J.1974), New Jersey terminated AFDC to recipients who had previously been convicted of criminal fraud in obtaining welfare. The plaintiffs maintained that this created an additional standard of eligibility inconsistent with the Social Security Act and that recoupment under the federal regulations was limited to "reasonable limits on the proportion of such payments that may be deducted so as not to cause undue hardship on recipients." 45 CFR 233.20 (12) (a) (12) (i) (f). The court concluded that termination of assistance would be contrary to the Social Security Act.

The precise status of recoupment or disqualification for fraud is discussed infra. § 36. The point here is simply that it is a procedure for determining financial eligibility which may itself amount to an additional *condition* of eligibility. If so, and if it is not authorized by federal statute or regulation, then such a practice is void under the Supremacy Clause analysis of the Supreme Court in Townsend v. Swank, supra.

That mode of analysis is essential to implementing Congress' scheme of cooperative federalism under the Social Security Act. But the enormity and complexity of the federal-state welfare relationship makes enforcement of federal supremacy very difficult. Supremacy may be enforced either by federal administrative agencies or by litigation by welfare beneficiaries. These two modes are discussed separately in the next two sections of this text. It should be noted here, however, with respect to both of these, that the state always remains free to decline the federal funds. Thus there is always the danger that enforcing federal supremacy may theoretically have the undesired consequence of persuading a state to withdraw totally from a federally-funded program.

§ 4.   Compelling Conformity: State Plans and Conformity Hearings

In federal welfare programs, states are often given important roles to play in administration, setting benefits and ascertaining eligibility. This is true of AFDC, Food Stamps and Medicaid. The federal government must then police and regulate the conformity of the states to federal requirements in these areas to assure the supremacy of federal legislation.

To some extent, the issue of federal supremacy has been relieved by the legislation creating SSI (Supplemental Security Income). The effect of this was to remove the adult categories, aid to the aged, blind and disabled, from state hands. Yet, federal supremacy and state non-conformity were never major problems in those programs. AFDC generated most of the federal-state conflicts. Since that program remains largely under state administration and continues to generate local criticisms and opposition, it may be assumed that challenges to, or evasions of, federal supremacy will continue.

Compliance by the states may be sought in two ways. The first involves litigation by individuals, such as that in Townsend v. Swank, discussed in the preceding section, invoking the Social Security Act and the Constitution to curb state misconduct through the judiciary. However, an alternative exists for the Department of Health, Education and Welfare to initiate a "conformity hearing". In such a hearing, initiated and conducted by HEW, the issue is whether the state involved has failed to adhere to the Social Security Act and the regulations enacted by HEW pursuant to it. Prior to 1970, there had been few conformity hearings. Since that time, the number has increased and a few have involved judicial review. The frame of reference for a conformity hearing is provided by the detailed requirements imposed on states by the Social Security Act and HEW regulations.

To receive federal funds, a state must prepare a "state plan," a comprehensive statement submitted by the state agency describing the nature and scope of its program and giving assurance that it will be administered in conformity with federal requirements, 45 CFR 201.2. The plan must contain "all information necessary" for HEW to determine whether the plan can be approved. Review is initially by the state governor and then HEW's regional office, which must act within 90 days. Quarterly statements of expenditures are also required.

A state plan must provide for adequate hearing procedures prior to termination of benefits. 42 U.S.C. § 602. It must also provide for procedures to minimize payment errors. Opportunity must be provided for every eligible person to apply for assistance and "prompt action," usually within 30 days, must be taken. Provision must be made for social services, including family planning, work training and protective services. Applicants must be required by the state plan to register for work incentive (WIN) program purposes.

The state plan must designate the classes of people who are eligible and may not impose eligibility criteria beyond those authorized by the Social Security Act. HEW regulations require a state plan to identify clearly and equitably those people who are eligible. 45 CFR 233.10. A state must impose every condition of eligibility required in the Social Security Act. A state may impose other criteria to assist "in the efficient administration of its public assistance programs or further an independent state welfare policy" if the criteria are "not inconsistent" with the provisions and purposes of the Social Security Act.

A state plan must establish a single state agency to administer federally-assisted programs throughout the state. 45 CFR 205.100 et seq. It must provide for separation of services and assistance payments functioning independently with separate lines of authority. The state plan must be in effect throughout the state, administered through a system of local offices and made mandatory for all political subdivisions. State and federal funds must be apportioned equitably to all political subdivisions. For certain federally-funded programs, such as AFDC, advisory committees must be established. Eligibility and need criteria must be in effect throughout the entire state.

Equitable funding administration must apply throughout a state. 45 CFR 205.130(a). State funds in Medicaid may not total less than 40% of the non-federal share; the balance may come from local funding. Local funding is not necessary, but if a state chooses to require such participation it must be on an equalization or apportioning basis assuring that lack of local funds will not jeopardize the "amount, duration, scope or quality of care and services or level of administration under the plan in any part of the state." 45 CFR 205.130(c)(2).

The Social Security Act, 42 U.S.C. § 1316, provides that a state plan shall be reviewed within 90 days of submission to HEW. Reconsideration may be sought by a state of HEW's decision, with ultimate review in the United States Court of Appeals. The findings of fact of the Secretary are conclusive, "if supported by substantial evidence." The court may remand for further proceedings or reverse or affirm HEW, in whole or in part.

If a state is found to be deviating from federal requirements, a "conformity" hearing may be conducted. 45 CFR 213.1 et seq. The records and proceedings are public. The hearing will concern such issues as the Administrator designates, which may have to be in the Federal Register. In addition to HEW and the State, other interested parties may participate if their "interest is within the zone of interests" protected by the governing statutes. All parties may participate through counsel, conduct discovery, and conduct evidentiary examinations. "Technical rules of evidence" do not apply. Post hearing briefs and exceptions may be filed. The decision constitutes "final agency action" under 5 U.S.C. § 702 for purposes of judicial review.

The Social Security Act, 42 U.S.C. § 604, provides that HEW shall end payments to a state which is not in conformity with the Act. Funds may be withheld if a state is found in non-compliance with its plan or federal requirements, 45 CFR 201.6, including new federal regulations. Reduction may be from 50% to 75% for generalized instances of non-compliance. Judicial review is in the United States Court of Appeals. 28 U.S.C. § 2112; 45 CFR 201.7.

The relationship between HEW and the states in conformity hearings is typified by the facts involved and the result obtained in State Department of Public Welfare of Texas v. Califano, 556 F.2d 326 (5th Cir. 1977). There the state of Texas had sought $92,000,000 in matching funds from HEW for services which local agencies had provided during the preceding year. HEW refused reimbursement. Claiming this was a "disallowance", HEW argued there was no need for a conformity hearing and no provision for judicial review. However, the state maintained that HEW had in effect found that its plan was not in conformity with federal requirements. It therefore sought a conformity hearing pursuant to 42 U.S.C. § 1316(a). HEW maintained that it was simply disallowing a state expenditure and that, at most, it was required to reconsider its decision but not to afford a hearing. Further, any reconsideration was not subject to judicial review.

The Court of Appeals ruled against HEW. It found that, in effect, HEW had denied the requested funds on the basis that the state had no plan in effect providing for the services involved. Such a finding amounted to nonconformity, not disallowance of funds for services within an approved plan. In drawing the distinction, the Court was guided by the history of the 1965 amendments to the Social Security Act, whose purpose was to put "the States on a more equal basis with the Federal Government in the administration of the public assistance program" and thereby reduce intergovernmental friction. 556 F.2d at 331. It noted that the Congressional history reflected a policy of court review prior to implementation of a proposed change in a state's plan in order to avoid the necessity for withholding or recouping federal funds. While minor areas of disagreement might escape administrative hearing and judicial review, the Court held that a large scale denial of funds amounting to a finding of nonconformity required a hearing which might later lead to court challenge.

Where a conflict with federal requirements does in fact exist HEW may initiate a conformity hearing with the ultimate sanction being termination of funds. Obviously this is a draconian and unwieldly sanction and such proceedings were therefore rare until the 1970's. Conformity hearings are further unsatisfactory procedurally because they allow little role for the welfare recipients, who have the greatest stake in the outcome. Conformity hearings can be initiated only by HEW, not private litigants. Although recipients may be allowed to participate, National Welfare Rights Organization v. Finch, 429 F.2d 725 (D.C. Cir. 1970), they cannot broaden the issues beyond those selected by HEW. From the perspective of welfare recipients, therefore, conformity hearings are an ineffectual means of assuring that states will offer the benefits mandated by the Social Security Act.

An example is reflected in Arizona State Department of Public Welfare v. Department of Health, Education and Welfare, 449 F.2d 456 (9th Cir. 1971). The decision in that case illustrates both the procedures and limitations of conformity hearings. HEW initiated the proceeding, raising four issues: improper residency requirements, improper calculation of financial eligibility, the failure of the state to appoint advisory committees and improper legal custody requirements. Significantly, welfare recipients and groups sought to add seven additional issues for consideration. These were rejected by HEW, although the welfare recipients were permitted to participate in the hearing itself. This ruling by HEW was upheld by the Court of Appeals.

Ultimately the case was settled and AFDC funding continued. This has been the result in every conformity proceeding brought by HEW. Indeed, in Rosado v. Wyman, 397 U.S. 397 (1970), Chief Justice Burger, in dissent with Justice Black, noted that this result is almost inevitable. Consequently, conformity hearings have substantially diminished value. Inevitably, they lead to settlement and compromise and the threat of termination of funding is unrealistic. While the proceeding is pending, benefits are lost beyond recall and there is relatively little incentive for a state to comply quickly with federal requirements. The impact of non-compliance is borne by the individual welfare recipients before and during the conformity hearings.

Still, a conformity hearing has advantages for private litigants. It is possible that welfare groups may participate in a conformity hearing even though they could not produce a member who had been hurt by a state welfare practice. For example, in the Arizona case, an issue related to the failure to appoint advisory committees. It would be difficult to maintain private litigation as to that issue, since no single individual would have standing to raise it. Nevertheless, that issue as well as others, for example hiring practices or training practices by welfare departments, are appropriately reviewed in conformity hearings.

Participation in a conformity hearing is not limited by other constraints involved in private litigation. Evidentiary considerations and the expense of counsel in private litigation are minimized in conformity hearings. Also, mootness is less of a problem in such hearings than in private litigation. These and other considerations make a conformity hearing an important, albeit limited, opportunity for welfare recipients to challenge failure of a state to abide by federal requirements. The ineffectiveness of conformity hearings has also been of concern to HEW, which has sought more effective means to insure state compliance with federal requirements.

As an alternative to conformity hearings, promulgate under the Social Security Act. The funds, HEW has attempted to prescribe "quality control" guidelines which will lead only to reductions in funding. In the 1970's, HEW provided that a state could have an error factor of only 3% in providing assistance to people who were ineligible for assistance. Further, a state could have a 5% error factor in the *amount of assistance paid*. If these factors were exceeded, an amount equal to the improper payments by the state would be withdrawn from the federal finan- where the only sanction is total withdrawal of cial participation. No guidelines were established for *under-payments* to otherwise eligible people; nor were penalties attached to under-payments.

These guidelines led to litigation, as reflected in Maryland v. Mathews, 415 F.Supp. 1206 (D.D.

C.1976). In that case, the State of Maryland was joined by other states in claiming the tolerance guidelines were beyond the scope of HEW to states further claimed that the precise guidelines published were arbitrary and unreasonable, when measured by the Act. Finally, the states maintained that there was no factual basis for the figures of 3 and 5 percent.

The court rejected the first two arguments. It held that the Secretary of HEW could promulgate guidelines concerning quality control and, further, could use specific figures. However, the court found that there was no factual basis for the particular figures prescribed. A study had in fact been undertaken but it specifically disclaimed use for quality control purposes and further noted that the smallest appropriate figure would be 9%, not 3 or 5 percent. Therefore, the court invalidated the particular regulations involved in Maryland v. Mathews.

That case, however, involved evidence that the regulations had been effective during their two years existence. In the first year, 1974, only a handful of states were in compliance. By 1975, approximately 20% of the states were in compliance or very nearly so. It remains open, then, for the Secretary of HEW to prescribe quality control figures based upon a legitimate study and thereby require the states to tighten their eligibility screening process.

However, federal policing of the states is an unwieldy, slow process. It is not well calculated to vindicate the specific interests of individual welfare beneficiaries. For them, compelling state compliance is best sought through private litigation, the subject of the next section of this text.

§ 5. Compelling Conformity: Private Litigation

The most effective device, from the welfare recipient's perspective, for forcing state conformity to federal requirements has been private litigation in federal court. Often such litigation claims that the states are violating both federal statutes and the federal Constitution by denying fair or equal treatment. A civil rights claim is thus stated under 42 U.S.C. § 1983. Jurisdiction may be invoked under 28 U.S.C. §§ 1331 and 1343. By these devices, welfare recipients are able to initiate their own proceedings, framing whatever issues they choose and fashioning direct relief without danger that federal funding will be terminated or that relief will be delayed or compromised by HEW. Most of the significant court decisions discussed earlier and subsequently within this text are the product of private litigation by welfare beneficiaries. In those suits, the beneficiaries obtained court orders which precluded future deviations by the states—and often the federal agencies, too—from Congressional or constitutional requirements. See generally § 37, infra.

But a significant limitation on private litigation in federal court was imposed by the Supreme Court in its decision in Edelman v. Jordan, 415 U.S. 651 (1974). There, welfare beneficiaries in the State of Illinois had sued the state for failure to process applications as promptly as required by HEW. 42 U.S.C. § 602(a)(10) requires prompt action; HEW had interpreted this to mean approval within 30 to 45 days. Illinois, in many instances, had delayed months. The beneficiaries sought injunctive relief to require swifter processing and damages for benefits which had been wrongfully withheld by the past delay.

The Supreme Court of the United States held that injunctive relief was proper but damages were not. The Eleventh Amendment to the United States Constitution provides that no federal court may hear a suit against a state brought by a citizen of another state. The plaintiffs in *Edelman* argued that the State of Illinois had waived this limitation on federal jurisdiction by participating in the Social Security Act. Put somewhat differently, receipt of federal funds should be deemed consent to be sued when the state misspent the funds. The plaintiffs sought to rely on 42 U.S.C. § 1983 as Congressional authority for their lawsuit.

The Supreme Court rejected these arguments. It distinguished earlier cases where waivers had been found because, in those instances, Congress had specifically created a right to sue on the part of the beneficiaries. No such right had been created under the Social Security Act. Further, the Court said that any recovery of past welfare benefits would have to come directly from the state treasury. This was precisely what the 11th Amendment was designed to prevent.

Justices Douglas, Brennan, Marshall and Blackmun dissented in the decision in Edelman v. Jordan. Justice Douglas argued that the impact on the state treasury was minor compared with that in school desegregation cases and was present, in any event, in any injunctive relief in a welfare case. Justice Brennan argued that the 11th Amendment, by its terms, did not apply to a suit by Illinois citizens against Illinois. Justices Marshall and Blackmun argued that voluntary participation in a system of cooperative federalism necessarily implied consent to be sued; if not, states would wilfully violate federal requirements. All of these arguments failed.

The decision in Edelman v. Jordan represents a significant limitation on the value of private litigation in federal court as a means of checking state irresponsibility. There are, however, means of employing such litigation to compel state conformity. Edelman v. Jordan explicitly recognizes the continued viability of injunctive relief, even though it may require a state to appropriate funds in the future. Consequently, *Edelman* is a limitation only on damages for *past* irresponsibility. The decision therefore puts a premium on seeking preliminary injunctive relief in any federal court welfare suit so that the passage of time in litigation will not preclude obtaining benefits at the conclusion of the litigation. *Edelman* also leaves open lawsuits for past benefits where a state has abolished sovereign immunity comprehensively, so as to permit a suit in federal court. A federal court suit would also be feasible in a welfare context where it could be shown that the specific funds involved were insulated or separate from the general state treasury or where, similarly, the funds were held by a local unit of government. Justice Rehnquist also noted in *Edelman* that individual damages from welfare officials could be sought and are not barred by the Eleventh Amendment. This individual liability provides an incentive to comply with federal requirements.

In reviewing the impact of *Edelman,* two other aspects should be noted. By its terms, it did not include a constitutional claim. Rather, it was simply a claim that the State of Illinois was not complying with federal regulations. In their dissent, Justices Marshall and Brennan noted this distinction. Thus, it may well be that a constitutional claim against a state for past benefits wrongfully withheld in violation of the Constitution might survive the defense of the Eleventh Amendment. Further, the challenge in Edelman

v. Jordan was based upon the Social Security Act. A welfare claim based upon a separate act, as with Food Stamps, might succeed in making the argument that participation by the state involved a waiver because of specific provisions imposed by Congress of a more demanding nature than those present in the Social Security Act.

Despite these considerations, Edelman v. Jordan remains a substantial impediment to federal court litigation in the welfare area where past benefits are sought. It is, however, only a limitation on federal court jurisdiction. *Edelman* did not insulate state treasuries from suits in *state* court. A majority of states have abolished, in varying degrees, sovereign immunity. Hence, a suit would be appropriate in state court. Further, the Eleventh Amendment does not bar welfare suits against *federal* agencies, who are often defendants in suits concerning joint state-federal welfare programs.

Because of *Edelman,* the chief value of private welfare litigation in federal court is *prospective,* to compel states to abide by federal requirements in the future. For these purposes, federal injunctive relief is available. This may mean bypassing HEW administrative procedures and it may mean extensive, detailed changes in state welfare procedures. Nevertheless, federal court power for such purposes has been upheld. Examples may be found in Townsend v. Swank and King v.

Smith, discussed supra § 3, establishing the supremacy of federal requirements under the Social Security Act. Where the cost of state compliance may—unlike those cases—be massive, however, the state may argue that a welfare recipient must "exhaust administrative remedies" *before* bringing suit. And the state may argue that, in any event, the state can withdraw from the federal program rather than comply with federal requirements or a court order implementing them.

These arguments were advanced by the State of New York in Rosado v. Wyman, a protracted litigation concerning the levels of benefits in New York. See 397 U.S. 397 (1970) and 402 U.S. 991 (1971). There, unlike King v. Smith and Townsend v. Swank, the issue was not merely whether eligibility was being improperly denied a few AFDC recipients but whether higher benefits were due all or most AFDC recipients. The Supreme Court granted relief, despite the potential for greatly increased costs to the state. It held clearly that a welfare litigant suing a state is not required first to seek relief through federal agencies; nor are litigants relegated to HEW conformity hearings for relief.

Although the Court reaffirmed the right of the federal judiciary to scrutinize state welfare programs and to order compliance with federal statutes, it noted that remedial problems were posed where injunctive relief might involve substantial state expenditures. It therefore ordered the district court to retain jurisdiction to compel compliance by the state or, if the state chose not to comply with federal statutes, to "issue its order restraining the further use of federal monies pursuant to the present statute." The Court added the comment that it viewed "with concern the escalating involvement of federal courts in this highly complicated area of welfare benefits." But the Court found not "the slightest indication that Congress meant to deprive federal courts of their traditional jurisdiction to hear and decide federal questions in this field." The Court concluded that it was the responsibility of federal tribunals, "no less in the welfare field than in other areas of the law," to resolve disputes concerning federal funds.

In Rosado v. Wyman Justice Douglas concurred, observing that the fact that HEW was studying the New York program was "irrelevant to the judicial problem." He noted that statutory provisions for review by HEW of state AFDC plans do not permit private individuals to initiate or participate fully in those compliance hearings. Further, Justice Douglas noted that HEW had been extremely reluctant to apply:

> "the drastic sanction of cutting off federal funds to states which are not complying with federal law. Instead, HEW usually settles its differences with the offending states through informal negotiations." 397 U.S. at 426.

Justice Douglas concluded that there was little to support the State's argument that the court should abstain from deciding welfare litigation and leave primary jurisdiction to HEW.

Supremacy of federal statutory requirements, some defendants still argue, can be enforced only through HEW conformity proceedings. This argument was rejected in Rosado v. Wyman. However, it continues to recur in the case law. In T–H v. Jones, 425 F.Supp. 873 (D.Utah 1975), the State of Utah required that family planning services be given only to children whose parents consented. The court held that this violated the Social Security Act, which required states to provide such services as a part of Medicaid and AFDC. The state argued that the only available sanction was termination of federal funding, as provided in the Act. The court rejected this, citing Rosado v. Wyman.

The same argument was also rejected in Stanton v. Bond, 504 F.2d 1246 (7th Cir. 1974). There, Indiana had been deficient in complying with federal requirements under Medicaid. The only penalty in the Social Security Act was a loss of one percent of the Medicaid funding. The State apparently was willing to suffer this. The Court held, however, that the plaintiffs were entitled to injunctive relief:

"Declaratory and injunctive relief at the behest of those individuals most directly affected by the administration of a program are available should the state not develop a conforming plan within a reasonable period of time when using federal funds." 504 F.2d at 1251.

The holding in *Rosado* is significant for relieving litigants of the obligation of exhausting administrative remedies prior to welfare suits against states under the Social Security Act. It should be noted, however, that Congress may require such exhaustion of remedies prior to suit. It has done so with suits against HEW in, for example, OASDI and SSI cases under 42 U.S.C. § 405(g). See Weinberger v. Salfi, 422 U.S. 749 (1975). But it has not done so with federal suits requiring states to comply with federal welfare requirements; *Rosado* thus remains governing law. The result is that private litigation, despite the obstacle raised in *Edelman* through the Eleventh Amendment, remains a powerful tool for compelling states to assure welfare benefits.

The injunctive relief available to private litigants may therefore involve far-ranging relief. Often, this will relate to benefits. But increasingly it relates to procedures. An example of the latter is Class v. Norton, 376 F.Supp. 496 (D. Conn.1974), aff'd in part 505 F.2d 123 (2d Cir. 1974). There, in 1972, the district court had ordered the Connecticut Commissioner of Welfare to comply with federal regulations and act upon AFDC applications within 30 days. If no action were taken, the Commissioner was ordered to presume eligibility. The Commissioner was further ordered to supply bi-monthly reports. Nevertheless, two years later the court found that AFDC applications were not acted upon within 30 days in 1,300 instances during the preceding 12 month period. Some 20 percent of all applications took longer than 30 days for processing. The state argued that these delays were due to a lack of personnel.

The court held that non-compliance with the court's orders would not be excused because the welfare department had failed to assign sufficient personnel to the task. The court reasoned that no economies accrued to the state by delays and that delays meant a greater drain upon General Assistance from towns which had to support applicants who were being denied federally-assisted state welfare. The court also rejected the procedure in several of the state welfare offices of delaying two weeks between an applicant's initial request for assistance and the appointment at which an application could be completed. Because further verification would require an additional four to six weeks, the 30 day requirement was violated. This meant that the state was denying retroactive benefits even where it found eligibility. The court found these delays and denials unacceptable.

The court took the extraordinary steps of ordering that within 15 days the defendant welfare

director assign at least four full-time office workers to review inactive cases and submit monthly
reports to the court reflecting retroactive payments. With respect to active cases, the defendant was ordered immediately to institute procedures to review records to determine whether
such recipients were eligible for retroactive payments. Future determinations of eligibility
would be made within 30 days from the date of
application whether "by telephone or in person."

Similarly, in Perez v. Lavine, 422 F.Supp. 1259
(D.N.Y.1977), a federal district court ordered
New York City's Welfare Department to provide
an application form on the date of a person's first
or second visit. The court further ordered that
application forms be provided at alternative locations throughout the community. The court then
took the extraordinary step of listing such organizations and requiring the Commissioner of New
York's Department of Social Services to publicize
the availability of application forms through such
organizations. Further, the court required provision of an "application kit" containing a complete
set of instructions in English and Spanish. The
court mandated that signs be posted at all income
maintenance centers notifying people requesting
an application of their rights in both English and
Spanish; the court incorporated the language of
the sign in its order.

The court orders in *Class* and *Perez* are re-
markable in their detail and in the extent of in-

trusion by the courts into the functioning of welfare offices. They are atypical in not dealing with simple questions of eligibility, but they serve to illustrate the breadth of judicial relief available to welfare litigants as an alternative to HEW conformity hearings in forcing state conformity to federal welfare requirements. It is just such litigation which, since 1960, has generated the statutory and constitutional caselaw comprising the content of this text.

§ 6.   Preemption of State Welfare Programs

The preceding sections of this text have described the increasing dominance of federally-funded programs in the field of welfare. Federal law is supreme and states receiving such funds are constitutionally bound to comply with federal requirements. But some states may also choose to offer their own programs, as they have for over two centuries, or they may argue that they cannot be compelled to give up essential state interests as a price of participating in federal programs. In either instance, the question may arise as to whether Congress has preempted—or may preempt—a state's legitimate concerns.

Supremacy and preemption are distinct concepts. Both support federal dominance and both turn upon Congressional intent to dominate. But while supremacy means that a cooperating state must accept federal conditions or requirements, preemption may apply even where the states receive no benefits from the federal government. Preemption would then preclude independent or parallel action by the states. Preemption usually arises as an aspect of legislation affecting peculiarly national concerns. Thus, in Hines v. Davidowitz, 312 U.S. 52 (1941), Pennsylvania's alien registration statutes were held void, on the basis that they would undercut national policies reflected in Congressional legislation. A similar argument was made—but rejected—in a welfare context in New York Department of Social Services v. Dublino, 413 U.S. 405 (1973), upholding New York's work rules despite Congress' creation of work incentive programs. The Court held Congress had not preempted the field; hence, the state could act.

The argument of the plaintiffs in *Dublino* was that the Social Security Act "preempted" the field of legislative activity concerning work requirements for welfare recipients. The federal WIN program, they maintained, left no room for state work programs. This argument of preemption is different from the supremacy argument in Townsend v. Swank, where the Supreme Court held that a state eligibility requirement in addition to those permitted by the Social Security Act impermissibly violated that Act. The principle involved in *Townsend* was supremacy, not preemption. And the difference was crucial in *Dublino*. The Court in *Dublino* ultimately remanded for consideration of whether certain aspects of the New York Work Rules conflicted with certain aspects of the federal WIN program, under Townsend v. Swank. But the Court rejected the broad, sweeping preemption argument of the plaintiffs.

On a literal level, the reason that the Court rejected the preemption argument in *Dublino* was that Congress had not indicated an intent to occupy the field. However, more fundamentally it may be questioned whether preemption could ever apply to the field of welfare. Ordinarily, the doctrine of preemption operates in matters of peculiar importance to the national government. These might include national security, immigration and naturalization, bankruptcy or interstate commerce. Even in such areas, courts have been reluctant to find that Congress intended to exclude the states absent a clear declaration of intent to do so. The nature of the fields in which preemption ordinarily operates suggests that the field of welfare would be a highly unlikely area for preemption. This was undoubtedly a factor in the Supreme Court's decision in *Dublino*.

It has also been a factor in the thinking of other courts. In Doe v. Maher, 414 F.Supp. 1368 (D.Conn.1976), the court upheld a Connecticut statute which punished mothers who failed to seek support from the fathers of AFDC children. It held that the statute was consistent with the

Social Security Act and that Congress had not preempted the field. The Connecticut statute furthered the Congressional legislation. And, the court noted, welfare is not a subject which, by its nature, is of exclusive importance to the federal government.

Historically, federal welfare legislation has been sensitive to local concerns. The Social Security Act reflects a deliberate and conscious acknowledgement of this, as encapsulated in the principle of "cooperative federalism." The political realities of adopting the Social Security Act in the 1930's compelled an approach assuring that states would continue to play a role in welfare through their own programs and also through setting levels of benefits and eligibility for federally-funded programs. Hence a role was created for state administration. While recent legislation, such as SSI, has reflected a tendency to move welfare to the federal level, it is equally true that significant federal legislation of recent origin has continued the principle of cooperative federalism, as with the Food Stamps program and Medicaid.

The legislative deference to the states has constitutional roots. During the Depression, the Supreme Court invalidated federal welfare and economic legislation which impinged on areas left to the states under the Interstate Commerce Clause, invoking the concept of "substantive due process". See supra, § 2 and infra §§ 8–13. While that concept has fallen into disuse, deference to states has recently been given new life under the Tenth Amendment to the Constitution, as interpreted in National League of Cities v. Usery, 426 U.S. 833 (1976). There the Supreme Court upheld state challenges to Congressional extension of federal minimum wage legislation to state employees. The states argued that this invaded powers left to the states under the Constitution.

The Court invalidated the Congressional legislation under the Tenth Amendment, protecting the integrity of the states, on the ground that the legislation would:

" . . . significantly alter or displace the states' abilities to structure employer-employee relationships in such areas as fire prevention, police protection, sanitation, public health, and parks and recreation. These activities are typical of those performed by state and local governments in discharging their dual functions of administering the public law and furnishing public services. Indeed, it is functions such as these which states have traditionally afforded their citizens. If Congress may withdraw from the states, the authority to make these fundamental employment decisions upon which their systems for performance of these functions must rest, we think there would be little left of the states' separate and independent existence." 426 U.S. at 838.

The Court emphasized, in *National League of Cities,* that the state's power to determine wages of employees involves determinations which are "essential to separate and independent existence." Arizona estimated a 2,500,000 dollar impact. The State of California estimated that a budgetary increase of between 8,000,000 and 16,000,000 dollars would be required by the federal legislation. California argued that it would not be able to comply with the overtime costs required by the Act to be paid to highway patrol cadets and would be forced to reduce academy training programs from over 2,000 hours to only 960 hours. The city of Inglewood, California, maintained that it would be forced to curtail its affirmative action program for providing employment opportunities to men and women.

Significantly, the arguments advanced successfully by the states in *National League of Cities* were very similar to those which had been used forty years earlier—and which had failed—in challenging the Social Security Act. See supra, § 2 and Steward Machine Co. v. Davis, 301 U.S. 548 (1936). This does not suggest a reversal of those earlier cases, which had upheld federal legislation under the broad federal welfare powers, in contrast to the narrower Interstate Commerce Clause involved in *National League of Cities.* But it does suggest that there are limits on how far Congress may go even in the welfare field. While Congress may assist the states or even dominate the entire welfare field, it may not preclude altogether legitimate, time-honored state programs of local, General Assistance. To date, this problem has been considered in only one welfare case.

In Dupler v. City of Portland, 421 F.Supp. 1314 (D.Me.1976), the City argued that it could reduce locally-funded General Assistance by the bonus value of Food Stamps. The Food Stamp Act specifically forbade reducing welfare payments by reason of the receipt of Food Stamp benefits. The City maintained that this provision, 7 U.S.C. § 2019(d):

> ".   .   . impermissibly infringes on the exclusive domain of state and local governments, in violation of the Tenth Amendment."

The City relied upon the historic concerns and functions of localities, reaching back hundreds of years, in providing local welfare. It argued that the federal government could not, consistent with state and local autonomy, forbid the City to consider federal benefits as income in reducing local benefits, citing National League of Cities v. Usery.

The district court distinguished *National League of Cities*. It noted that the legislation imposed on the states there, minimum wage and maximum hour requirements of the Fair Labor Standards Act, had the effect of forcing "directly upon the states [Congress'] choices as to how essential decisions regarding the conduct of integral government functions are to be made." The court also noted that the legislation in *National League of Cities* was founded upon the Interstate Commerce Clause; in contrast, the Food Stamps Act was founded upon that clause as well as the Spending Power Clause. Art. 1, § 8, Cl. 1. The court commented:

> "Federally imposed restrictions on state and local government activities which accompany federal grants administered by the states have long been regarded as unobjectionable exercises of the spending power . . . the imposition of the requirement of Section 2019(d) that state and local governments not reduce welfare grants to food stamp recipients is clearly and reasonably in furtherance of Congress' intent to raise the nutritional levels of low income persons. As such, it is a valid, unexceptional exercise of the spending power." 421 F.Supp. at 1320.

The court concluded that "the operation and practical effect of the federal statute is very different here than in *National League of Cities.*"

While the court in *Dupler* was unpersuaded by the City's Tenth Amendment argument, it might succeed in other contexts. If Congress' purpose were less rationally tailored to its legitimate authority or if the local interest were more compelling, then *National League of Cities* might have greater relevance. This would be true where the impact of federal legislation totally precluded local programs of General Assistance. More realistically, a Tenth Amendment argument might be available where federal legislation permitted state programs—or state participation in a federal program—conditioned on relinquishing a fundamental state prerogative or concern. *National League of Cities* indicated that these include police, fire and welfare powers. Federal legislation has carefully avoided preempting such areas in federal-state welfare programs, as with AFDC, by—for example—leaving the funding of abortions at state option. Eliminating such options at the price of receiving federal funds, particularly those essential to the welfare of the poor, might run afoul of legitimate state interests as *parens patriae* under the Tenth Amendment.

The reality is that states will not be preempted from welfare. They will continue with local programs. And they will continue in joint federal-state programs. Congress has chosen to eliminate some of these cooperative programs, as with SSI, but to create others, as with Food Stamps and Medicaid. The supremacy of federal statutes in such cooperative programs is assured, although it continues to be a subject of litigation. Preemption of local welfare programs, in contrast, seems unlikely. They have historical roots and present day viability, the subject of the next section of the text.

§ 7. Local Welfare: General Assistance

Historically, welfare has been primarily a local matter. This was true during the Colonial period in the United States and continued to be true until the mid-1930's. The enactment of the Social Security Act represented a federal presence of massive proportions in the field of welfare. That presence has grown over the succeeding decades, augmented by programs in housing, food supplies, medical services and legal services.

Nevertheless, local welfare continues. Federal programs are usually directed toward categories of people, such as the aged, the blind, the disabled, and dependent children. Those who do not qualify must look elsewhere for assistance. In each state there are programs for the poor who do not qualify for categorical assistance. Those programs are called General Assistance or, in some states, "Home Relief".

General Assistance often is used for short-term, emergency needs which must be met while a person is awaiting federally-funded categorical assistance. A distinction should be drawn, however, between such local, short-term payments and the federally-funded program of Emergency Assistance. The latter program is created by 42 U.S.C. § 606(e) of the Social Security Act and is optional for states participating in other categorical programs. Emergency Assistance is not limited to such programs, however.

General Assistance constitutes a major category of welfare in the United States. The roots of these programs are deep: They represent the direct descendants of the programs established under the Elizabethan Poor Laws. Their function remains important, since the General Assistance programs fill the interstices left by categorical assistance programs. Thus, if a person is *not* aged, blind, disabled or a dependent child there is no federal assistance available. Public assistance, if it is available at all, must be sought through locally funded programs of General Assistance.

General Assistance, by definition, does not involve federal funding. Consequently, the requirements of federally subsidized programs do not apply. Such provisions of the Social Security Act as uniformity throughout a state, prompt action on applications, fair hearings upon termination of assistance and centralized administration are not applicable to general assistance. The only federal limitations are those embodied in the Constitution.

In some states the programs of General Assistance are administered by Overseers of the Poor, elected by towns or counties. Often these boards also operate a hospital for the poor or a home for the aged. The General Assistance program may consist of unrestricted cash grants or may operate on a voucher system for such necessities as food or clothing. Occasionally, General Relief may take the form of vendor payments, as with rent, or in-kind assistance, as with clothing.

In practice, General Assistance programs have varied widely from place to place within each state. Levels of benefits are set by local governmental authorities. Procedures often are poorly developed. Standards often are not articulated. The opportunity for arbitrariness and discrimination thus created is precisely the reason for the provisions in the Social Security Act requiring state-wide administration and uniformity.

The contours of General Assistance are well reflected by the decision of the New York Supreme Court in Wilkie v. O'Connor, 25 N.Y.S.2d 617 (App.Div.1941). The plaintiff sued for old age assistance. The commissioner's answer alleged that petitioner, despite all efforts to dissuade him, "insists upon his right to sleep under an old barn, in a nest of rags to which he has to crawl upon his hands and knees." Despite an offer of "suitable living quarters and an increase in pension sufficient to enable him to maintain a so-called civilized standard of living," the petitioner insisted upon his mode of living. The court upheld the denial of benefits. It said:

> "Appellant also argues that he has a right to live as he pleases while being supported by public charity. One would admire his independence if he were not so dependent, but he has no right to defy the standards and con-

ventions of civilized society while being supported at public expense. This is true even though some of those conventions may be somewhat artificial . . . After all he should not demand that the public, at its expense, allow him to experiment with a manner of living which is likely to endanger his health so that he will become a still greater expense to the public." 25 N.Y.S.2d at 619.

The Court concluded that "in accepting charity, the appellant has consented to the provisions of the law under which charity is bestowed." The approach of the Court in Wilkie v. O'Connor reflects assumptions of the General Assistance system which remain true today: that welfare is a charity and may be conditioned largely as local officials choose.

The absence of written standards and fair hearing procedures in state or locally funded programs of General Assistance raises due process problems. A number of courts have held that a fair, evidentiary hearing must be afforded before local General Assistance may be terminated. White v. Roughton, 530 F.2d 750 (7th Cir. 1976). This is true even where the local assistance is in the form of rent or food vouchers. See Brooks v. Center Township, 485 F.2d 383 (7th Cir. 1973), cert. denied 415 U.S. 911 (1974). It has also been held that the absence of standards denies due process. In White v. Roughton, the court noted that state and federal programs of public assistance are governed by written statutes and regulations. It said further:

> "Defendant Roughton as administrator of the general assistance program has the responsibility to administer the program to ensure the fair and consistent application of eligibility requirements. Fair and consistent application of such requirements requires that Roughton establish written standards and regulations. At the hearing in the district court on the preliminary injunction, defendant Roughton admitted that he and his staff determine eligibility based upon their own unwritten personal standards. Such a procedure, vesting virtually unfettered discretion in Roughton and his staff is clearly violative of due process." 530 F.2d at 753–54.

Decisions such as *Roughton* and *Brooks* tend to force rationality and fairness upon local programs of General Assistance. Those programs, drawing upon the traditions of the Elizabethan Poor Laws, tend to resist change. The need for precision and clarity is further illustrated by another case, Baker-Chaput v. Cammett, 406 F. Supp. 1134 (D.N.H.1976). There, the plaintiff challenged the lack of standards in the New Hampshire General Assistance program. The New Hampshire statute provided that:

> "Whenever a person in any town shall be poor and unable to support himself he shall

be relieved and maintained by the overseers of public welfare at such time, whether he has a settlement there or not."

The New Hampshire program of public assistance or General Assistance was wholly funded by local taxation and administered by local authorities. The plaintiff challenged the failure to publish standards defining the meaning of the terms "poor and unable to support himself". The court stated that:

"This is essentially a question of substantive due process. I believe that procedural due process and substantive due process are inextricably intertwined . . ." 406 F.Supp. at 1137.

It noted that the statutes created no precise guidelines for administration and that the plaintiff was only asserting a basic right to be free from unguided administration of the local welfare programs. The court held that she had such a right.

The decision in *Baker-Chaput* was necessitated by the historically vague nature of General Assistance or Poor Relief. But its significance reaches beyond those programs. For the court was saying that it is not enough for a state to mandate assistance; nor is it enough for an individual to receive such assistance. Rather, due process requires that a program of assistance be sufficiently clear and precise that people may know who is entitled to benefits and what those benefits are. Such a requirement of precision inevitably runs counter to the traditions of General Assistance. Moreover, the resulting standards would then, because of their precision, be susceptible to equal protection and due process challenges to the extent that arbitrariness or discrimination—previously obscure—becomes apparent.

In addition to constitutional pressures, economic and social pressures are forcing changes in General Assistance. The concentration of the poor in cities has made local funding impossible in many settings. Equally important is the rising level of expectations as to what must be afforded the poor. Increasingly, General Assistance is becoming a state-funded matter. With this shift has come centralized control and standards, akin to those in the AFDC program. The result is a tendency to view local assistance from a statewide perspective and to eliminate traditional variations in benefits and practices.

This is illustrated by the decision in Robinson v. Rhodes, 424 F.Supp. 1183 (E.D.Ohio 1976). There, Ohio's program of General Assistance was administered by counties. The Summit County Commissioners terminated funding for their program in order to avoid supporting strikers in a local labor dispute. The state, therefore, withdrew its funding for General Assistance. The plaintiffs sued, however, under a state statute which required the Ohio Department of Public Welfare to "administer Poor Relief in any local area where no local relief department has been established or in operation." Other state statutes required the state department to establish standards for local departments and authorized the state department to supersede a county if it was in violation of state law.

The court ordered the state to replace the Summit County Welfare Department and to provide General Assistance. It held that the state statutes were mandatory. Further, denial of General Assistance to residents of Summit County, while other residents elsewhere in the state received assistance, violated the equal protection guarantee of the United States Constitution.

In Robinson v. Rhodes, the structure of General Assistance was different from that in New Hampshire. State statutes had, in effect, changed the General Assistance from a purely local matter to a largely state matter. The consequence was that failure to provide assistance to the residents of one county could be viewed as a denial of benefits by the state, not just the county. Hence, denial of equal protection could be found. See infra, § 31.

The different structure in the Ohio system thus led to a difference in result. Because the New Hampshire state statutes left General Assistance largely to the localities, they would be free—in the tradition of the Elizabethan Poor Laws—to vary or discontinue assistance as they choose. The only limitation was that of due process, requiring published standards. By shifting General Assistance to *state control,* it became possible for the plaintiffs in Robinson v. Rhodes to argue that intrastate variations denied equal protection of the laws. To the extent that argument prevails, the local traditions of General Assistance are substantially diminished and local variations in benefits become impermissible. It remains true, however, that the unique quality of General Assistance is its local funding of local programs for local residents.

In many parts of the United States, local benefits remain limited to local residents. This is primarily true of in-kind services, such as hospitalization or nursing home care. This is becoming less true as such services become federally funded. However, in Memorial Hospital v. Maricopa County, 415 U.S. 250 (1974), the United States Supreme Court purposely left open the question of whether a county might limit hospital services to county residents where services were wholly funded by county taxpayers. In that case, the county residency rule was held void as to a person who had moved from New Mexico, since the residency requirement infringed the right to travel *inter*state. But there as yet has been no right found in the Constitution for *intra*state travel. And the Elizabethan Poor Law traditions of local settlement support limiting locally funded services to local residents.

To some extent support for this is also found in the Supreme Court decision in Sosna v. Iowa, 419 U.S. 393 (1975). The precise issue there was whether Iowa could require a person to reside within the state for one year before being eligible for a divorce. The Supreme Court held that such a durational residency requirement was permissible, since divorce is peculiarly a matter of local state concern. If such a residency requirement could withstand a challenge based on Constitutional rights of interstate travel, then the peculiarly local concerns of locally funded services could, arguably, be reflected in a limitation of those services to local residents.

Requirements of local residency remain viable chiefly as to in-kind services, such as nursing home facilities or hospitalization. The reason is that such facilities have limited capacities. Preference is therefore given to local residents. But even here the policy has been slowly eroded as federal funding through Medicaid and Medicare has become available to relieve the burdens on local funding of services involving facilities. Nevertheless, where funds are purely local, it would appear that county residency requirements may still be permissible.

The pressures upon locally funded General Assistance tend to cause the programs to become state administered and funded. This is in part due to the changing needs of urban populations and changing concepts of constitutional entitlement. But increasing centralization also flows from the federal requirements in federally-funded programs, such as AFDC. These require state administration and state-wide uniformity, accompanied by partial local funding. The demands thus created tend to eliminate local funds for local programs. Indeed, municipalities are increasingly seeking to shift the cost of welfare from local funds to state or federal sources. See supra, § 3 and infra, § 31.

In Lindsay v. Wyman, 372 F.Supp. 1360 (S.C. N.Y.1974), the Mayor of the City of New York sued the State, challenging division of the State into Social Service Districts, which required the City to pay 25% of the amount of AFDC received by welfare beneficiaries within its borders. The State would pay 25% and the remaining 50% would come from federal funds. The city maintained that it was being forced to pay more than its share of the New York welfare burden simply because the poor chose disproportionately to move to and live in New York City. While the City had only 45% of the state population, it was responsible for 75% of the state welfare burden. In 1972, 16% of the City's residents received welfare, compared with 5% elsewhere. In 1971, New York City spent $151.47 per inhabitant on welfare, against $44.23 elsewhere.

The court rejected the City's argument that this denied equal protection of the laws. It relied upon the Supreme Court's opinion in San Antonio Independent School District v. Rodriquez, 411 U. S. 1 (1973), which had rejected a similar argument concerning state and local funding of schools. Discrimination, the court noted, was not against beneficiaries, all of whom received the same benefits, but against the city and taxpayers. It held the state could properly look to the city because of the historic role of localities in funding welfare programs. As a counterweight, the state legislature had granted the city separate taxing and special revenue powers. Also, the City not only had a greater percentage of the welfare burden, but also of the taxable wealth in the state.

The presence of federally-funded state programs nevertheless creates structural pressures on local funds. In addition, those programs generate constitutional pressures on the way local programs are run. Traditionally, local benefits have been far less than state and federal benefits. This discrimination has generally been upheld. See § 31, infra. But the guarantee of equal protection of the laws under the Constitution increasingly calls such disparities into question. Thus, in Lee v. Smith, 43 N.Y.2d 453 (Ct. of App.1977), the New York Court of Appeals held that the State could not deny General Assistance to SSI recipients of federal benefits where they were receiving *less* than General Assistance. Whether the reverse would be true, requiring increasing General Assistance to SSI levels, was not decided, but litigation raising that possibility will undoubtedly be brought. If successful, it would further erode the local traditions of General Assistance.

Local or state-funded programs of public assistance will undoubtedly continue parallel to, and independent of, the federally-assisted programs. This is particularly true of in-kind services, such as hospitals, housing and homes for the aged. The cash-grant General Assistance programs will also continue, in the tradition of the Elizabethan Poor Laws. But increasingly they will conform to the models of state-federal programs, such as AFDC, responding to the pressures of changing constitutional concepts concerning welfare. These are the subject of the next sections of this text.

II. CONSTITUTIONAL ENTITLEMENT

§ 8.   The Right/Privilege Distinction

The historical and structural development of the American welfare system has created a system of legislative programs at the state and federal levels. Without such legislation, there would be no welfare, since there is no "right" to welfare under the Constitution. Welfare is unlike speech, religion or association, all of which are specifically guaranteed by the Constitution. However, the Constitution has been important in preventing arbitrary granting or denying of benefits. Welfare is thus more than a "privilege" or charity and has become protected in much the same way as other "rights". This is a dramatic change from early judicial attitudes toward welfare.

Until recently, courts were willing to protect rights such as speech and religion from arbitrary governmental infringement but were unwilling to extend similar protections to public benefits, no matter how essential to life. This anomaly makes historic sense. The guarantees of the Constitution are, by and large, restrictions on the scope and activities of government. They do not require funding or administrative agencies or physical facilities. All they require is judicial enforcement. In contrast, programs of public assistance are not restrictions upon government but affirmative undertakings. A court is hardly in a position to mandate or guarantee such undertakings, since it is the legislature and not the judiciary which controls finances. Thus the Elizabethan Poor Law notions of charity and the "dole" dominated thinking about welfare until the 1930's and the adoption of the Social Security Act.

The Social Security Act represented a declaration by Congress of quite a different philosophy. Assistance was provided for categories of the poor, the aged, blind, disabled and dependent, to enable them to achieve at least minimal dignity. States were thus required to extend minimal fairness. A state plan had to be uniform in dealing with those eligible for assistance and assistance had to be provided throughout the state. Hearings had to be afforded when benefits were denied, giving reasons for any denial. Prompt action had to be taken upon applications. Since this represented a legislative declaration of entitlement or protection for welfare beneficiaries, in contrast to the pre-existing notion of welfare as a dole or charity, it inevitably influenced a similar shift in constitutional interpretation by the Supreme Court. See, supra, §§ 1–2.

This shift in attitude, influenced by legislative policy-making, is best illustrated by Edwards v. California, discussed supra § 2. There the Supreme Court held that California could not prevent in-migration by poor people during the depression. The Court, in thus rejecting ancient notions of settlement in dealing with the poor, specifically rejected the policies of the Elizabethan Poor Laws and relied instead upon the Congressional findings underlying the Social Security Act, to the effect that poverty was a matter of national cognizance. The poor were constitutionally protected in their right to travel in order to improve their lives.

The decision in *Edwards* constituted a major departure from the pre-existing conception of welfare. It established, in a constitutional framework, the importance of public assistance. And, influenced by Congressional action, the Supreme Court protected the poor from discriminatory state legislation of a kind which had been tolerated for centuries. But *Edwards* did not elaborate on the guarantees attendant upon welfare; indeed, it did not specifically address the issue of public benefits. Before the Court confronted those issues in the 1960's, a framework for analysis was developed in a related area of crucial public benefits: education.

Education, like welfare, is not constitutionally mandated. Government need not provide it. Yet it has been generally available as a governmental benefit since the mid 1800's. The Supreme Court early upheld the right to be free from religious discrimination in education. Pierce v. Society of Sisters, 268 U.S. 510 (1924); Abington School District v. Schempp, 374 U.S. 203 (1963); Wisconsin v. Yoder, 406 U.S. 205 (1972). In a landmark decision, the Court also held that racial discrimination in education is impermissible.

Brown v. Board of Education, 347 U.S. 483 (1954). More recently, the Court has held that freedom of speech may not be denied by schools, Tinker v. Des Moines School District, 393 U.S. 503 (1969), nor may they expel students without due process. Goss v. Lopez, 419 U.S. 565 (1975).

By thus protecting education, the Supreme Court altered the constitutional status of public benefits generally. Privileges become akin to "rights" if they are protected. The same approach has been developed with respect to welfare. There, the Supreme Court rejected the proposition that welfare is a property right, but has nevertheless held that—like education—it is protected by the Constitution. This developing framework for analysis began with the decision in Flemming v. Nestor.

Flemming v. Nestor, 363 U.S. 603 (1960), involved the termination of OASDI benefits for a Bulgarian who had resided in the United States since 1913 and had become eligible for benefits in 1955. In 1956, he was deported for having been a Communist in the 1930's. This ground of deportation was enacted by Congress in the 1950's and made a basis for denying Social Security benefits. In the course of its opinion, the Supreme Court held that OASDI, although a program of social insurance which workers earn and contribute to, was not "an accrued property right." Hence, denial did not constitute a "taking" of property. Congress' legislation needed only a "minimal rationality" in order to be sustained constitutionally.

The Court in Flemming v. Nestor, while refusing to view Social Security benefits as constituting "accrued property rights" commented further:

> "This is not to say, however, that Congress may exercise its power to modify the statutory scheme free of all constitutional restraint. The interest of a covered employee under the Act is of sufficient substance to fall within the protection from arbitrary governmental action afforded by the Due Process Clause." 363 U.S. at 611.

By this language, the Supreme Court clearly indicated that public benefits could be protected from arbitrary denials and that constitutional protections surround such benefits. Conceptually, this was a major advance. *Flemming* was disappointing in its result, however, for it found the denial of benefits to be rational in the light of Congress' purpose to conserve funds. While this weakened the value of the constitutional protections, nevertheless the status of public benefits had been recognized as warranting some constitutional cognizance.

The issue of whether welfare benefits are "property" was also addressed in Richardson v. Belcher, 404 U.S. 78 (1971). There, the appellee had established entitlement to OASDI payments under the Social Security Act in 1968. In 1969, the payment was reduced when it was determined that the appellee was receiving state workmen's compensation benefits. The district court held that this denied due process. The Supreme Court disagreed, citing Flemming v. Nestor, 363 U.S. at 611 for the proposition that "a person covered by the Act has not such a right in benefit payments as would make every defeasance of accrued interests violative of the Due Process Clause of the Fifth Amendment." In *Belcher,* the Court added:

> "The fact that Social Security benefits are financed in part by taxes on an employee's wages does not in itself limit the power of Congress to fix the level of benefits under the Act or the conditions upon which they may be paid. Nor does an expectation of public benefits confer a contractual right to receive the expected amounts." 404 U.S. at 80.

The Court further commented that the analogy drawn between welfare and "property" "cannot be stretched to impose a constitutional limitation on the power of Congress to make substantive changes in the law of entitlement to public benefits." Id. at 81.

The Supreme Court has deliberately and specifically declared that the distinction between rights and privileges has little bearing in determining constitutional protection of welfare benefits. Thus, the Court in Shapiro v. Thompson,

394 U.S. 618 (1969) and Goldberg v. Kelly, 397 U.S. 254 (1970), invalidated state legislation limiting AFDC to residents and denying hearings prior to termination of benefits. Welfare, the Court said, was not a mere privilege. While it may not be a "right" or an accrued property interest, it is nevertheless constitutionally protected. While *Nestor* had also expressed this view, that case had afforded little realistic protection to welfare recipients. *Shapiro* and *Goldberg,* in contrast, imposed significant substantive and procedural limits upon government and required a compelling showing of necessity to justify breaching those limits.

In Goldberg v. Kelly, the Court commented concerning welfare and poverty that a hearing prior to termination of benefits would advance "important governmental interests." It said:

> "From its founding the nation's basic commitment has been to foster the dignity and wellbeing of all persons within its borders. We have come to recognize that forces not within the control of the poor contribute to their poverty. This perception, against the background of our traditions, has significantly influenced the development of the contemporary public assistance system. Welfare, by meeting the basic demands of subsistence, can help bring within the reach of the poor the same opportunities that are available to others to participate meaningfully in the life

of the community. At the same time, welfare guards against the societal malaise that may flow from a widespread sense of unjustified frustration and insecurity. Public assistance, then, is not mere charity but a means to 'promote the general welfare and secure the blessings of liberty to ourselves and our posterity. The same governmental interests which counsel the provision of welfare, counsel as well its uninterrupted provision to those eligible to receive it; pretermination evidentiary hearings are indispensible to that end.' " 397 U.S. at 264–265.

In *Goldberg*, the Court said further:

"Appellant does not contend that procedural due process is not applicable to the termination of welfare benefits. Such benefits are a matter of statutory entitlement for persons qualified to receive them. Their termination involves state action that adjudicates important rights. The constitutional challenge cannot be answered by an argument that public assistance benefits are a "privilege" and not a "right". Relevant constitutional restraints apply as much to the withdrawal of public assistance benefits as to the disqualification for unemployment compensation; or to denial of a tax exemption; or to discharge from public employment." 397 U. S. at 261–262.

Goldberg required government to follow proper procedure before denying benefits; *Shapiro* dictated substantive limits. Similarly, in Sherbert v. Verner, 374 U.S. 398 (1963), the Supreme Court held that a state could not deny freedom of religion by requiring a woman to violate her religious beliefs by working on Saturday or lose her unemployment compensation. The net result of these cases is a significant increase in the constitutional protections available to welfare recipients, based on a recognition that welfare—although not a "right"—is a constitutionally protected interest.

Despite these developments, the nature of welfare as a protected interest remains to some extent related to pre-existing notions of what is "property." The Supreme Court in Flemming v. Nestor held that OASDI was not a property interest, but it still represented an interest which is protected by the Constitution. That distinction has been repeated in subsequent cases. See, e. g., Weinberger v. Wiesenfeld, 420 U.S. 636 (1975) and Califano v. Goldfarb, 430 U.S. 199 (1977). But the question remains as to how minor a welfare interest may be before it loses all constitutional protection.

The Fourteenth Amendment to the Constitution protects "property" and "liberty." Therefore, if an asserted interest does not fit within these two categories, there is no right to a hearing prior to governmental intervention. In many instances the interest clearly qualifies. A driver's license may not be withdrawn without a hearing, Bell v. Burson, 402 U.S. 535 (1974); nor may welfare benefits, Goldberg v. Kelly, supra, nor may public utility services, Memphis Light & Power Co. v. Craft, 98 S.Ct. 1554 (1978). At the other extreme, however, the United States Supreme Court has held that due process does not protect a citizen against the action of a city police chief in defaming the citizen as a criminal. See Paul v. Davis, 424 U.S. 693 (1976). And employment may be terminated by a public agency where the employee was on solely probationary status, Bishop v. Wood, 426 U.S. 341 (1976), with no legitimate expectation of continued employment.

The spectrum thus framed was addressed in a context related to welfare in Smith v. Organization of Foster Families, 431 U.S. 816 (1977). There, foster parents sued the State of New York to prevent removal of foster children without a hearing into the grounds and necessity for removal. Natural mothers of children in foster care intervened. The district court held that the existing state procedures were constitutionally defective. The Supreme Court noted that the freedom of personal choice in family life is protected by the Fourteenth Amendment but concluded that the limited recognition accorded to the foster family by New York statutes and contracts argued against "any but the most limited constitutional liberty" in the foster family. In the end, the Court did not resolve the difficult question of whether and what "property" or "liberty" interests the foster parents had, since it found that the procedures afforded by the state of New York prior to removal were, in any event, adequate to protect whatever interests the foster parents might assert.

In a number of welfare cases courts have looked to the Supreme Court decisions in Board of Regents v. Roth, 408 U.S. 564 (1972) and Perry v. Sinderman, 408 U.S. 593 (1972) to determine whether welfare interests are protected by due process. *Roth* and *Perry* held that teachers are entitled to notice, hearing, and reasons for discharge. The Court's reasoning was akin to that protecting property interests although the teachers, in a classical sense, had no "property" interests in their jobs. These cases, in effect, tend to revive the distinction between property and civil rights as a limitation on constitutional protections.

This distinction is particularly troublesome in welfare cases. Based as it is on case law involving property interests, the extension of *Roth* and Perry v. Sinderman to welfare cases could mean denial of protections to non-propertied people who are far less able to bear the loss of privileges than was true of the middle-income litigants in *Roth* and *Perry*. Thus, in Torres v. Butz, 397 F. Supp. 1015 (N.D.Ill.1975), the Court held that failure to extend breakfast programs to all eligible children denied due process under *Roth* and Perry v. Sinderman. But in Dodson v. Parham, 427 F.Supp. 97 (N.D.Ga.1977), the Court held that *Roth* protections did not embrace the expectation of Medicaid recipients that a specific list of drugs would remain available. By looking to *Roth*, courts tend to lose sight of the "brutal needs" of welfare recipients, recognized by the Supreme Court in Goldberg v. Kelly: a need which distinguishes them from others who may depend upon public benefits, but to a lesser degree than welfare recipients. The importance of protecting the poor was underscored by the Supreme Court in Memorial Hospital v. Maricopa County, 415 U.S. 250 (1974), invalidating a residency requirement for a county hospital, where the Court commented:

> ". . . It is at least clear that medical care is as much 'a basic necessity of life' to an indigent as welfare assistance. And, governmental privileges or benefits necessary to basic sustenance have often been viewed as being of greater constitutional significance than less essential forms of governmental entitlements." 415 U.S. at 259.

It seems apparent that the status of welfare as a constitutionally protected interest is in a stage of confusing development, caught in the cross-currents of traditional concepts such as "right", "privilege", "property" and "entitlement". These are shifting, fluid concepts and treatment of welfare as a form of entitlement reflects this. Yet due process does recognize that, however characterized, welfare is a protected interest in many—if not all—cases. These cases become clearer when a claim of entitlement invokes other concepts, such as the doctrine of unconstitutional conditions, discussed in the next Section.

§ 9.   Unconstitutional Conditions

Constitutional claims concerning welfare benefits may arise in any case where benefits are denied or conditioned unfairly or irrationally. The difficulty with such claims is analyzing what is "fair" or "rational." The most compelling arguments are those which refer to a specific constitutional guarantee, such as speech or religion. Under the Constitution, these rights may not be denied. Nor may they be infringed by requiring that a person give up such rights as the price of receiving welfare. That would constitute an "unconstitutional condition," contrary to the Fourteenth Amendment guarantee of due process.

Due process analysis of denial of benefits is most rigorous when that denial infringes other constitutional guarantees, such as those concerning race, speech or religion. Such guarantees cannot be conditioned upon receipt of governmental largesse. Thus, in Sherbert v. Verner, 374 U. S. 398 (1963), a Seventh Day Adventist could not be denied unemployment compensation where her refusal to work on Saturday was religiously motivated. Similarily, in Speiser v. Randall, 357 U.S. 513 (1958) a tax exemption could not be conditioned upon loyalty oaths. In either instance, the restraint on freedom, although indirect, constituted an unconstitutional condition. Such conditions can be justified, the Court said, only by a "compelling state interest."

The significance of this is that an unconstitutional conditions mode of analysis subjects the asserted state interests to "strict scrutiny." The state legislation failed in Sherbert v. Verner because there were alternative means of obtaining the objective: prevention of fraud. Further, requiring people to work on Saturday was "over-inclusive" because it would affect fraudulent and religious persons equally. It was also "*under*-inclusive," since some fraudulent claimants would not be reached. These concepts, requiring exhaustion of alternatives and requiring that means chosen not be over or under-inclusive, are the hallmarks of a "strict scrutiny" test.

The unconstitutional condition line of analysis raises one persistent problem, that of knowing *when* a right is conditioned. Obviously, an express denial of a right is easily resolved, but—for the same reason—rarely occurs. Sherbert v. Verner, was, in this sense, an easy case: Ms. Sherbert could not collect unemployment compensation because she insisted upon practicing her religion. The impact of the state's regulation was clear, even if the legal remedy was in doubt. But often the impact is not so clear. In Shapiro

v. Thompson, 394 U.S. 618 (1969), a waiting period of one year for welfare benefits was invalidated because it infringed the right to travel. But the impact on that right was far from clear. The recipients argued that the state need not fear a great influx of people seeking higher benefits. If so, the dissent responded, it could not be said that the right was really infringed or its exercise deterred. A partial response came in Memorial Hospital v. Maricopa County Hospital, 415 U.S. 250 (1974), dealing with a similar waiting period: a condition may be impermissible either because the exercise of the right is deterred *or* because a penalty is put upon exercise. Accord: Dunn v. Blumstein, 405 U.S. 330 (1972).

The doctrine of unconstitutional conditions is conceptually difficult, not only because the indirect influence upon constitutional guarantees is often unclear but also because the content of those guarantees may itself be unclear. Thus, in Wyman v. James, 400 U.S. 309 (1971), it was argued that requiring home visits by caseworkers as a condition of receiving AFDC was an unconstitutional condition on Fourth Amendment guarantees concerning searches and privacy. The Supreme Court rejected the argument on three levels. First, the effect on the Fourth Amendment was indirect and remote. Secondly, it was unclear whether a caseworker visit was a "search" within the meaning of that Amendment. Finally, unlike *Sherbert* and *Speiser,* there was a compelling state interest in caseworker visits: to protect the children receiving the AFDC and to guard against fraud. No other means, the Court held, would suffice for these ends.

One way of reconciling *James* and Sherbert v. Verner is to assess the impact of the condition on the right. The denial in Sherbert v. Verner was absolute. There was no way for the religious person to comply without abandoning her religious tenets. In Wyman v. James, on the other hand, the incursion on privacy would be transient and limited. Further, it was tailored to maximum convenience for the welfare recipient. Thus, to a certain extent, the impact of the unconstitutional conditions was different.

There is still a further consideration. The unconstitutional condition in Sherbert v. Verner was not essential to the unemployment compensation program. Requiring people to work on Saturday would not assist in detecting fraud, nor was it necessary for funding the program. In contrast, the State of New York made at least a tenable argument in Wyman v. James that home visits were indispensable to detecting fraud, preventing child abuse and rehabilitating or serving the welfare recipient and her children.

At bottom, the difference between *Sherbert* and *James* may lie in the right asserted by the welfare recipient. Freedom of religion weighs more heavily on constitutional scales than does the right of privacy asserted in *James*. The content of the Fourth Amendment is also less clear. Thus unconstitutional conditions analysis was successful in *Sherbert* yet failed in *James* not because the analytical frameworks were different but because the constitutional rights were of unequal dignity. The implications of this are serious for welfare recipients, for whom the right of privacy is frequently compromised as the price of receiving public assistance.

This suggests that unconstitutional conditions analysis will rarely be of help to welfare recipients. To the extent that the system *needs* personal control, privacy is lost. In *James,* home visits were deemed necessary to prevent fraud. In other areas, such as work rules or eligibility recertifications, the welfare system makes continuing demands upon the persons and privacy of recipients. They are thus at a distinct disadvantage in asserting that the cost of benefits is unconstitutionally high in those cases where the price is loss of privacy, a constitutional guarantee of recent origins and uncertain contours. This is nowhere more true than in legislation dealing with sexual privacy.

The doctrine of unconstitutional conditions was rejected in the Supreme Court cases holding that a state need not provide elective abortions under their Medicaid programs. In Beal v. Doe, 432 U. S. 438 (1977), and Maher v. Roe, 432 U.S. 464

(1977), the Court held that the Medicaid statute did not require that a state provide funds for elective abortions and that refusal to do so did not violate the Equal Protection Clause of the Constitution. The states were providing funds for therapeutic abortions and for full-term delivery. They were, to that extent, discriminating against women who chose elective abortion rather than live births to terminate their pregnancies. This, the Court held, was permissible because it furthered the state's interest in life and because it did not constitute a bar to the right to *seek* an abortion.

The unconstitutional condition analysis of Sherbert v. Verner, however, would seem to indicate that a different result would have been appropriate. In *Sherbert,* a woman who chose to exercise her religious freedom was forced to do so at the price of forfeiting her unemployment compensation. Similarly, the women in *Maher* and *Beal* were forced to choose between their right to seek an abortion and their right to Medicaid funds. The unconstitutional condition analysis, upheld in *Sherbert,* would have seemed equally appropriate in *Maher* and *Beal,* where the right of privacy in seeking an abortion, affirmed in Roe v. Wade, 410 U.S. 113 (1973), was clearly being compromised.

The Supreme Court held otherwise. First, it distinguished *Sherbert* on the ground that it involved First Amendment guarantees. Historically, the Supreme Court has treated other constitutional guarantees as being of lesser dignity than the First Amendment. Nevertheless, Shapiro v. Thompson, which involved the right to travel, would also have supported an unconstitutional conditions analysis. The Court distinguished *Shapiro* on the ground that there the complainant's welfare benefits had been totally terminated, whereas in *Maher* and *Beal* only the additional funding for obtaining the abortion was lost. Hence, the Court said, the state had simply made childbirth a more attractive alternative, but it had imposed no restriction on access to abortion that was not already there.

Justice Brennan in dissent commented that this reflected a "distressing insensitivity to the plight of impoverished pregnant women . . ." He argued that the case involving elective abortions was even stronger than Sherbert v. Verner, because by definition the plaintiffs in *Maher* and *Beal* were indigent and "even more vulnerable" than the plaintiff in *Sherbert,* who might well have been able to survive and exercise her rights without the unemployment compensation which she was losing. Justice Marshall in his dissent in *Beal,* argued that the effect of the decision upholding exclusion of elective abortions would be that the poor would simply not obtain abortions. He noted that in 1975, eight out of ten counties lacked an abortion provider in the United States; only 18% of American public hospitals performed even a single abortion; and in several states only a handful of abortions were performed at all. Further, the Court's decision would have a racial impact, since 40% of minority women relied upon Medicaid for their medical services.

The argument of the dissents in *Maher* and *Beal* was essentially that over a large range of individuals the pattern of coercion and pressure would be made clear. A significant number of women would choose to forego elective abortions. Although in a strict sense no bar had been erected, a clear channel had been. That channel would result in non-exercise of the important rights mandated and protected by the decision in Roe v. Wade. This is discussed further, infra, as an aspect of Medicaid, but warrants emphasis here: the legislative rewards for live births would, in all probability, diminish the constitutional value of the right to an abortion.

This consideration of statistical probabilities is an important one. If the state or federal government had erected an explicit barrier to obtaining abortions, then the legislation involved would fall under an equal protection analysis. However, the unconstitutional conditions analysis involved in *Sherbert* and Shapiro v. Thompson is calculated to reach less explicit, more subtle conditions on important rights. There was, in fact, no showing that *anyone* had been deterred from exercising the right to travel in *Shapiro*; nor was there any

showing that freedom of religion had been fore-
gone because of the unavailability of unemployment compensation, which was at issue in Sherbert v. Verner. But the high probability that a
substantial percentage of individuals would be influenced by the legislation involved in those cases
to choose *against* exercise of constitutional rights
was sufficient to invalidate the legislation there
involved. A similar analysis would have seemed
appropriate in Beal v. Doe and Maher v. Roe.

In the light of *James* and the Medicaid abortion decisions, it seems fair to say that unconstitutional conditions challenges will rarely be useful to welfare recipients. It remains available as
a tool for analysis. But the conditions and demands of welfare are sufficiently subtle and pervasive to escape challenge, at least under the
present state of the doctrine concerning such conditions. More useful concepts are available, and
these are the subject of the next sections.

§ 10. Equal Protection: Traditional Standards

The Fifth and Fourteenth Amendments to the
United States Constitution protect individuals
against denials of equal protection of the laws.
The essence of an equal protection argument is
that the legislature has acted in favor of—or
against—only part of a class of eligible people.
Such discrimination violates the Equal Protection
Clause unless it is reasonable. Since most wel-

fare legislation affects only a segment of the poor, for example, the aged, the blind, the disabled or dependent children, it is by its very nature discriminatory. The important question then is whether and when such discrimination is reasonable and will withstand a challenge under the Equal Protection Clause.

The answer, briefly, is that discrimination will be constitutional if it is minimally rational and does not affect fundamental constitutional guarantees. Providing welfare to those whose income is below $3000 per year or whose age is below 21 would pass muster, since a legislature might rationally define them as most necessitous. Similarly, denying welfare to those who can work is permissible. But denying welfare because of race or residence or sex raises profound constitutional concerns and would be constitutional—if ever—only where a legislature could show a "compelling state interest". Absent such concerns, a state need show only "minimal rationality" for the many choices made in limiting specific welfare programs.

In the field of welfare, examples abound. The federal categorical programs, by limiting aid to the aged, blind, disabled and dependent, exclude many others. Even within categories, such as AFDC, there are exclusions, as with the families having dependent children whose parents are both at home. Similarly, aid to the aged reaches only those above certain ages. Retirement insurance under OASDI is provided only for those who have worked a certain number of quarters or years in their lives and who have limited earnings. At the state level, distinctions in terms of benefits are drawn from state to state and even within a state. It was not uncommon for a state to pay 100% of need for those receiving aid to the aged, but only 60% of need to AFDC recipients. Such line-drawing is constitutional, whether tested under the Due Process Clause or—more recently—under the Equal Protection Clause.

Obviously, legislation such as that in Sherbert v. Verner, 374 U.S. 398 (1963), creates two classes of people: those who will work on Saturday and receive unemployment benefits and those who will not. The Court invoked the Due Process Clause, but this discrimination could be treated as a matter of equal protection. Indeed, in a similar case, Shapiro v. Thompson, 394 U.S. 618 (1969), an equal protection analysis was used to invalidate residency requirements denying AFDC to non-residents. The reasons for choosing equal protection rather than due process are not wholly clear. It may be because the Due Process Clause fell into disrepute during the 1920's and 1930's, the era of "substantive" due process, during which the Supreme Court took a highly controversial view of social legislation. The Equal Protection Clause has no similar historical taint. Or it may be that equal protection analysis seems more mechanical: the inquiry is not what a State *must* do, only whether it may distinguish between two classes when it makes choices.

While equal protection analysis avoids the political dangers of assessing legislative objectives, the focus on means inevitably raises the same dangers. Whether a distinction is reasonable in equal protection terms inevitably involves questions of objectives. To avoid these, courts have traditionally deferred to legislative choices as to means, subjecting them to only "minimal scrutiny" and requiring only "minimum rationality". The legislature may choose among alternatives and need not choose the best one. The leading Supreme Court decision exemplifying this is Dandridge v. Williams, 397 U.S. 471 (1970), permitting states to set upper limits on the amount of AFDC which would be paid to families, regardless of size. See infra, § 30.

The Court held that the legislation should be tested under "traditional" concepts of equal protection. The Court referred to Williamson v. Lee Optical Corp., 348 U.S. 483 (1955), for the proposition that a legislative classification only needs "some reasonable basis" and does not offend the Constitution simply because the classification "is not made with mathematical nicety or because in practice it results in some inequality." The Court further quoted from McGowan v. Mary-

land, 366 U.S. 420 (1961), for the principle that
"a statutory discrimination will not be set aside if
any stated facts reasonably may be conceived to
justify it."

The Court found that there were rational
objectives to be served by the maximum grant
legislation.   Such legislation encourages employment and avoids discrimination between welfare
families and the families of the working poor.
By keying the maximum grants to the minimum
wage, a steadily employed head of household receives parity with the benefits paid to the non-
working poor.   While the legislation might nevertheless deny AFDC to welfare recipients who
could *not work*, and while AFDC benefits would
be paid to those in small families who *could*
work, these imprecisions were not of concern to
the Court:

> "For here we deal with state regulation in
> the social and economic field, not affecting
> freedoms guaranteed by the Bill of Rights,
> and claimed to violate the Fourteenth
> Amendment only because the regulation re-
> sults in some disparity in grants of welfare
> payments to the largest AFDC families.   For
> this Court to approve the invalidation of
> state economic or social regulation as 'over
> reaching' would be far too reminiscent of an
> era when the Court thought the 14th
> Amendment gave it power to strike down

state laws because they may be unwise, improvident, or out of harmony with a particular school of thought." 397 U.S. at 484.

This mode of analysis, imposing minimal scrutiny on legislative judgments, has continued to be the prevailing view of the Supreme Court in welfare cases, as a brief review of cases subsequent to *Dandridge* will illustrate.

In Richardson v. Belcher, 404 U.S. 78 (1971), the Supreme Court considered whether reduction of disability benefits because a recipient was also receiving workmen's compensation might deny equal protection of the laws. The Court held that Congress could rationally find that reducing disability benefits would avoid duplication with workmen's compensation programs. This would encourage continued funding of those programs. It would also provide an incentive to the worker to return to the job. These objectives were legitimate and the Court therefore upheld the legislation, concluding that it was not part of its responsibility "to consider whether the legitimate purposes of Congress might have been better served by applying the same offset to recipients of private insurance or to judge for ourselves whether the apprehensions of Congress were justified by the facts." 404 U.S. at 84.

In Geduldig v. Aiello, 417 U.S. 484 (1974), the Court upheld a California program of disability insurance which did not cover pregnancy. It noted that the program covered many risks, but not all. The Court found that the state was not denying equal protection of the laws, saying:

> "This Court has held that, consistently with the equal protection clause, a state 'may take one step at a time, addressing itself to the phase of the problem which seems most acute to the legislative mind. The legislature may select one phase of one field and apply a remedy there, neglecting the others . . .' Williams v. Lee Optical Corp., 348 U.S. 483, 489 . . . [p]articularly with respect to social welfare programs, so long as the line drawn by the state is rationally supportable, the courts will not interpose their judgment as to the appropriate stopping point. 'The equal protection clause does not require that a state must choose between attacking every aspect of the problem or not attacking the problem at all.' Dandridge v. Williams, 397 U.S. 471, 486–487." 417 U.S. at 495.

Two other cases upholding discrimination against equal protection challenges should be briefly noted. In Jefferson v. Hackney, 406 U.S. 535 (1972), the Supreme Court upheld the widespread practice of paying a lesser percentage of need to AFDC recipients than to recipients of other categories of assistance. And in San Antonio Independent School District v. Rodriguez, 411

U.S. 1 (1973), it similarly upheld differentials in state funding of school districts according to taxable property. In both cases, only "minimum rationality" was required for the discrimination and it was found in legislative intent to limit and distribute funds in traditional ways.

The dissents in the cases discussed above all argued that the legislation was sufficiently imprecise that it should be invalidated. A "stricter scrutiny" would have shown that the means chosen served the ends poorly, if at all, and better alternatives were available. However, "strict scrutiny" is available under the Equal Protection Clause only in limited circumstances. Those are the subject of the next Section.

§ 11. Equal Protection: Strict Scrutiny

Traditionally, courts are reluctant to question legislative discretion in social legislation. All such legislation involves some drawing of lines and some discrimination. This is permissible and will generally survive challenge under the Equal Protection Clause of the Fourteenth Amendment. But a two-tier system of equal protection analysis has emerged, leading to a "strict scrutiny" of legislation where it affects "fundamental rights" or involves "suspect criteria." Although this development has been attended by confusion it is clear that where strict scrutiny is appropriate, legislation will survive only where it serves a "compelling state interest." And—to date—none has.

The most demanding form of equal protection analysis is that represented by Shapiro v. Thompson, 394 U.S. 618 (1969). There the Supreme Court invalidated state legislation requiring a one year waiting period of non-residents before they could be eligible for AFDC benefits. The Court conceded that there might be minimal rationality for such legislation, designed to protect state finances and long-time residents, deter those who came seeking higher welfare benefits and permit budget predictability. While these might be minimally rational, the Supreme Court held that such legislation must be justified by a "compelling state interest," not the traditional equal protection standard of minimal rationality.

The reasons for this more demanding standard were two-fold. First, waiting periods which favor residents deter travel, infringing a fundamental right deemed to be crucial to a federal union. Secondly, legislation which discriminates along lines of race, religion or alienage employs "suspect criteria." Impliedly, although the court did not so hold squarely, residence is such a criterion. Under either of these principles, the Equal Protection Clause would invalidate legislation unless it is shown to be justified by a compelling state interest.

A compelling state interest will be found only if four elements can be met by the State. First, the legislation cannot serve certain impermissible objectives, such as deterring travel or religion. The *Shapiro* Court held squarely that people may move for better governmental programs, be they welfare, education or parks. Secondly, the legislation must not be overinclusive or underinclusive; it must embrace the whole class. In *Shapiro,* the waiting period requirement was overinclusive in barring assistance to some residents who were returning after only a short or temporary absence. Thirdly, there must not be other means of achieving the asserted State objective. The waiting period requirement was thus faulty, since other means could be devised to establish residency or to deter fraud or to effect budget predictability. Finally, if an objective such as budget predictability were asserted to justify legislation then that objective must *in fact* be pursued. In *Shapiro,* the Court found that budget planning was not in fact based on waiting periods.

Perhaps it should be noted that the mode of analysis in *Shapiro* was akin to that required under the unconstitutional conditions doctrine discussed supra, § 9. As there, *Shaprio* demanded that conditioning a fundamental right must serve a compelling interest and be effected by precisely tailored means. It added, however, the principle that such "strict scrutiny" would also be required where suspect criteria were involved. *Shapiro,* in its demanding standard, drew upon the due process traditions of Sherbert v. Verner, 374 U.S. 398 (1963) and departed from the relaxed approach of Flemming v. Nestor, 363 U.S. 603 (1960). As with *Sherbert,* however, *Shapiro* left open important questions concerning what criteria are "suspect," which rights are "fundamental" and when they are deterred.

In Dunn v. Blumstein, 405 U.S. 330 (1972), invalidating a residency requirement for voting, the Court held that requiring an actual showing of deterrence was a "fundamental misunderstanding of the law" and stated further:

> "*Shapiro* did not rest upon a finding that denial of welfare actually deterred travel. Nor have other 'right to travel' cases in this court always relied on the presence of actual deterrence. In *Shapiro* we explicitly stated that the compelling state interest test would be triggered by 'any classification which serves to penalize the . . . right to travel.' " 405 U.S. at 339–340.

To some extent, then, *Dunn* resolved the question left open in *Shapiro* as to when a right—if involved—is deterred. The answer, briefly, is that actual deterrence is not required: a "penalty" is sufficient. See also, Memorial Hospital v. Maricopa County, 415 U.S. 250 (1974).

However, the question of when a fundamental right is involved remains problematical. The right to travel was implicated in *Shapiro*. But in Dandridge v. Williams, discussed in the preceding section, the Supreme Court found that the right of procreation was not affected by legislation which placed maximum limits on AFDC. And in Maher v. Roe, 432 U.S. 464 (1977), the Court also found that the right to an abortion was not affected by legislation limiting Medicaid to live births. Perhaps these cases only suggest that lack of clarity as to the content of rights will affect a determination, in *Shapiro* terms, of when a fundamental right is implicated.

Similar questions remain with respect to the issue of *what is* a fundamental right. The Supreme Court held in Shapiro v. Thompson that the right to travel qualifies. But in Wyman v. James, 400 U.S. 309 (1971), the Supreme Court held that a welfare recipient could be required to submit to home visits as a condition of receiving public assistance, even though the plaintiff maintained that this was an abrogation of her rights under the Fourth Amendment. Similarly, in Maher v. Roe, supra, the Supreme Court held that states might deny funds for elective abortions, while providing funds for therapeutic abortions and full-term delivery, despite the plaintiffs' argument that this penalized the right of privacy. In *Maher* the Court not only found that there was no fundamental right in the *Shapiro* sense, but also that the residency requirements in *Shapiro* actually denied the right to travel whereas withholding benefits in *Maher* simply made other alternatives more attractive. The Court distinguished *Shapiro* by saying that it did not hold in *Shapiro* that a state must provide the bus fare for people to travel in order to receive public assistance.

What constitutes a suspect criterion also remains unclear. In San Antonio School District v. Rodriguez, 411 U.S. 1 (1973), the Supreme Court upheld a property-based system for funding education, despite the argument that this meant discrimination because of wealth. The Court rejected reliance on *Shapiro*, in part because education is not a fundamental right but also because wealth is not a "suspect criterion." It noted that "social importance is not the critical determinate for subjecting state legislation to strict scrutiny," Id. at 32, quoting from Lindsey v. Normet, 405 U.S. 56, 74 (1972) for the following proposition:

> "We do not denigrate the importance of decent, safe, and sanitary housing. But the constitution does not provide judicial remedies for every social and economic ill. We are unable to perceive in that document any constitutional guarantee of access to dwellings of a particular quality or any recognition of the right of a tenant to occupy the real property of his landlord beyond the term of his lease without the payment of rent . . . absent constitutional mandate, the assurance of adequate housing, and the definition of landlord-tenant relationships are legislative, not judicial, functions."

A number of possibilities for "suspect criteria" exist. Race clearly qualifies, as does alienage. But sex, illegitimacy and age are more difficult and troublesome criteria. For this reason, and because these criteria are widely used throughout the welfare system, they will be treated as separate subjects, infra §§ 22–24.

The strict scrutiny analysis in Shapiro v. Thompson has been sparingly employed by the Supreme Court in subsequent cases. In Graham v. Richardson, 403 U.S. 365 (1971), the Court invalidated a 15 year waiting period imposed by the state of Arizona on aliens to qualify for welfare. But the strict scrutiny analysis which the Court has most frequently employed since *Shapiro* has been recast into a due process model, rather than, as in *Shapiro,* an equal protection approach. The due process approach has been to invalidate legislation which discriminated against people by creating an irrebuttable presumption contrary to fact. In a sense, this was involved in *Shapiro,* since the waiting period was designed to deter fraud and thereby presumed fraud on the part of all new residents.

This due process approach has been employed, for example, in Cleveland Board of Education v. LaFleur, 414 U.S. 632 (1974), where pregnant teachers were required to leave employment at the end of the third month of pregnancy, thereby creating an irrebuttable presumption of inability to perform their duties. The Supreme Court held that this was a denial of due process since some teachers were able to perform their duties during later stages of pregnancy. Similarly, irrebuttable presumptions that women are more likely to be dependent than men were rejected as denying due process in public assistance programs which extended benefits to widows but not widowers; the Court denominated it a denial of due process to the deceased woman wage earner who had generated the benefits for her surviving husband. See Weinberger v. Wiesenfeld, 420 U.S. 636 (1975) and Califano v. Goldfarb, 430 U.S. 199 (1977). Similar reasoning led to a holding that due process had been denied by a presumption in Frontiero v. Richardson, 411 U.S. 677 (1973), that male dependents of service women were unlikely to be sufficiently dependent upon the female wage earner to necessitate dependency allowances which were routinely granted to the female dependents of service men. See infra, § 24.

These cases could have been decided under a *Shapiro* equal protection analysis but the use of a due process approach permits a more flexible test for legislation to meet. This is a "middle-range" form of scrutiny, somewhere between Flemming v. Nestor and Dandridge v. Williams minimum scrutiny on the one hand, supra, §§ 8–10, and the strict scrutiny of *Shapiro*. This middle range approach has been employed in dealing with discrimination based on illegitimacy and sex under both equal protection and due process labels. See infra, §§ 22–24. It avoids having to decide whether sex or illegitimacy is a "suspect criterion" and concentrates instead on balancing the public and private interests affected by legislation. Such an approach is at once more sensitive and more difficult than the "traditional" and "strict scrutiny" approaches.

The confusion that is thus created is exemplified by the recent decision in Zablocki v. Redhail, 98 S.Ct. 673 (1978). There, eight Justices of the Supreme Court agreed that Wisconsin could not prohibit a person from marrying simply because he could not pay support for his children. But they could not agree upon a rationale. Justices Marshall and Stevens relied upon the Equal Protection Clause, finding a fundamental right to marry. Justice Stewart found a denial of due process on the ground that the right to marry had been unconstitutionally conditioned. Justice Powell also relied upon due process, apparently because inability to provide support was improperly presumed. Justice Stevens cited the Equal Protection Clause for much the same reason.

It is at least clear after *Zablocki* that courts will examine some forms of social legislation closely, whether under equal protection or due process analysis, where important interests are at stake. The rigidity of the *Shapiro* approach has given way to a more flexible mode of equal protection analysis, represented by cases dealing with sex or illegitimacy, discussed infra §§ 22–24. And due process may also support such close analysis where legislation reflects false factual presumptions, the subject of the next section. In either instance, however, this middle-range of scrutiny involes the kind of analysis of means undertaken in *Shapiro*: legislation will fail if it is overinclusive, underinclusive or fails to employ more precisely tailored alternatives.

§ 12. Substantive Due Process and Presumptions

The Fifth and Fourteenth Amendments of the Constitution protect the property and liberties of citizens against denials of "due process." This at least means that property may not be *taken* for public use without proper procedure and compensation. More difficult issues arise, however, when the question is how much government may *regulate* the activities of citizens in such areas as zoning, licensing, labor laws and economic legislation. The Supreme Court in the 1920's and 1930's invalidated many legislative efforts on the ground that they denied "freedom of contract," contrary to the Due Process Clause. See Lochner v. New York, 198 U.S. 45 (1905). This doctrine of "substantive due process" generated intolerable conflicts with Congress during the Great Depression and the New Deal and has fallen into disuse.

Due process, as a constitutional protection, remains significant in two respects. First, it is still a check, albeit minimal, on legislative latitude in business, economic and social regulation. This has received new vigor under recent decisions striking down improper legislative presumptions of facts concerning individuals or groups in the welfare field. Secondly, the Due Process Clause continues to assure fair procedure in governmental dealings with citizens. This doctrine of "procedural" due process will be discussed in the next section; the present discussion will focus on "substantive" due process and the recent developments concerning legislative presumptions.

The Due Process Clause limits the extent to which government may deny rights to its citizens. One of the earliest applications in a welfare setting came in Flemming v. Nestor, 363 U. S. 603 (1960). There, the Supreme Court upheld denial of OASDI to a man who had worked in America since 1920 but who was deported to Bulgaria in the 1950's for having been a Communist in the 1930's. The ground of deportation, for having been a Communist, was created in the 1950's. Deportation was then made a basis for denial of OASDI.

The Supreme Court upheld denial of benefits on the ground that there had been no "taking of property" since welfare—even the social insurance represented by OASDI—is not "property" in the sense of an insurance policy or an annuity. Secondly, although welfare is protected by the Due Process Clause it may be conditioned on reasonable grounds. The Court found that such grounds existed since Congress might well have believed that OASDI should not be paid to persons who have been deported because such payments would not be circulated within the United States economy, depriving that economy of the use of such expenditures to create jobs and generate tax revenues. The Court said:

> "For these purposes it is, of course, constitutionally irrelevant whether this reasoning in fact underlay the legislative decision, as it is irrelevant that the section does not extend to all to whom the postulated rationale might in logic apply . . . nor, apart from this, can it be deemed irrational for Congress to have concluded that the public purse should not be utilized to contribute to the support of those deported on the grounds specified in the statute."   363 U.S. at 612.

There are several aspects of Flemming v. Nestor which are most troublesome. In fact, the reasoning ascribed to Congress was not the motivation of Congress; clearly, Congress denied benefits to Ephraim Nestor because he had been a Communist. Thus the Court's reasoning in Flemming v. Nestor is deficient in two respects. The Court did not inquire into the *actual* reasoning of

Congress. And it did not evaluate seriously the reasoning which it imputed to Congress. The imputed reasoning—preserving the economy—had little validity, since the amounts of money sent to overseas recipients were small and monies were denied overseas recipients only if they had been deported, not if they chose—as many do—simply to live outside the continental United States.

Flemming v. Nestor has had a checkered career. The standard in the case is frequently cited where the Supreme Court wishes to uphold welfare legislation. But the case is rarely cited where legislative motivation in reality is aimed at punishing a specific political group. For example, in United States Department of Agriculture v. Murry, 413 U.S. 508 (1973), Congress defined "household" in determining eligibility for Food Stamps to exclude homes containing unrelated individuals. It was clear from the Congressional history that this was aimed at "hippies" and communes. The Court could have taken the same approach as that in Flemming v. Nestor and ignored Congressional motivation. In fact, it chose not to do so, invalidating the legislation. So also, in some of the Supreme Court decisions invalidating welfare legislation which discriminates against women, the Court has declined to fabricate rationales and has recognized the underlying realities of biased motivation. See § 24, infra.

To the extent that the Supreme Court will look at the reality of Congressional intent or purpose, the holding in Flemming v. Nestor is invalid. But the "minimum rationality" standard articulated in that case continues. See supra, § 10. Thus, in Weinberger v. Salfi, 422 U.S. 749 (1975), the Supreme Court upheld a limitation on OASDI which required a wife to be married nine months prior to her husband's death in order to qualify for survivor benefits. Ms. Salfi had been married only six months; she was, therefore, denied survivor benefits.

The Supreme Court upheld this requirement, relying upon Flemming v. Nestor. The Congressional intent was clearly to prevent fraudulent marriages. The Court held that limiting benefits to those who had been married for longer than nine months was a legitimate way of achieving this goal. It was true, of course, that such limitations would deny benefits to many—such as Ms. Salfi—whose marriages were *not* fraudulent. In this sense, the legislation was *over*inclusive. It would also mean that some fraudulent marriages would lead to benefits; in this sense, the legislation was *under*inclusive. But these imprecisions are permitted under the standard in Flemming v. Nestor.

In enacting laws, a legislature draws lines which may be based on policy judgments, such as how much money it chooses to spend on welfare or what is the most effective means or area for reducing poverty. This may determine levels of benefits, kinds of services or the kinds of people reached. Or the legislature may draw factual lines, with similar effect. Unlike policy judgments, the latter lines may deny equal protection or due process. This may be achieved by creating presumptions which are employed for administrative convenience. For example, in Shapiro v. Thompson, 394 U.S. 618 (1969), Connecticut had decided to limit its welfare benefits to residents. It therefore denied AFDC to all those who had not been in the state for at least a year. In effect, this created a presumption that all those who had not been in Connecticut for a year were not residents. This was false and, the Court held, denied equal protection of the laws to excluded residents. Significantly, *Shapiro* required that the legislative means be precisely tailored to the objective—preventing fraud—and not be over or underinclusive, in contrast to Flemming v. Nestor.

Residency requirements are frequently employed by state educational institutions. In Vlandis v. Kline, 412 U.S. 441 (1973), the Supreme Court held that a state cannot irreversibly or irrebuttably classify a non-resident as such for tuition purposes. The court held:

> "[It] is forbidden by the due process clause to deny an individual the resident rates on the basis of a permanent and irrebuttable presumption of nonresidence, when that presumption is not necessarily or universally

true in fact, and when the state has reasonable alternative means of making the crucial determination." 412 U.S. at 452.

A student must be given an opportunity to show that he or she is a bona fide resident qualified for in-state tuition. Where this opportunity is provided, a residency requirement for educational purposes has been upheld. See Hooban v. Boling, 503 F.2d 648 (4th Cir. 1974). Significantly, while *Shapiro* cited the Equal Protection Clause, *Vlandis* relied upon due process.

While *Shapiro* was decided on equal protection grounds, the Supreme Court has continued to invalidate presumptions on due process grounds. Thus, in Cleveland Board of Education v. LaFleur, 414 U.S. 632 (1974), the Supreme Court invalidated a school board policy forcing pregnant women to leave teaching at the end of the fourth month. The Court said that the:

> "[Q]uestion is not whether the school board's goals are legitimate, but rather whether the particular means chosen to achieve those objectives unduly infringe upon the teacher's constitutional liberty." 414 U. S. at 648.

The permissible goal was to assure effective teaching; the infringed liberty was that involving privacy, marriage and family. The maternity leave policies were held unconstitutional because of their use of unwarranted conclusive presumptions. The school board was free to conduct hearings into fitness or to require medical certificates or require teachers to wait until the next semester to return. But individualized determinations of fitness could not be avoided by false, conclusive presumptions.

The *LaFleur* decision is noteworthy for several reasons. First, it did not invalidate all presumptions: only those burdening fundamental rights where alternatives, such as hearings, would suffice. In this dual focus, the case closely resembles the strict scrutiny test of Shapiro v. Thompson, protecting the right to travel and requiring a state to pursue alternatives where fundamental rights would otherwise be unduly burdened. And, like *Shapiro, LaFleur* emphasized overinclusiveness: if the objective is to exclude teachers who are not fit, a conclusive presumption relating to pregnancy will surely exclude some who are perfectly competent.

Analysis under the due process clause concerning impermissible presumptions invokes "strict scrutiny." The chief significance of this is that it enables a court to examine the means chosen by a legislature to achieve admittedly permissible objectives. If the means are overinclusive or underinclusive or if there are alternatives, the means will fail. This is the chief difference between "strict scrutiny" and traditional due process or equal protection analysis. Under the latter modes of analysis courts customarily say that the choice of means is for the legislature. Once an acceptable objective is established, the legislature is free to choose any means available to achieve it.

The divergent opinions in *LaFleur* illustrate the difficulties inherent in the due process/presumption line of analysis. But most of the difficulties seem manageable. Despite the dissents, a concern for presumptions does not invalidate all legislative line-drawing, only those affecting fundamental rights and based on factual assumptions which are substituted for facts which *could* be found. Thus, presumptions of fitness to vote may be tied to age since no standard or facts may be articulated determining electoral fitness. But fitness to teach could clearly be found as a matter of fact and presumptions are unnecessary. Still, they may be tolerable, as with forced retirement at a certain age. Massachusetts v. Murgia, 427 U.S. 307 (1976).

What is unclear is when and whether the due process/presumption approach differs from the strict scrutiny approach of *Shapiro*. In many respects, the two are similar: both are triggered by line-drawing which affects fundamental interests and both require a State to meet a rigorous standard of justification. In a sense, *LaFleur* represents only a single application of *Shapiro*: that where the classification is overly broad and a hearing can narrow it. *Shapiro's* test would reach other instances, for example, where the means was perfectly tailored but the end illegitimate, e. g., excluding outsiders. Thus, the test in *LaFleur*, at least as applied there, is a strict *means* test and the dissenters' criticisms are wide of the mark.

To some extent, the due process/presumptions approach does, however, involve inquiry into legislative policy-making and goals, as argued by the dissenters in *LaFleur*. For example, the majority assumed that the purpose of the school board regulation was to determine fitness. As such, it was imperfectly drawn and was inferior to other alternatives, such as a factual, individualized hearing. Yet it is highly likely that the regulation was the result of quite a different determination to exclude pregnant teachers for reasons of community mores or taste, much as pregnant women in former times went into "confinement." None of this is discussed in *LaFleur*. By positing a different legislative objective and finding only the means inadequate, the Court was able to avoid passing judgment upon those objectives. Yet, implicitly, it rejected moralizing as a legitimate legislative objective.

Due process/presumptions analysis has a further difficulty. The legislature may treat something as true not because it *is*, but because such treatment *encourages* it to become true. This is a policy judgment, presumably within legislative discretion. Yet a court may mischaracterize the judgment as being based on a misconception of existing facts and improperly creating an inaccurate presumption. In the welfare area, this has been apparent in cases dealing with "men in the house" rules. By imputing the assets of such men to AFDC mothers, thereby rendering them ineligible, the legislature may be seeking to encourage them to support the women or to leave the household, rendering it eligible again. These would, arguably, be legitimate objectives. But such rules imputing assets are customarily viewed as presumptions that assets are in fact available; since this is inaccurate, the rules are invalidated. By mischaracterizing the legislative objective, courts are, in effect, passing judgment on what objectives are permissible. See King v. Smith, 390 U.S. 309 (1968), discussed in §§ 3 and 25.

In cases subsequent to *Shapiro*, the Supreme Court has used an unconstitutional presumptions mode of analysis rather than the *Shapiro* equal protection test. For example, in United States Department of Agriculture v. Murry, 413 U.S. 508 (1973), the plaintiffs challenged a provision of the Food Stamps Act which rendered an entire household ineligible if a single member was claimed as a tax dependent by a non-member.

Two of the plaintiffs in *Murry* were rendered ineligible for Food Stamps because their former husbands claimed their children as dependents, quite without regard to whether they in fact provided support. The impact was not only on the individual claimed as a dependent; it was the *entire* household which was rendered ineligible.

The Supreme Court invalidated this provision. It did so on the ground that it created "a conclusive presumption that the tax dependent's household is not needy and has access to nutritional adequacy." The Court said further that the provision in the Food Stamps Act was:

> ". . . not a rational measure of the need of a different household . . . and rests on an irrebuttable presumption often contrary to fact. It therefore lacks critical ingredients of due process . . ." 413 U.S. at 514.

Significantly, the constitutional provision invoked was the Due Process Clause, not the Equal Protection Clause involved in Shapiro v. Thompson. Justice Marshall, concurring, noted that the case was equally subject to an equal protection analysis.

In *Murry*, the Supreme Court relied heavily upon its earlier decision in Stanley v. Illinois, 405 U.S. 645 (1972). There it had invalidated an Illinois statute barring an unmarried father from accepting custody of children. The Court said in *Stanley* that:

> ". . . it may be argued that unmarried fathers are so seldom fit that Illinois need

not undergo the administrative inconvenience of inquiry in any case, including Stanley's. The establishment of prompt efficacious procedures to achieve legitimate state ends is a proper state interest worthy of cognizance in constitutional adjudication. But the Constitution recognizes higher values than speed and efficiency. Indeed, one might fairly say of the Bill of Rights in general, and the due process clause in particular, that they were designed to protect the fragile values of a vulnerable citizen from the overbearing concern for efficiency and efficacy that may characterize praiseworthy government officials no less, and perhaps more, than mediocre ones." 405 U.S. at 656.

The application of the due process/presumptions approach has not been consistent since United States Department of Agriculture v. Murry. In a similar case, United States Department of Agriculture v. Moreno, 413 U.S. 528 (1973), the Court employed a traditional equal protection test in invalidating Food Stamp legislation which denied assistance to a household having unrelated people living with it. Presumably, the Court might instead have used a presumptions analysis.

Justice Douglas concurred in *Moreno* on the ground that the *Shapiro* standard of equal protection should be invoked since unrelated households were exercising the fundamental right of freedom of association. The fact that Justice Douglas was alone in this view illustrates the problems inherent in identifying the nature of fundamental rights or their presence in any particular case as a means for invoking the *Shapiro* analysis. The difference between the analysis in *Murry* and *Moreno* suggests the dividing line between cases where due process/presumptions analysis will be available and those where only equal protection analysis will apply. In a case where only a legislative *policy* judgment is involved, only equal protection is available as a test. This was true in *Moreno*, where the legislature had simply chosen not to provide assistance to unrelated households. There was no factual assumption involved, at least on the surface. The Court noted that the legislation was motivated by ". . . a bare Congressional desire to harm a politically unpopular group," to wit, hippies or communes, but it tested that objective under the Equal Protection Clause, not due process.

In United States v. Murry, in contrast, the outer limits of governmental benefits were clear: whole households were eligible for Food Stamps. The only requirement was that they be needy. If the exclusion because of the claim of tax dependency had any meaning, it had to be as a test of need. Yet it was wholly deficient as such a test. Indeed, the only effective means available would be a factual hearing. Such a hearing would be neither overinclusive nor underinclusive and would be a reasonable alternative to the factual presumption. Hence, the Court, finding that a hearing would serve the legislative purposes, could reason backwards to conclude that the decision challenged was based upon or expressed in terms of an irrebuttable presumption. Such a presumption denied the due process right to a hearing.

When viewed in this light, it would seem that Justice Rehnquist was unduly alarmed when he dissented in Cleveland Board of Education v. LaFleur, supra, saying:

> "The court's disenchantment with 'irrebuttable presumptions,' and its preference for 'individualized determination,' is in the last analysis nothing less than an attack on the very notion of lawmaking itself."   414 U.S. at 660.

Rather, the decisions in *Shapiro, Murry,* and *Moreno* would seem to suggest that a due process/presumption analysis will operate only where the legislation challenged is based on assumed facts and not policy decisions and, further, where those facts can be tested in a hearing and, finally, where conducting such a hearing is feasible.   This is illustrated by the Supreme Court's decision in *LaFleur.*   Justice Stewart for the majority in *LaFleur* emphasized, in passing, that a conclusive presumption *might* be permissible at the end of a pregnancy.   The reason, simply, would be that there might be no time for an individualized determination to establish competency. Or, alternatively, disability might become sufficiently common in the last few weeks of a pregnancy among all teachers so that a conclusive presumption would be legitimate.

This would explain the Supreme Court's decision in Weinberger v. Salfi, supra, upholding a provision of OASDI which denied survivor's benefits unless the surviving spouse had been married for more than nine months to the deceased. On one level, it could be said, as the majority asserted, that this was simply a definition of the scope of benefits. But the legislative line drawn was similar to that invalidated in *LaFleur*. And the government had defended this provision as a means of dealing with fraudulent marriages. In that sense, the nine month requirement was a presumption of fraud and clearly overinclusive, since many marriages which were terminated by death prior to nine months would not have involved fraudulent intent. A hearing, however, would hardly have been feasible in *Salfi*, since it would have inquired into the subjective states of mind of two people—one of whom was dead—concerning an arrangement effected weeks or months before as to which no objective evidence existed. In contrast, hearings as to fitness or a license or guardianship or the need for Food Stamps, all involved in the cases employing a due process/presumptions analysis, would relate to present facts readily ascertainable.

On this basis, the due process/presumptions cases could be distinguished from *Salfi*. The majority in *Salfi* attempted to distinguish those cases, however, on a different ground. Justice Rehnquist, writing for the majority, characterized *Stanley* and *LaFleur* as involving fundamental rights. However, the dissent seems more accurate in rejecting that element as an essential part of the due process presumptions test. Certainly, the presence of "fundamental rights" was not essential to the reasoning of the Court in United States v. Murry, which clearly involved due process/presumption analysis.

Still, *Salfi* represents a re-working of earlier due process doctrine. Justice Rehnquist wrote in *Salfi* that what Congress had done was to limit the scope of coverage, not create presumptions. But this was unlike other limits of coverage which had been upheld under the Due Process or Equal Protection Clauses. For example, the maximum grant limitation in Dandridge v. Williams, 397 U.S. 471 (1970) or the intercategorical discrimination in Jefferson v. Hackney, 406 U.S. 535 (1972), represented only legislative policy and fiscal choices, not presumed facts. In contrast, *Salfi's* exclusion of recent marriages is sensible only as a way of reaching—and hence, presuming—fraud. By treating this as a matter akin to *Dandridge* or Flemming v. Nestor, however, the Court expanded the doctrine of those cases and *pro tanto*, the latitude of the legislature to limit benefits by exclusion of groups.

The decision in *Salfi* must therefore be viewed as a substantial limitation upon due process/presumptions doctrine because of the majority's characterizing earlier applications as involving fundamental rights. Earlier cases, such as *LaFleur,* Stanley v. Illinois and Vlandis v. Kline, did involve important interests. But the *Salfi* majority seems to have exaggerated their importance, elevating them to a limited range of *fundamental* rights, in order to limit the future application of due process/presumptions analysis. The result has been that, since *Salfi,* the due process/presumptions approach has had reduced utility in Supreme Court decision-making.

In Mathews v. Lucas, 427 U.S. 495 (1976), the Supreme Court upheld imposition of a burden of proof upon illegitimate children to show entitlement to survivor's benefits under OASDI; similarly, in Lavine v. Milne, 424 U.S. 577 (1976), the Court upheld a requirement that recipients who left employment within seventy-five days of applying for welfare rebut a presumption of fraud. Again, in Burns v. Alcala, 420 U.S. 575 (1975), the Court held that pregnant women could be denied AFDC despite their argument that this "presumed" they were not "needy." All three cases could have been resolved differently under a due process/presumptions analysis. But *Salfi* has obviously limited the scope of that doctrine to irrebuttable presumptions where fundamental rights are at stake, unlike those in *Lucas* and *Milne*.

Within these limits, due process/presumptions analysis remains viable. The Supreme Court most recently employed it in Zablocki v. Redhail, 98 S.Ct. 673 (1978). There, the Court invalidated Wisconsin legislation which barred remarriage by a man who was not supporting his children from the dissolved marriage. Although the Justices disagreed as to a rationale, eight of them in varying ways rejected the presumptions in the legislation that failure to support was willful or that re-marriage would divert funds from the previous children. Because marriage is a fundamental interest, the Court rejected the legislation as over-inclusive, under-inclusive and unnecessary in the light of more precisely tailored alternatives. These are the hallmarks of strict scrutiny, see supra, § 11, whether under equal protection or due process analysis.

Due process/presumptions analysis, at bottom, reflects a judgment that instead of *presuming* facts, the legislature should create a procedure for *determining* them. This was true of *LaFleur*, where pregnant teachers could not be presumed unfit but were entitled to a hearing before discharge. Thus presumptions analysis is closely related to the due process right to a hearing, the subject of the next section.

§ 13. Procedural Due Process and the Right to a Hearing

The early concept that governmental benefits were a privilege akin to private charity meant that those benefits could be terminated at any time without explanation. The facts might be mistaken, the policy may have been misapplied, or, indeed, the policy itself might be wrong. Nevertheless, the recipient would have no opportunity to show any of this. The Social Security Act rejected this concept by providing for a fair hearing after termination and for prompt action on an application. See supra, §§ 1–3. Thus, both applicants and recipients were granted a form of protection amounting to limited entitlement. But the limitations were significant: these procedures did not apply to programs lacking federal funds, they did not assure a full range of procedural protections, such as right to counsel at hearings, and they did not require a hearing before termination of benefits. The issue which remained unclear was whether the Constitution required any form of hearing prior to denial of benefits.

This issue was raised and resolved in Goldberg v. Kelly, 397 U.S. 254 (1970). In that case, recipients of General Assistance and of AFDC sued the State of New York, challenging its failure to afford a full hearing explaining the reasons why benefits were terminated *prior* to a hearing. During the pendency of the case, several of the plaintiffs were afforded "fair hearings" *after* the termination. Nevertheless, the Court held that the case had not been mooted because several of the plaintiffs remained liable, in the future, to having their benefits terminated without a prior hearing. The issue thus posed remained alive and of obvious importance.

The Court found that the New York procedures were deficient. It said:

> "Appellant does not contend that procedural due process is not applicable to the termination of welfare benefits. Such benefits are a matter of statutory entitlement for persons qualified to receive them. Their termination involves state action that adjudicates important rights. The constitutional challenge cannot be answered by an argument that public assistance benefits are a 'privilege' and not a 'right'. Relevant constitutional restraints apply as much to the withdrawal of public assistance benefits as to the disqualification for unemployment compensation; or to denial of a tax exemption; or to discharge from public employment. The extent to which procedural due process must be afforded the recipient is influenced by the extent to which he may be "condemned to suffer grievous loss" and depends upon whether the recipient's interest in avoiding that loss outweighs the governmental interest in summa-

ry adjudication." (Citations omitted) 397 U.S. at 263.

In weighing the need of welfare recipients for a hearing prior to termination of benefits against the government's interest in administrative efficiency, the Court in *Goldberg* said further:

> "For qualified recipients, welfare provides the means to obtain essential food, clothing, housing, and medical care. Thus the crucial factor in this context—a factor not present in the case of the blacklisted government contractor, the discharged government employee, the taxpayer denied a tax exemption, or virtually anyone else whose governmental entitlements are ended—is that termination of aid pending resolution of a controversy over eligibility may deprive an *eligible* recipient of the very means by which to live while he waits. Since he lacks independent resources, his situation becomes immediately desperate. His need to concentrate upon finding the means for daily subsistance, in turn, adversely effects his ability to seek redress from the welfare bureaucracy." 397 U.S. at 264.

In view of the interests to be served and of the importance to the recipient, the Court in Goldberg v. Kelly held that a recipient must be afforded a hearing before welfare benefits may be terminated. The Court held, however, that the hearing "need not take the form of a judicial or quasi-judicial trial." A complete record and comprehensive opinion would not be necessary. Instead, only minimum procedural safeguards were required. The essence of due process, the Court said, "is the opportunity to be heard." Therefore, the seven day notice required by the New York provisions was held to be sufficient. The form of notice, advising of the reasons for termination and the opportunity for a hearing, was also held to be sufficient. However, the Court held that a recipient must be afforded the right to appear personally, with or without counsel. There must also be an opportunity to confront and cross-examine adverse witnesses, as well as to present favorable witnesses. A recipient could not be limited to written submissions.

The Court held, further, that "the decision-maker's conclusion as to a recipient's eligibility must rest solely on the legal rules and evidence adduced at the hearing." To assure this, the decision-maker must state the reasons for the decision and indicate the supporting evidence. An impartial decision-maker was "essential." A welfare official might qualify, but not if he or she had "participated in making the determination under review."

In Goldberg v. Kelly, Mr. Justice Black dissented from the holding that a welfare recipient was entitled to a hearing before benefits could be terminated. Essentially, Justice Black's dissent rested upon a fundamental disagreement concerning the nature of welfare benefits. While the majority in Goldberg v. Kelly had viewed those benefits as being a matter of statutory entitlement, Justice Black viewed them as "gratuities". He commented:

> "The court . . . in effect says that failure of the government to pay a promised charitable installment to an individual deprives that individual of his own property, in violation of the Due Process Clause of the 14th Amendment. It somewhat strains credulity to say that a government's promise of charity to an individual is property belonging to that individual when the government denies that the individual is honestly entitled to receive such a payment." 397 U.S. at 275.

Justice Black went on to comment that the majority's interpretation of the Due Process Clause of the 14th Amendment was not supported by the history of that amendment or by the constitutional limitations on the role of the judiciary.

A fundamental question left open in Goldberg v. Kelly was the extent to which the holding there, to the effect that there was a right to a hearing prior to termination of public assistance, would apply to other forms of governmental benefits such as social insurance. Public assistance, by definition, is available only to "the needy." This was an important consideration in Goldberg

v. Kelly.   The Court emphasized that loss of benefits would have serious, if not grievous, consequences for the recipient.   In contrast, a recipient of social insurance may not be "needy."   Entitlement to benefits such as unemployment compensation, workmen's compensation or OASDI is based upon past work and contributions to the system of insurance.   Benefits are paid whether a person is needy or not.

In Mathews v. Eldridge, 424 U.S. 319 (1976), the Supreme Court held that due process applies to social insurance, as well as public assistance, although it held that the procedures in *Eldridge* —unlike those in *Goldberg*—were constitutionally sufficient.   This holding was akin to that in other areas extending the right to a hearing under the Due Process Clause to other important governmental benefits.   Thus, a driver's license may not be revoked without a hearing, Bell v. Burson, 402 U.S. 535 (1971) nor may the privilege of purchasing liquor, Wisconsin v. Constantireau, 400 U.S. 433 (1971).   A creditor may not attach property prior to suit without a due process hearing. Fuentes v. Shevin, 407 U.S. 67 (1972); Mitchell v. W. T. Grant, 416 U.S. 600 (1974).   Discharge from public employment may also require a public hearing, Perry v. Sinderman, 408 U.S. 593 (1972), as may discharge from school, Goss v. Lopez, 419 U.S. 565 (1975) and the termination of public utility service, Memphis Light & Gas Co. v. Craft, 98 S.Ct. 1554 (1978).

These cases, as well as *Goldberg* itself, establish an important limitation on governmental action. However, important questions are left unanswered: what interests are protected by due process, from what kinds of action and what procedure is adequate? Because these issues are better treated as an aspect of the procedures of the welfare system, they are reserved for treatment, infra, § 33.

III. WELFARE PROGRAMS

§ 14. Poverty: A Definition

Basic to any system of public assistance is a definition of poverty. This is sometimes treated in terms of who is poor, in the sense of who needs assistance. It may also be treated in terms of why they are poor and what strategies will best alleviate causes of poverty. Or poverty may be treated in terms of the resources society is willing or able to allocate to assist the needy. Obviously, these approaches vary significantly in the people reached, the kinds and levels of assistance afforded and the total resources allocated.

One approach to defining poverty would be extrapolating from a food or nutritional budget to calculate the remaining needs of a poor family. Clothing, housing, health, transportation and education must all be considered. It has been suggested that these may simply be a coefficient factor of the food budget. But this is at best an arbitrary computation, since these other needs have no precise relationship to nutrition. The most that can be said is that undernourished people are likely to have greater health needs and diminished capacities for work or education. There is no way, however, to determine, from nutritional needs alone, what an adequately nourished family needs, for example, for housing or transportation or other vital services.

Then, too, all areas of need involve value or policy choices. How good should housing be in quality or space? What should the quality of clothing be, in style, durability and variety? Is public transportation enough and, if not, how expensive and reliable should private transportation be? And what of other needs, such as communication and recreation: should the poor be subsidized sufficiently for telephones or televisions? With such questions, the definition of need shifts visibly into one of ultimate goals—shall the poor be limited to subsistence or moved towards middle class parity?

Federal agencies have established data-gathering activities with a view toward setting standards of need in connection with specific programs. But there was no official statistical poverty measure until the mid-1960's. The "War on Poverty" was announced January 8, 1964, in the President's Annual Message to the Congress on the State of the Union. In order to indicate the number and types of families that might be classified as "poor" under the various new anti-poverty programs, the Council of Economic Advisors (CEA), in its *Annual Report 1964*, designated as poor any family of two or more persons with an annual income of less than $3,000 or any person living alone (or with nonrelatives only) on less than $1,500. In assigning these as the critical thresholds, the Council cited a Social Security Administration (SSA) study appearing in the

July, 1963 Social Security Bulletin which estimated $3,165 as the minimum income needed in 1961 for a non-farm family of two adults and two children.

In January 1965, the Social Security Bulletin contained a study by Mollie Orshansky, *"Counting the Poor: Another Look at the Poverty Profile,"* which developed a sliding scale of income requirements for different family sizes and compositions. Although the total number of poor persons was nearly the same as that obtained by using the CEA's single-dollar income cutoffs, the characteristics of the two populations differed greatly. Small families with requirements exceeding $3,000 were included. The number of children counted as poor increased substantially, while the number of childless couples, young and old, decreased.

According to the Orshansky method, the set of poverty thresholds vary according to family characteristics such as size, sex of household head, number of related children, and farm or nonfarm residence. When considering the poverty threshold, a nonfarm family of four is the usual standard. In 1966 the threshold for such a family was $3,317 or 40 percent of the median income of such a family. By 1974 the poverty threshold was $5,038, but because of the rapid increase in nonpoverty family income, this poverty threshold had dropped to 34 percent of the median family income. The poverty threshold in 1976 had increased to $5,674. U. S. Department of Health, Education and Welfare, *The Measure of Poverty* (1976).

These thresholds were based on the cost for the Department of Agriculture's "economy food plan," originally developed in 1961 as the least costly of the USDA's family food plans at four levels of cost—economy, low-cost, moderate-cost and liberal. The economy plan specified, for men, women, and children of different ages, quantities of eleven different food groups that together made up a nutritious diet. In 1967, procedures for estimating the cost of food plans were revised to reflect food use from the USDA's 1965–66 survey. Because of demographic problems with the 1965–66 data for very low-income households, however, the cost of the economy plan was estimated at 80 percent of the low-cost plan between 1968 and July, 1975, when the plan was replaced by the "thrifty" food plan. The USDA economy plan specified quantities of food for twenty age-sex categories, reflecting each category's nutritional and caloric requirements. Costs for any family could be figured by totaling costs for plans for the age and sex of family members and adjusting the total by "economy-of-scale" factors for families of different sizes.

By 1968, there was concern about updating the poverty concept. The poverty cutoffs had been updated with the increasing price of the food budget, but the cost of other consumer items as measured by the Consumer Price Index did not always change at the same rate. The 1960–61 Bureau of Labor Statistics (BLS) *Consumer Expenditure Survey,* published in 1965, suggested that a smaller proportion of total income was spent on food than was reflected in the original Orshansky calculations. In addition, the Department of Agriculture urged lowering the differential between farm and nonfarm poverty lines. The poverty measures, and the poverty population they delineated, remained quasi-official numbers until August, 1969, when the Budget Bureau designated them as the official statistical series to be published regularly by the Census Bureau.

A measure of the adequacy of such calculations is provided by comparing them to the income necessary for a moderate standard of living. The Bureau of Labor Statistics estimates an "urban intermediate budget" for a four person family in selected metropolitan areas. In 1975 this "intermediate" budget ranged from approximately $13,500 to $18,000. The cost of food for the "intermediate" budget alone averaged between $3,500 and $4,000. Thus a middle income family was spending almost as much for food as the entire budget of a family living at the level of poverty.

The major data source providing annual poverty counts is the Current Population Survey conducted in March of each year by the Census Bureau. In addition, the Decennial Census provides detailed information on the low-income population at 10-year intervals, but the results will vary. For example, the 1970 Census and the 1970 Current Population Survey (CPS) yield different estimates of the poverty population for 1969; the number reported in the Census is 27.4 million poor persons, compared with 24.1 million in the CPS. The apparent inconsistency has two explanations. Although both surveys use a similar concept of income and the same definition of poverty, the income collected in the CPS by trained interviewers is more accurate than the less detailed income reported by self-enumeration in the 1970 Census. Furthermore, college students, who are generally enumerated at their family home in the CPS, are enumerated at their college residence in the Decennial Census, tending to increase the number of low-income persons in that data source. In both surveys there is an undercount of persons and some sources of income are known to be substantially underreported.

The definition of poverty is obviously a difficult task, varying not only with economic or social factors but also with the purpose of the definition. No single universal definition can be formulated. It is necessary therefore to consider a defintion of poverty in context, rather than in the abstract, because the context will add substance to the definition. The result varies among agencies and programs. Who is poor is a different question with a different answer in SSI, Food

Stamps and legal services programs, with further
differences in each state for AFDC and Medicaid.
And it is still further a different matter with local programs, such as General Assistance and
public housing.

The federally-established Income Poverty
Guidelines used to determine eligibility for School
Lunch and Breakfast Programs set poverty levels
as follows: for a family of 1, $2,940; 2, $3,860;
3, $4,780; 4, $5,700; 5, $6,550 to a maximum of
$11,680 for a family of 12. Such figures leave
open many questions, such as what is included as
"income" and what variations should be allowed
for urban and rural variations. Further, the *utility* of the figures is a separate question. Eligibility for free meals is extended to families whose
income is 125% of poverty level, suggesting that
in a functional sense "poverty" exists *above* the
"poverty line." Indeed, eligibility for reduced-
price meals is extended even to families whose income is 195% of the poverty level.

The complexity of calculating poverty is illustrated by the eligibility figures used with Food
Stamps. In a sense, the Food Stamp program is
directed at "the poor." But its objective is assuring adequate diet. Hence, eligibility may more
properly be designed to reach not only the poor
but also those who are nutritionally deprived.
However that may be, income levels are prescribed and, for example, a family of four with a
monthly income of $553 is eligible for $166 in

food coupons. But that does not mean $553 (or $6636 annually) is a "poverty" figure, for two reasons. First, the income figure excludes many items, such as irregular or children's earnings or a shelter deduction. Secondly, the family must *pay* for the coupons, implying that—while it gets a net "bonus"—it nevertheless is sufficiently affluent to accumulate some liquid assets. See infra, § 16.

The Food Stamp program illustrates the way in which financial eligibility standards become complicated by diverse objectives. Programs such as those involving food, housing or medical care are designed to reach the poor. But, to some extent, they are designed to assist the providers, be they farmers, builders or physicians and hospitals. To expand the cash flow to these "middlemen," it becomes necessary to broaden their economic and population base. Expanding eligibility for tax-supported programs is one device for doing this, with the consequence that middle-income people become eligible for benefits along with the poor.

The preceding discussion explores the difficulty and variety in defining poverty as an "eligibility" test for benefits. Such definitions also have an "allocative" use, to determine allocation of federal funds for distribution at the state or local level based on the number of "poor" people in a given area. This has been true, for example, of federal aid to education. At this level of abstraction, poverty definitions clearly become wedded to legislative and policy objectives or goals. And poverty then becomes less an individual, economic test than a demographic characterization of population. The questions become not what is poverty but what are the characteristics of the poor, how many are there, what are their problems and how effective are welfare programs in relieving poverty.

Examining the distribution of poverty among the population reveals significant patterns. Poverty discriminates against the very old and the very young. It is also disproportionately high among large families, women, racial minorities and those employed in marginal industries. See Tables 9–14, Annual Statistical Supplement, Social Security Bulletin. Strategies aimed at relieving poverty, particularly among future generations, must seek to correct these biases. Improvement in education and family planning are two areas receiving current emphasis among social services. Legislative responses are calculated to eliminate racial and sex discrimination and to improve minimum wages and working conditions.

The Bureau of Census attempts to estimate the number and distribution of the poor in the United States. In 1974, its figures estimated that twenty-four million were poor, down from twenty-seven million in 1967. Racial poverty remained constant at approximately one-third of the total. Put differently, while only 11% of whites were poor nearly one-third of minorities were so classified. The 1970 census indicated that the poor were concentrated in the industrial and Southern states, with the latter having a higher percentage of their population qualifying as poor.

About 12 percent of all families have a family head who is nonwhite. Although the poverty incidence is greater for nonwhites than for whites, the relative effect of public assistance in alleviating poverty is slightly greater for whites. Poor whites benefit more from the social insurance programs because of their higher earnings records, while cash assistance and in-kind transfers result in a relatively larger reduction in poverty among nonwhites.

More than a quarter of all poor "families" are single persons, most of whom are either aged or young. Of these, about 48 percent are poor before taxes and government assistance, and about 80 percent of these poor individuals have incomes that are less than half the poverty level. The incidence of poverty for other families (those with two or more persons) is less than half that for single persons, about 19 percent. The inclusion of social insurance as income has similar impact for both these family types, resulting in a 41 percent reduction in poverty for single persons and 43 percent for other families. In-kind transfers, on the other hand, have a relatively greater impact on the multiple-person families, even though the medical programs on the average are targeted more effectively to single persons.

The current programs of assistance benefit families headed by an aged person (65 or over) more than families headed by a younger person. About 16 million families (20 percent of all families) have a head who is 65 or over; more than one out of every two of these families is in poverty. For the rest of the families, the incidence of poverty is less than 19 percent. After taxes and assistance (including in-kind), however, the poverty count of the aged is substantially reduced; only about 6 percent would be counted among the poor. Social insurance, which is dominated by OASDI, lifts about 64 percent of the aged poor over the poverty line. As would be expected, the impact of social insurance on those under 65 is modest by comparison: 24 percent are moved out of poverty by receipt of social insurance.

The effectiveness of public programs in reducing poverty is relatively greater for families residing in the Northeast and North Central regions than in the South and West regions. About 46 percent of the poor families in the North Central region are moved out of poverty through social insurance, compared to roughly 37 percent in the South. This disparity reflects not only the types of programs and families residing in the different regions, but also the differences in the relative wage structures which affect the benefits in wage-related programs such as social security and unemployment insurance.

A demographic view of poverty thus suggests racial, geographic, social and sexual variations. A fuller exploration is beyond the scope of this text. But such considerations lead naturally to a consideration of strategies for assisting the poor. Those strategies may be grouped roughly into two categories: in-kind services and cash grant assistance. The policy objectives and potential of each are quite different. But the legal framework is quite similar and is the subject of the next sections of this text.

§ 15. In-Kind Welfare Benefits: An Introduction

Most public assistance in the United States is in the form of cash grants. At least, this is true of programs under the Social Security Act. However, in the last two decades programs involving "in-kind" benefits have proliferated. Medicaid, housing programs, legal services programs and Food Stamps are examples. The choice of in-kind benefits necessitates a structure which involves several layers of government as well as, oftentimes, private enterprise. Medicaid is an example, as is the Food Stamp program. These programs will be discussed individually in the next sections; at this point, some common themes will be developed.

In-kind programs represent a significant departure from the basic policy of the Social Security Act, favoring cash grant benefits. Cash grants place maximum emphasis upon the freedom and responsibility of the recipient to meet his or her own needs. To some extent, in-kind programs imply a distrust of the recipient's competence, as with vendor payments to landlords. Often, however, such programs are a realistic acknowledgement that individual recipients cannot bring about massive provision of needed services, such as public housing or medical services. Too, some in-kind services are designed to support the providers as well as the welfare recipients, as with Food Stamps and Medicaid.

Because of these characteristics, in-kind benefit programs may often serve or create competing interests. This is clearest with the use of vendors. For example, Medicaid and Food Stamps both use existing private facilities in the community, such as hospitals and stores. But these private entities have purposes of their own, including the generation of income to maintain their existence. This compels extensive regulation by public assistance agencies to assure that the poor are adequately served and not over-charged. Analogous problems exist in the housing area.

Conflicts may also exist where in-kind benefit programs use existing public agencies for delivery purposes. For example, school lunch programs are offered through existing educational facilities. However, the primary goal of those facilities is education. Consequently, the public assistance agencies are burdened with the responsibility of assuring that the public assistance programs are not compromised or discredited in the educational administration.

A chronic problem with in-kind programs is assuring full use by the eligible population. This is true of the food programs, such as Food Stamps and school breakfast or school lunch. It is also true with some aspects of medical services. The problem is a direct consequence of the complexity of in-kind programs. Cash grant benefits may be delivered by the simple means of mail. But in-kind programs, by definition, require moving people and services and publicizing the availability of benefits. The result often is that only a limited percentage of a target population is reached. This may be illustrated by reference to specific programs.

In Tyson v. Norton, 390 F.Supp. 545 (D.Conn. 1975), mod. 523 F.2d 972 (1975), Food Stamp recipients sued to enforce a provision of the Food Stamps Act which required Connecticut to inform families about the Food Stamp program and to *insure* full participation. The Food and and Nuitrition Service Regulations only required *informing* eligible recipients. As a result, only 43 percent of eligible households in Connecticut participated in the Food Stamps Program.

The court held that the federal regulations were deficient in requiring only that a state inform potential recipients. A state must go further and *insure* their participation. Further, Connecticut was deficient in informing potential recipients because it was making only seventeen contacts per year and even these were with groups not likely to contain the maximum number of potential recipients. Further, the media most likely to reach the poor were not being employed. Nor was Connecticut monitoring or evaluating the success of its informational programs. The court ordered the state to make more vigorous outreach efforts. See infra, § 16.

Another example of the difficulty of implementing in-kind programs is afforded in Torres v. Butz, 397 F.Supp. 1015 (N.D.Ill.1975). School breakfast programs in Chicago did not reach the neediest schools. The reason was that their principals had not requested participation. The state superintendent looked to local school authorities who in turn deferred participation to their individual principals. As a result, two-thirds of Chicago's eligible children did not participate.

In *Torres,* the court held the system of low level local option to be invalid. Participation by a *state* was voluntary. But once a state had choosen to participate, the statute required that the school board and state superintendent make an effort to enroll all needy children. The school board had a duty to apply on behalf of all children, not only a few. Not only was the federal statute violated, but delegation of uncontrolled discretion to principals was held to deny equal protection of the laws.

Yet another example may be found in Stanton v. Bond, 504 F.2d 1246 (7th Cir. 1974), cert. den.

420 U.S. 984 (1975). There, the Medicaid Act required state officials to undertake early periodic screening, diagnosis and treatment (EPSDT) of eligible minors. They had failed to implement this requirement, which would have made the in-kind medical benefits available to many who were not taking advantage of Medicaid. The court held that EPSDT must be implemented and it mandated the necessary personnel and procedures. See infra, § 17 as to Medicaid generally.

In-kind programs necessarily involve creating a means for controlling quality of services. This may be done, as with legal services, by creating the agency providing the service and then hiring the practitioners. Another approach, as with builders or grocery stores, is to control them through contract or license, subject to federal requirements. Problems of quality control become most difficult in delivering health services.

Various devices have been used. One is to look to existing professional associations to certify or license practitioners for reimbursement. This approach was challenged in Rasulis v. Weinberger, 502 F.2d 1006 (7th Cir.1974). There, physical therapists qualified for medicaid reimbursement only if they had graduated from a curriculum approved by the American Physical Therapists Association or if they had been members of the association prior to 1966. Thus, the Association controlled Medicaid reimbursement, eligibility for which was crucial to obtaining employment. The

Court upheld this arrangement. The Medicare
Act authorized the Secretary to issue regulations
concerning disciplines and providers of service,
with the exception of the practice of medicine.
It was reasonable, the Court found, for the Secretary to rely upon membership in a professional
association or that association's certification of
curriculum. By this device, the Secretary could
avoid legislating by regulation in areas of expertise.

Another approach to assuring quality of services is to establish an association of practitioners
independently of those already existing. This approach was upheld in Association of American
Physicians v. Weinberger, 395 F.Supp. 125 (N.D.
Ill.1975) aff'd, 423 U.S. 975 (1975). There, HEW
was contracting with Professional Standards Review Organizations to determine what medical
services were necessary in particular kinds of
cases and which cases were appropriate for Medicaid reimbursement. The PSRO's were non-
profit corporations composed of physicians and
funded to examine the necessity, quality and ap-
propriateness of services in a particular case.
The court said:

> "In summary . . . the professional
> standards review law is a massive piece of
> legislation which represents, for the first
> time, a nationwide program of medical utili-
> zation review." 395 F.Supp. at 131.

The physicians maintained that the legislation posed a danger to their right to practice and to the physician-patient relationship. The court rejected these arguments on the ground that the physicians remained free to practice their profession; the federal government also remained free to determine what services it would reimburse. There was no discrimination and procedural due process was afforded in the form of a hearing.

Perhaps the most obvious approach for controlling quality of in-kind services is to prescribe statutorily those which will be reimbursed. This will not, however, deal with the difficult problems of quality in the services for which reimbursement is available. Further, categorical exclusion of particular services or providers may be sufficiently imprecise or overly broad as to constitute impermissible discrimination. This issue was raised in Rastetter v. Weinberger, 379 F.Supp. 170 (D.Ariz.1974), aff'd 419 U.S. 1098 (1975), by chiropractors who were eliminated from Medicare reimbursement unless the services rendered had been limited to spinal manipulation. The chiropractors maintained that they were competent to render services of a much broader nature.

The court upheld the limitation on reimbursement. It noted that Congress is entitled to proceed a step at a time in social programs. The limitation or exclusion of chiropractors was reasonable in the light of a Congressionally commissioned study which indicated that chiroprac-

tors lacked sufficient training or theoretical ori-
entation. That same study indicated that those
deficiencies were not true of other independent
practitioners, such as occupational therapists and
speech pathologists or clinical psychologists.
While the equal protection challenge of the practitioners in *Rastetter* failed it might well be that
challenges by more soundly based practitioners
would succeed.

Quite apart from the problems of policing in-
kind programs, the success of such programs depends on the reliability and quality of the providers. If they founder, the program founders.
Thus, in Sasse v. Ottley, 432 F.Supp. 440 (S.D.N.
Y.1977), a union attached funds due a nursing
home from the City of New York for services
rendered to Medicaid patients. The attachment
was for employees' wages. The nursing home argued that the attachment was barred by 42 U.S.
C. § 1396(a)(18), which prohibits a lien against
the property of any individual on account of medical assistance. The court held that this protected patients, but not "providers." Otherwise, employees and creditors of nursing homes would not
do business with them and the entire program
could fail. But the same consequence may follow
if the creditors are able to deprive the provider of
funds necessary to continue services to the beneficiaries.

Problems in policing providers are important
not only for agencies such as HEW but also for

beneficiaries, who may bring law suits to obtain benefits. But in-kind programs pose peculiarly difficult issues concerning standing to sue for enforcement. Ordinarily, standing is viewed as a procedural matter which can be easily satisfied if the plaintiff demonstrates injury or a substantial likelihood of injury. However, the plaintiff must also show that the legislature intended a right to sue. This is sometimes treated as a matter of "implying a remedy." With in-kind programs legislative action may be intended to benefit both providers of services as well as recipients. Litigation by the recipients may thus be challenged on the ground that they lack standing.

The problems posed by the use of vendors or private entrepreneurs in delivering welfare programs is typified by Simon v. Eastern Kentucky Welfare Rights Organization, 426 U.S. 26 (1976). There, poverty litigants sued the Secretary of the Treasury, challenging his granting charitable exemptions from the Internal Revenue Code to hospitals on the basis that they were serving the poor when—in fact—they were not. It was clear that the exemptions were designed to encourage such service. By this device, Congress intended to deliver medical services for the poor; however, the system was not working.

The Supreme Court held in *Simon* that the poverty litigants lacked standing to sue. They could not show, the Court reasoned, that denying the charitable exemptions would in fact lead to delivery of the services sought. Put another way, the litigants could not show that granting the exemptions had led to denial of the services. Either way, the required "nexus" between the offending conduct and the injury for standing was missing.

The standing aspect of the *Simon* decision is not particularly troublesome. While the validity of the Court's reasoning may be questioned, the impact is limited to those programs where the private entrepreneur is merely *encouraged* to deliver services. In contrast, most programs—such as Medicaid and Food Stamps—pass governmental funds along to the entrepreneur and it is the direct or indirect denial of these funds to the intended beneficiary which confers standing upon them. See § 37 infra, as to litigation generally.

However, another aspect of *Simon* is more troublesome. In the course of its decision, the Supreme Court found that the plaintiffs in *Simon* not only lacked standing but also that Congress had not intended to confer a cause of action upon them. Put somewhat differently, the Court would not "imply" a remedy on behalf of the litigants even if they had standing. The reason, the Court said, was that Congress had not expressly created a right to sue and—absent Congressional intent—the Supreme Court would not do so. Yet the charitable exemptions scheme was clearly designed and intended for the benefit of the poor. The unwillingness of the Court to imply a remedy for the poor is a danger inherent in the system of delivering public benefits through cooperation between government and private entrepreneurs.

The Court's holding in *Simon* as to implying a remedy is probably unique to the facts of that case. In other contexts involving governmental benefits through private entrepreneurs, courts have been willing to imply remedies on behalf of the poor. Thus, in Gomez v. Florida State Employment Service, 417 F.2d 569 (5th Cir.1969), the Court upheld a right to sue on behalf of farmworkers who had traveled to Florida to work on farms under an interstate employment service authorized by the Wagner-Peyser Act. The service involved federal and state authorities working in cooperation with farmers to provide the latter with laborers in return for which the laborers were to receive decent wages and working conditions. The farmworkers sued because of breach of this promise.

The farmers claimed that there was no right to sue on the part of the farmworkers because only the state or federal government could enforce the Wagner-Peyser Act. It was true that Congress had not created an express right to sue. Nevertheless, the Court rejected this argument. It "implied" a remedy on behalf of the farmworkers from the Congressional intent to benefit them especially as a class and from the necessity of sustaining their law suit as a means of *enforcing* Congressional intent.

The Court's reasoning in *Gomez* is essentially the same as that of the Supreme Court in Cort v. Ash, 422 U.S. 66 (1975). There the Supreme Court said that four factors would determine whether a cause of action would be "implied" where Congress had not expressly created one. These factors were, essentially, that the legislation conferred benefits on a special class; that it could be inferred that Congress intended that lawsuits could be maintained by members of the class; that granting relief would be consistent with the legislation; and, finally, that the relief was not of the kind usually left to state courts. These criteria will most often be met by poverty litigants. When they bring actions against private entrepreneurs who frustrate Congressional legislation intended for the benefit of the poor, such litigation invariably would further Congressional intent and be consistent with legislation even where no express right to sue had been created. This was true of *Gomez* and would seem equally true elsewhere. See supra § 5 and infra § 37.

This introduction to in-kind benefits illustrates the difficulties inherent in such programs. Essentially, policing the providers and the products creates unavoidable problems in administration, with a consequent denial of benefits. Even more basically, in some programs such as housing, there may be no providers or the financial rewards may be insufficient to motivate them.

While such programs may be wise and indeed necessary, still the problems are significant. The next sections will review in detail the content of the more significant in-kind programs.

§ 16. Food Stamp and School Lunch Programs

The present Food Stamp program has roots in the wartime food coupons, but more recently its origins lie in the Food Stamp Act of 1964, with significant amendments in 1971. 7 U.S.C. § 2011 et seq.; 7 CFR 270 et seq. During this development, the program's emphasis has shifted from agricultural subsidies to income transfer. It has become a significant element in the national welfare scheme, complicated in various ways by administration having been left with the Department of Agriculture (Food and Nutrition Service), rather than the Department of Health, Education and Welfare. The summary which follows is necessarily tentative, since Congress amended the Food Stamp Act in 1977, Public Law 95–113, and implementation of these significant changes —which are discussed infra—turns upon adoption of regulations. See 43 Fed.Reg. 47, 846.

No welfare program attempts to pay 100% of need. Even in those states where AFDC benefits are set at 100% of "need", the standard of need is often out-of-date. Moreover, particular items may be excluded. The only program of assistance approaching adequacy on a routinely updated basis is the Food Stamp Program. Initially, the program mandated providing "an opportunity *more nearly* to obtain a nutritionally adequate diet". As amended in 1971, the Act provided that it was the duty of the Secretary of Agriculture to provide Food Stamp recipients "with an opportunity to obtain a nutritionally *adequate* diet . . .". 7 U.S.C. § 2013(a). The latest change dilutes somewhat the 1971 amendment, mandating "an opportunity to obtain a *more* nutritious diet . . .". However phrased, the standard is unique in the welfare field in approaching adequacy and doing so on a routinely updated basis.

States participate voluntarily by submitting a state plan, with actual administration usually being left to local welfare departments. Applications are made at local welfare offices; eligibility for most applicants is certified for three months. Food Stamps are printed coupons with designated dollar values and are used in lieu of money to buy food. They may not be used for other consumer goods, such as tobacco or soap. Any store approved by USDA may accept Food Stamps. A number of court decisions have upheld USDA suspensions of stores which have accepted Food Stamps for other household goods, such as cleaners. See Berger v. United States, 407 F.Supp. 312 (D.R.I.1976).

The benefit to recipients is that they pay less for the stamps than they are worth in purchasing power: this is the "bonus value" of the stamps. The actual purchase of the stamps may be at the welfare office in some states; in others, community organizations, banks and post offices handle the sales transactions. An identification card indicates the amount of the coupon allotment and the purchase price. As noted later in this Section, recent legislation has eliminated the purchase mechanism from Food Stamps, while retaining—in different form—the "bonus value" benefit.

The amount of stamps received by a household is determined by its size, but the amount paid depends on its adjusted net income after all deductions. The higher the income, the more the stamps cost. For a household of four in 1977 the maximum monthly income would be $553 and the coupon allotment would be $166. If the household's income were $553, it would pay roughly $140 for the stamps. If the income were $200 (roughly what an AFDC family might be receiving), the purchase price would be $53, leaving a substantial bonus value of roughly $110. As another example, a household of five with a monthly income of $240 would pay $66 for $198 worth of food stamps.

Food stamps are issued to a household. This may be a single person, family or group of unrelated people if they live together as a single "economic unit," share common cooking facilities and usually buy food together. Many such households will be receiving public assistance, including SSI, but a household may qualify for Food

Stamps even if its income is above welfare guidelines. Eligibility in any specific case involves a fairly detailed computation of assets and income, since certain items are disregarded and others are deducted. Once a household is deemed eligible, the amount it pays for stamps is determined by its precise income.

In United States Department of Agriculture v. Murry, 413 U.S. 508 (1973), the Supreme Court upheld a challenge to Food Stamp amendments which denied benefits where a member of a Food Stamp household had been claimed as a tax dependent in a preceding year by a person who was not also a member of the household. The justification offered was that tax dependency tended to establish the absence of "need." The Court rejected this argument. And in a companion case, United States Department of Agriculture v. Moreno, 413 U.S. 528 (1973), it similarly invalidated legislation which would have denied benefits to households comprised of unrelated individuals, on the ground that it was directed at "communes" and "hippies." In both instances, the Court held that eligibility must turn on present need, actually existing, not presumptions aimed at unpopular groups. See supra, § 12 and infra, § 27.

The basic test of eligibility for Food Stamps is financial and determined by income. There are, however, exclusions and inclusions which have generated litigation. Knebel v. Hein, 429 U.S. 288 (1977) involved a challenge to Food Stamp regulations which counted governmental benefits as income. This included the tuition grants and transportation allowances for the plaintiff in that case to pursue training as a nurse. The Supreme Court held that this was permissible. And in Patrick v. Tennessee Department of Public Welfare, 386 F.Supp 944 (D.Tenn.1974) the plaintiffs challenged a provision under the Food Stamp regulation which reduced eligibility because the plaintiffs were receiving a rent supplement under programs of the Department of Housing and Urban Development. The Secretary of Agriculture defined income as including public assistance, General Assistance "or other assistance programs based on need." Benefits were excluded, however, if they were "not in money." The court rejected the argument that this definition was wholly within the discretion of the Department of Agriculture, but then upheld the provisions on the basis that "income" under the statute could include governmental benefits.

While Food Stamps may count governmental benefits as income, Food Stamps themselves may not be so treated. In Dupler v. City of Portland, 421 F.Supp. 1314 (D.Me.1976), the court held that General Assistance could not be reduced due to receipt of Food Stamp benefits. 7 U.S.C. § 2017(d) specifically prohibited reducing "welfare grants or other similar aid." The Congressional purpose of Food Stamps, the court held, was to meet previously unmet needs. If General Assistance could be reduced, Food Stamps would simply be paid in lieu of other benefits and the net result would be a shifting of burdens from local or existing programs to the Food Stamp program, without any enhancement of the position of recipients. See supra, §§ 6 & 7.

One consequence of the Food Stamp program has been to reduce the disparities in income of AFDC families living in different states. The reason is that food stamp allotments are greatest for the poorest families. For example, in Michigan AFDC benefits for a family of four are $360 compared with $60 in Mississippi, a six-fold difference. But the Mississippi family would receive a $142 Food Stamp bonus value, compared with only $53 in Michigan, reducing the differential in total resources to two-fold. Still, the difference exists, heightened by the restriction that the Food Stamp value is limited to food purchases and is not available for general needs.

The Food Stamp program represents an affirmative effort to assure adequate diets on a national basis. It is estimated, however, that only 40 to 50% of those eligible actually receive Food Stamps. Federal statutes therefore impose a duty on states to adopt plans informing families of the program and insuring full participation. The latter requirement is unique among welfare statutes. In Tyson v. Norton, 390 F.Supp. 545 (D.Conn.1975), a federal court held that Connecticut had not complied with either requirement when it had delayed eighteen months in drafting a plan which assigned only one official for the entire state, who contacted only seventeen people per year. No provision was made for monitoring, use of media or foreign languages and interviews were delayed for weeks after the applicant first came to an office. The court ordered the State to correct these deficiencies. See supra, § 15.

The Food Stamp program as described above remains in effect, but Congress made significant changes in 1977 in Public Law 95–113. While this legislation was effective in October, it did not go into effect until implementing regulations were adopted. Department of Agriculture Regulations implementing and interpreting this new legislation are now in final form but a review of these regulations would be premature at this time. Full implementation is not expected before late 1978 or early 1979. But a review of the underlying legislation reflects a re-working of important features in the Food Stamp program. See generally, 1977 U.S.Code, Cong. & Admin. News, 1704 et seq. (particularly pages 1971–2444, and 2490–2507) final regulations which have been adopted may be found at 43 Fed.Reg. 47,846.

The new legislation will eliminate the present requirement that low-income households must pay cash for their stamps. This had meant that lump sums of cash were necessary to "buy into" the program in order to receive the benefit of the bonus value. This was a serious hurdle for many poor people. Under the new legislation, households will simply be provided a benefit amount in stamps according to need, the approach taken with most public assistance programs, with the stamps issued directly to the household. The value of the allotment to a household shall equal the "thrifty food plan" for its size, reduced by 30 percent of the household's income. 7 U.S.C. § 2017(a).

Need will be determined according to income, which will be calculated somewhat more simply than—but with many of the exclusions—in the past. 7 U.S.C. § 2014(d). There will be three basic monthly deductions: a $60 standard deduction for all households, a 20 percent deduction from earned income to reflect tax and OASDI deductions, and a maximum $75 deduction for high shelter and daycare costs. 7 U.S.C. § 2014(e). As with any system of flat deductions or flat grants, see infra, § 29, standardized deductions tend to eliminate those whose needs exceed prescribed limits. Thus this new method of calculating income will inevitably reduce the number of people in upper income levels qualifying for Food Stamps. Those in lower income brackets will continue to qualify, but automatic eligibility will no longer be extended to people receiving AFDC or SSI, increasing the burden on the poor of establishing eligibility. 7 U.S.C. § 2020(i).

The new legislation will also reduce income eligibility at the higher levels, with the result that over 1,000,000 people presently eligible for Food Stamps will be eliminated. The net income will be tied roughly to the federal non-farm poverty level. 7 U.S.C. § 2014(c). See supra, § 14. For a family of four the new net income limit is $5,850, whereas previously it was $6,804. The result of these changes in income limits and in calculating income is to eliminate lower-middle income people from the Food Stamp program, which had been one of the few forms of public assistance aiding that sorely pressed segment of the population just above the "poverty" line. This may also result from more stringent limits on assets retention by otherwise eligible applicants. 7 U.S.C. § 2014(g).

The new Food Stamp legislation reflects current trends in policing public assistance more closely. 7 U.S.C. § 2015. Work requirements are introduced, akin to those in AFDC. See infra, § 28. Significant penalties are imposed for fraud and higher funding is available to states in pursuing fraud. 7 U.S.C. §§ 2024, 2025. Vendor abuse is reduced since recipients will no longer be paying cash to receive stamps. One change is particularly significant: the right to continued benefits at the end of a certification period, pending a fair hearing and hearing decision, has been eliminated. 7 U.S.C. §§ 2020(e)(4), 2019. While this may ease administrative losses due to fraud, it increases the burden on recipients from administrative error and raises questions concerning Constitutional due process. See supra § 13 and infra, §§ 33–36.

In many respects, the new Food Stamp program will be similar to the old. It will remain on a federal-state administrative structure. 7 U.S.C. §§ 2013, 2014, 2020, 2025. States must continue outreach efforts, on a bilingual basis where necessary, and provide same-day filing of applications, with thirty-day action to follow. 7 U.S.C. § 2020(e). No additional, local conditions of eligibility may be imposed. 7 U.S.C. § 2020(e)(5). Non-conformity by a state may lead to an injunction proceeding by the Attorney-General. 7 U.S. C. § 2020(g). See supra, § 4. The state agency will calculate household income and determine eligibility. Eligibility is still determined by household, with the resulting complexity noted earlier in computing entitlement. 7 U.S.C. § 2014. Food Stamps may not be considered as income for other welfare programs. 7 U.S.C. § 2017(b); see supra, § 7 and infra, § 27. Retail food stores will still require approval, and the items purchasable will remain limited to "food or food products for home consumption". 7 U.S.C. §§ 2012(g), 2018.

This review of the new Food Stamp legislation is admittedly cursory and must remain so since § 1303 of Public Law 95–113, 7 U.S.C. § 2011, provides that implementation must await new regulations. Those regulations have been adopted, 43 Fed.Reg. 47,846, but will require extensive interpretation. It seems clear that the new regulations will generate a confusing transition period, but the basic structure and value of the Food Stamp program will continue. The 1977 legislation appropriated funding at the $6,000,000,000 level through 1981. This means that this highly valuable program will remain available to the poor, with its unique capacity for equalizing the varying levels at which the poor are assisted in differing states and communities throughout the nation. An equally important program, which will also continue, is the School Lunch and breakfast program, which will be briefly summarized in the remainder of this section.

The National Lunch Program was created by Congress in 1946 and augmented in 1975 by establishing a School Breakfast Program. 42 U.S. C. §§ 1773–1776. These and related programs are administered by the Department of Agriculture, Food and Nutrition Service, with funding through state departments of education. USDA regulations concerning food programs, including the lunch, breakfast and WIC (Women, infants and children) programs appear at 7 CFR 210–246.

The School Lunch program is created by legislation designed "to safeguard the health and well-being of the nation's children and to encourage the domestic consumption of nutritious agricultural commodities and other food." 42 U.S.C. § 1751. The funds are disbursed through agreements with state educational agencies, 42 U.S.C. § 1756, on a matching fund basis. The agency in turn makes agreements with local schools. 42 U. S.C. § 1757. A school breakfast program, with similar purposes and structure, also exists. 42

U.S.C. § 1773. Income guidelines for eligibility are prescribed by the Secretary of Agriculture and the participating state, and the program is to be operated on a non-profit, nondiscriminatory basis. 42 U.S.C. § 1758.

Funding is determined by the number of meals actually served by a state school, according to whether it was a free, reduced or full price meal. Reimbursement covers food, labor, preparation and supplies. If this is inadequate as to breakfasts, a school may apply for higher reimbursement status as "especially needy." This status is usually accorded a school where 75% of the children qualify for free or reduced price meals. Reimbursement for free breakfasts is 37.5 cents and lunches 73.25 cents; for reduced breakfasts, 30.75 cents and lunches 63.25 cents; and for paid breakfasts 10.75 cents and lunches 13.25 cents. These figures are adjusted twice yearly for cost-of-living purposes.

The school lunch and breakfast programs can be administered and operated together. Public schools, private schools and many residential facilities are eligible. Funding is by matching three "local" dollars for each federal dollar. Under 1970 legislation, 10% of the local share was required to come from state funds; the rest may be provided by local funds or charges to the children. Children are eligible for free meals if their family income is below 125% of poverty level.

The reduced price can be no more than ten cents for breakfast or twenty cents for lunch. Thus, in 1977, the poverty level for a family of 4 would be $5,700; if actual income were below $7,130, a child would qualify for a free meal, or if income were higher but below $11,110, for a meal at a reduced price.

The child food programs have been plagued by problems. Of 18 million eligible children, only some 60% receive free or reduced price lunches and only 8% receive breakfasts. Only 40% of the eligible children in daycare are reached. Nationally, funding and programs have been delayed or threatened. Locally, outreach has been minimal and available funds have not been fully utilized. Delivery of meals has often been of poor quality in poor settings and in a discriminatory manner. See supra, § 15.

School lunch litigation has involved difficult problems of forcing state or local agencies to comply with Department of Agriculture guidelines. One area of particular concern has been assuring that school districts give equal treatment to children, with priority to the neediest schools or children as required by federal regulations. This is administratively difficult, for reasons relating both to local politics and facilities. Yet courts have issued injunctions requiring local schools not to choose to discontinue the school lunch programs. See Jones v. Board of Education of Cleveland, 348 F.Supp. 1269 (N.D.Ohio 1972) and Davis v. Robinson, 346 F.Supp. 847 (D.R.I.1972).

School food programs were originally established by 42 U.S.C. §§ 1751 et seq. to assist the neediest schools. Unlimited funds are now appropriated by Congress for breakfasts, lunch and milk without limitation as to the kind of school. Participation by a state is optional, by contract between the Department of Agriculture and the State Superintendent, who is required to approve local plans and make an effort to enroll all eligible children. In Torres v. Butz, 397 F.Supp. 1015 (N.D.Ill.1975), Chicago's plan was invalidated because it left participation up to each individual school. The result was that the neediest schools did not participate, excluding two thirds of eligible children. The court found this represented a pattern of discrimination violative of the statute and the Constitution.

The School and Food Stamps programs are both directed towards nutritional needs of welfare recipients. While they deviate from the cash grant principle allowing freedom of choice, they undoubtedly serve legitimate needs. And their value is demonstrated by the increasing numbers of people—poor, low, and middle income alike—who take advantage of these programs.

§ 17. Medical Services and Abortions

In 1965 Congress added Title XIX to the Social Security Act, creating a comprehensive program of medical assistance for the needy (popularly called Medicaid). 42 U.S.C. §§ 1396–1396g. Medicaid is financed jointly with state and federal funds, with the current federal contribution to the cost of the program ranging from 50 percent to 78 percent. It is basically administered by each state within certain broad federal requirements and guidelines. 42 CFR 448 et seq.

Medicaid is designed to provide medical assistance to those people who are eligible under one of the existing welfare programs established under the Social Security Act; that is, AFDC or the Supplemental Security Income (SSI) program for the aged, blind and disabled. In general, receipt of a welfare payment under one of these programs means automatic eligibility for Medicaid. 42 CFR § 448.201. In addition, states may provide Medicaid to the "medically needy." These are people who fit into one of the categories covered by the cash welfare programs but have enough income to pay for their basic living expenses and so do not receive welfare. They are eligible, nevertheless, as being "medically needy" if their medical expenses are so massive as to leave little or no income for daily living.

Since states determine eligibility and benefits for AFDC, they exercise a great deal of control

over the income eligibility levels for Medicaid. If
they cover the medically needy, they may establish the income level for eligibility at any point
between the maximum assistance level for an
AFDC family (adjusted for family size) and 133⅓
percent of the payment to such AFDC family.
All of these variations—in benefits offered, in
groups covered, in income standards, and in levels of reimbursement for providers—mean that
Medicaid programs differ greatly from state to
state.

All states require Medicaid patients in long-
term care institutions to contribute their excess
income (generally all income over the $25 they
require for personal needs) to help pay for the
cost of their care. Similarly, all medically needy
individuals who have income that exceeds the
amount set for Medicaid eligibility must use their
excess income to pay for their medical care until
they have spent their income down to the Medicaid level. Neither of these forms of paying for
one's own medical care is subject to the limitations on cost sharing in the Medicaid program.

Medicaid operates as a vendor payment program. Payments are made directly to the pro-
·vider of service for care rendered to an eligible
individual. Providers must accept the Medicaid
reimbursement level as payment in full. Individuals, however, are required to turn over their excess income to help pay for their care if they are

in a nursing home. Co-payments may also be required.

States are required by law to reimburse for in-patient hospital services on the basis of reasonable cost, following the reimbursement practices of Medicare, unless they have approval from the Secretary of HEW to use an alternate method of reimbursement. The Secretary will approve an alternate system which varies from the Medicare method only if satisfied that (1) reasonable cost is paid (although the state may develop the methods and standards for determining what reasonable cost is and (2) the reasonable cost does not exceed the amount which would be determined as reasonable by Medicare. As of January, 1977, five states had received approval from HEW to use a reasonable cost reimbursement system for in-patient hospital services which was different from the system used by Medicare.

For all other services, including physician services, out-patient hospital services and skilled nursing facility services, states are not required to use the Medicare method of payment. With the exception of skilled nursing facility services and intermediate care facility services, in fact, the only requirement is that the state Medicaid reimbursement may not exceed the amounts paid under Medicare. While there is an effective ceiling on payment, there is no corresponding floor. In the case of long-term care institutional services (skilled nursing facility services and interme-

diate care facility services), the state is subject to
the additional requirement that their payment
system must be reasonably related to cost.

A state participating in Medicaid must provide
at least the following five services to the categorically needy: inpatient hospital services (other
than tuberculosis and mental health), outpatient
hospital services, other laboratory and x-ray services, skilled nursing facilities for individuals over
21, early and periodic screening and diagnosis
and treatment (EPSDT) of individuals under 21
and physicians' services, whether in a home, hospital, skilled nursing home or elsewhere. 42 CFR
449.10. A state which provides medical services
to the medically needy must offer seven services,
including those above or non-physicians medical
care, home health services (including nursing or
therapy), private duty nursing, clinic services,
dental services, physical and occupational therapy, drugs and prosthetic devices (including den-
tures and eyeglasses), diagnostic or screening
services, inpatient tuberculosis or mental hospitalization for persons over 65, intermediate care
facilities, inpatient psychiatric care for persons
under 21, or other medical or remedial care recognized by the state and HEW.

States can impose limitations on their coverage
of both mandatory and optional services, such as
limitations on the number of days of care for in-
patient services, and limitations on the number of

outpatient visits. In addition, states can require prior authorization for certain services. As a result of the Social Security Amendments of 1972, states may impose certain cost sharing requirements under their Medicaid program. The law specifies that no cost sharing can be imposed on the mandatory services for cash assistance recipients, but allows states to impose "nominal" cost sharing requirements on optional services for cash assistance recipients, and on any services for the medically needy.

An enrollment fee, premium or similar charge may be imposed for mandatory services to the categorically needy, tailored to income, not to exceed $19 per month for a family of two whose monthly income exceeds $1000. Co-payments and deductibles may be imposed, usually not exceeding $3.00 per month. No lien may be imposed against real or personal property for medical assistance received prior to age 65. A state may contract with an insurer or other provider to be reimbursed on a capitation basis, 42 CFR 449.82.

Standards concerning the need for, and quality of, health care services are to be set by "professional standards review," as prescribed in the Social Security Act. 42 U.S.C. § 1320c. To this end, HEW may designate Professional Standards Review Organizations (PSRO). These may consist of physicians or other qualified groups who shall determine whether services are "medically necessary," meet "professionally recognized standards," and could be rendered outside a hospital setting. 42 U.S.C. § 1320 c–4. See § 15, supra.

The scope of services available under Medicaid is, as indicated, quite broad. Litigation has been generated by state efforts to curb that scope and conserve funds. Thus, in Dodson v. Parham, 427 F.Supp. 97 (N.D.Ga.1977), a court invalidated Georgia's list of reimbursable drugs. The list had been reduced by approximately one half, to five thousand items. Expert testimony indicated that this was inadequate for the purposes of the Medicaid program. The court therefore held that the list was not "sufficient in amount, duration and scope to achieve the purposes of medical services." The "amount, duration and scope" requirement has also been significant in measuring state provisions with respect to podiatry and eyeglasses under Medicare or Medicaid funding. For example, in White v. Beal, 413 F.Supp. 1141 (E. D.Pa.1976), the court held that Pennsylvania's provision of eyeglasses to "persons with eye pathology" and to school children with ordinary refractive errors "was inconsistent with the federal regulation defining the purpose of eyeglasses as "lens . . . to aid or improve vision." 42 CFR 449.10(b)(12)(v). Perhaps the most controversial area of coverage under Medicaid has been that concerning abortions.

In recent years approximately 300,000 abortions have been performed annually with funding through federal or state public assistance. The cost of this has been calculated at nearly $15,000,000, although no precise figures are available. Perhaps no other single welfare expenditure has generated as much controversy or conflict. Supporters have argued that abortion should be available to the poor as well as the wealthy, to avoid economic discrimination in a woman's right to family planning and sexual privacy. Opponents have responded that public funds should be employed to support life and not to destroy it, particularly where public support is available once a child is born. The tenor and bounds of the debate have reflected the moral and ethical concerns which surround abortion itself.

Abortion has, until recently, been illegal in most states except for "therapeutic" purposes, chiefly where necessary to avoid risk to the mother's health or life or to avoid birth of a defective child. Non-therapeutic or "elective" abortions were held by the United States Supreme Court in Roe v. Wade, 410 U.S. 113 (1973) and Doe v. Bolton, 410 U.S. 179 (1973) to be a matter of constitutional right in the first trimester of pregnancy. A state might regulate procedures in the second trimester, but it could limit abortions to therapeutic grounds only in the last trimester. The basis for the woman's right to an abortion the Court said, was her right to privacy and freedom of choice, which could be reasonably restricted by a state only towards the end of a pregnancy, when the state's interest in the potential for life becomes substantial.

Abortions may be funded through a variety of state or federal welfare programs. But the chief of these is Title XIX, extending Medicaid to those receiving public assistance or otherwise "medically" needy. 42 U.S.C. § 1396 et seq. Among the authorized services are hospital, nursing and physician's services. A full range of surgical procedures is available, including—on the face of the statute, at least—abortion. Lower federal courts were divided, however, on the question of whether a state which limited or denied Medicaid for abortions, while still participating in Medicaid, was adding a condition of eligibility to Medicaid, contrary to the supremacy of the federal statute. See supra, §§ 3–6.

In Beal v. Doe, 432 U.S. 438 (1977), the issue reached the United States Supreme Court. Pennsylvania had limited Medicaid funding to those abortions which were "medically necessary;" i. e. where the pregnancy threatened the health of the mother, would lead to a defective child or was the product of rape. The Supreme Court held that this did not conflict with Title XIX, which does not mention abortion or any other specific procedure. Indeed, at the time Title XIX was passed, elective abortions were illegal in most states. A state was therefore only required to provide "*nec-*

essary medical services," 42 U.S.C. § 1396. It may, the Court said, refuse to fund *"unnecessary"*—though perhaps desirable—abortion services. Such a refusal would be justified by the state's interest in preserving life by encouraging and funding childbirth, even though it might create a risk to the health of the mother or a cost to the state of supporting the child.

Justice Brennan's dissent argued that Title XIX should be interpreted otherwise, to leave freedom of choice as to what is "necessary" with the patient and physician. Otherwise, if a state could deny funding for non-therapeutic abortions it could similarly treat therapeutic abortions. Various aspects of Medicaid and its legislative history were cited as supporting abortion and the freedom of choice. Justice Marshall's dissent noted that the effect of the Court's holding would be felt most keenly by the poor and minorities, for whom the right to an abortion would be effectively denied. Justice Blackmun commented, in a similar vein, that

> "There is another world 'out there', the existence of which the Court, I suspect, either chooses to ignore or fears to recognize. And so the cancer of poverty will continue to grow." 432 U.S. at 463.

Beal v. Doe upheld Pennsylvania's legislation against a challenge that it violated the federal statute; a similar Connecticut statute was upheld against the challenge that it violated the federal constitution in Maher v. Roe, 432 U.S. 464 (1977). Connecticut, in a fashion similar to Pennsylvania, limited first trimester abortions to those certified as "medically necessary." The Supreme Court held that this was constitutional. Neither a suspect class, such as race, nor a fundamental right was affected, since a state—although it could not *deny* the right to abortion—need not *assist* it. Hence, no strict scrutiny of the state's reasons was involved, and only minimal rationality was required. See supra, §§ 9–12.

The state's interest in *Maher,* as in *Beal,* was deemed to be legitimately encouraging childbirth as an alternative to abortion. The wisdom of that legislative choice, the Court held, was not a matter for courts to resolve. In dissent, Justice Brennan argued that the decisions in Roe v. Wade and Doe v. Bolton had been effectively undercut. The legislative choice favoring normal childbirth reflected "a distressing insensitivity to the plight of impoverished pregnant women" and constituted a form of "coercion." So viewed, a fundamental right was at stake and the majority's use of the minimum rationality standard of scrutiny was improper. See supra, §§ 9–12.

Justice Powell, writing for the majority, argued that denial of funding for elective abortions did not deny the rights protected in *Roe* and *Doe.* There, criminal laws had prevented seeking an abortion. Withholding funding did not prevent seeking an abortion; it simply meant that the state would not assist in the search. In this sense, the majority argued that the case was different from Shapiro v. Thompson (supra, § 11) where all welfare benefits had been denied to deter exercise of the right to travel. Women in Connecticut would not *lose* their welfare benefits if they obtained an abortion; they simply would not receive the additional assistance needed for the abortion. Justice Powell noted that the Court in Shapiro v. Thompson, while concluding that the state could not interfere with the right to travel, did not hold that the state must provide the bus fare.

The opinions of *Beal* and *Maher* make certain things clear. States may decline to fund elective abortions. This does not violate either the Medicaid statute or the Constitution. They may conversely *choose* to fund medicaid for elective abortions. Although this is not self-evident, Justice Powell in his majority opinion in both *Beal* and *Maher* made that statement. It is also true that Congress could choose through Medicaid to require participating states to provide funds for elective abortions.

A question left open by both the *Beal* and *Maher* decisions is whether a state may choose to deny funding for all abortions, even those which are "medically necessary" or therapeutic. Under Title XIX, the answer would seem to be negative, despite Justice Brennan's dissent in *Beal*. Title XIX requires a participating state to fund "necessary" services. Elective abortions perhaps do not qualify, since a normal delivery is an available alternative. But, by definition, this is not true where the health of the mother is threatened. Whether this would be equally true of the other two categories of Pennsylvania's definition of therapeutic abortions is less clear, since a normal delivery might be available even where the child was defective or the pregnancy resulted from rape.

The question as to these latter pregnancies might therefore have to be resolved under the Constitution, not Title XIX. The result is far from clear. But an argument could be made that pregnancies involving defective children or rape reach vitally into the concerns for privacy and procreation which underlay the Supreme Court's decisions in Roe v. Wade and Doe v. Bolton, thus implicating fundamental interests which a state may not condition. This would perhaps be a means of distinguishing *Maher*, where no such issues were at stake. In *Roe* and *Doe*, the Supreme Court emphasized not only freedom of choice but the consequences of the birth of an unwanted child; perhaps this latter factor would be a basis for a constitutional holding that therapeutic abortions must be funded if a state provides medical assistance for normal births.

A separate question left open by the *Beal* and *Maher* decisions is the status of Public Law 94–439 § 209, the "Hyde Amendment" passed by Congress over Presidential veto in 1976, prohibiting expenditure of federal funds for nontherapeutic abortions. At least one court, in McRae v. Mathews, 421 F.Supp. 533 (E.D.N.Y.1976), enjoined enforcement of the Hyde Amendment. But the subsequent Supreme Court decisions call this action into question. It would seem that if Connecticut and Pennsylvania may limit their funds to therapeutic abortions, Congress may do the same.

The controversy concerning the Medicaid abortion cases—*Beal* and *Maher*—tends to distract attention from the vast and valuable impact which Medicaid has had upon welfare recipients. Funding for medical services now exceeds $15,000,000,000 annually. When coupled with Medicare, which provides medical insurance for the elderly, the result is a revolutionary national mandate of health care for all. While the problems of administration and coverage remain, the reality is nevertheless a dramatic improvement —in less than a decade—in the health care of the poor.

§ 18. Social Services: Health and Family Planning

In-kind benefits are usually thought to include programs, such as Food Stamps and Medicaid, which stand on their own in providing specific benefits for the poor. Coupled with these and with the cash grant programs are complementary clusters of supporting services which are of considerable significance. Among these are preventive health services, family planning, educational counseling and employment placement. This last will receive separate treatment, infra § 28; the others—primarily family planning—will be treated here.

Social services are provided by all states to a wide variety of needy people. Many such services are keyed to cash grant programs, such as AFDC and SSI. The Social Security Act provides for federal assistance in services to the aged, blind or disabled, 42 U.S.C. §§ 1397–1397(f). These adult categories of assistance are now a part of SSI and federally administered, but state services to recipients remain available and federal funding is available to states. Services to children are a part of AFDC, 42 U.S.C. § 601 et seq., which remains state-administered. In addition to specific provision in the AFDC program, the Social Security Act provides for federal funding for related services, such as those relating to maternal and child health. 42 U.S.C. § 701 et seq.

Service programs under federally financed welfare programs are included in state plans concerning Title IV (AFDC). Certain services are mandatory, while others are optional. 45 CFR 220. The mandatory services include those concerning employment, self-sufficiency, child care, and homemaker services, foster care, family planning and protective services. Child welfare services must be expanded, "on the basis of need for services and shall not be denied on the basis of financial need" nor shall they be limited to AFDC cases. Optional services may include additional support services designed to preserve or strengthen families, to care for neglected children or to provide day-care. Federal financial participation is generally available for both mandatory and optional services. Similar provisions exist concerning social services to SSI recipients, 45 CFR 222, including protective services, homemaker assistance, health care and self-support, and for low income people in other programs, pursuant to Title XX. 45 CFR 228.

The Social Security Act, 42 U.S.C. § 602(a)(15) requires states to develop a program "for preventing or reducing the incidence of births out of wedlock and otherwise strengthening family life." The state must further offer services on a voluntary basis "in all appropriate cases (including minors who can be considered sexually active)." HEW regulations require every state participating in AFDC to provide family planning services. 45 CFR 220.21. These must be offered to individuals "wishing such services," "without regard to marital status, age or parenthood." The regulations specifically provide that services shall include medical contraceptive devices, with "diagnosis, treatment, supplies and followup." Individuals must be assured choice of method and source.

Family planning intrudes upon a most sensitive area. Since it affects or reaches the parent-child relationship, family planning not only concerns the right of procreation but also freedom of association. In a most basic way, family planning touches upon the fundamental associations of our society. This was the touchstone of the decision in Doe v. Irwin, 428 F.Supp. 1198 (W.D.Mich. 1977), where the court held invalid the practice of a family planning center which provided contraceptive information and materials to minors without notice to their parents. The center was operated by a county, under contract with the Michigan Welfare Department which, in turn, was complying with the family planning requirements of Medicaid.

The court granted that the minors had a right of privacy. But, in the court's view, the central issue was their capacity to exercise that right. For guidance in that exercise, the court looked to parents, not the trained staff of the planning center. As to the parents, the court held that there was clear constitutional entitlement under the First, Fifth and Ninth Amendments to the United States Constitution for protection of parental interests in the raising of children. The court described the family as being the "primary, essential cell in our society" and "anterior to the state". The court could find no compelling state interest which would justify curbing parental rights to notice of family planning counselling by a publicly supported program. There was no legislative enactment mandating such services and the Social Security Act did not require excluding parental notice.

The holding in Doe v. Irwin, that notice had to be given to parents, was consistent with an earlier decision in T–H v. Jones, 425 F.Supp. 873 (D.Utah 1975). But the rationale and concern in the *Jones* case were different. There, Utah Planned Parenthood Association provided family planning services under contract with the Utah Welfare Department. The Department regulations precluded providing services to a child *without* parental consent. The court held that such consent was not required, although—as in Doe v. Irwin—the state might require that *notice* be given to parents.

However, the discussion in *Jones* was significantly different from that in Doe v. Irwin. The court rejected any pre-eminent role for parents. It focussed, instead, on the rights to privacy and access to contraception which it found emanating from the decisions in Roe v. Wade and Doe v. Bolton, (see supra. § 17). The court held, essentially, that the right to end a pregnancy includes the right to avoid one. It further held that these rights extended to minors. The court in Doe v. Irwin had argued that parents were the best means of protecting minors from injuring themselves through intercourse or contraception; the Court in T–H v. Jones held, in contrast, that the social workers and physicians of the family planning center were adequate for these purposes. Hence, parental involvement was not necessary.

The controversy concerning family planning becomes intense when the method includes abortion (see supra, § 17) or sterilization. Some 150,000 low income women are sterilized annually, approximately 3,000 between the ages of 13 and 21. The danger of abuse is substantial, particularly where the services are coupled with other programs, such as AFDC, or where the recipients are not competent to exercise a free choice. In Relf v. Weinberger, 372 F.Supp. 1196 (D.D.C. 1974), HEW regulations were invalidated to the extent sterilization of minors or incompetents was authorized. The court in Relf v. Wienberger noted that sterilization, birth control, and family planning are areas of rapidly developing technology and changing values. It therefore commented that clear statements by the Congress would be necessary before HEW or a state agency could proceed to fund or undertake medical procedures which would have permanent and profound impact upon the right of people to procreate. It specifically noted that there was no question in Relf v. Weinberger of whether Congress could fund *involuntary* sterilization and it noted that sterilization of minors or incompetents was tantamount to involuntary sterilization.

The provisions concerning adults and *competent* minors were more troublesome, however. On their face, they required that informed consent be obtained. This would include, under the HEW regulations, specific advice that the consenting person might withdraw his or her consent without losing benefits. This would reduce any potential economic pressure brought to bear upon or felt by the Medicaid or AFDC recipient. Nevertheless, in *Relf* the court found that prior instances of pressure and coercion had arisen and that the potential remained. Therefore, it required that the counseling and advice to the person who was considering sterilization include an early and affirmative statement that no benefits could be lost if the person declined sterilization.

Following the decision in *Relf*, HEW adopted regulations designed to implement the court's decision and it declared a moratorium on federally-funded sterilizations of women under age 21. 45 CFR 205.35. Non-emergency and non-therapeutic sterilizations were required to be voluntary, accompanied by advice that no benefits would be withdrawn if sterilization were refused, and pursuant to "informed consent." This last requirement required a documented explanation of the procedures, risks and benefits, signed by the patient and an "auditor-witness." A non-therapeutic abortion would not include one necessary to treat an existing illness or medically indicated as part of an operation on the female genito-urinary tract. Although the regulations were silent, federal funds presumably could be used—under less stringent procedures—for emergency sterilizations. In the latest chapter in the *Relf* litigation, HEW withdrew the regulations and undertook promulgating new ones.

The validity of sterlization has also arisen under state legislation. In North Carolina Association for Retarded Children v. State of North Carolina, 420 F.Supp. 451 (M.D.No.C.1976), the federal court upheld a North Carolina statute authorizing compulsory sterilization of mental defectives who could not manage their own affairs and required supervision, including persons known as feebleminded, idiots or imbeciles. In a wide ranging opinion, the court noted that involuntary sterilization would rarely be prescribed by physicians and that retardation is very complex, with varied genetic, environmental and, possibly, nutritional causes. The court noted that "while mentally retarded persons may be entitled to express themselves sexually . . .," at least some are not able to understand the consequences of sexual activity. 420 F.Supp. 455. A hearing was required in every case before involuntary sterilization could be ordered, surrounded by a full range of protections.

A final area of social services, perhaps more accurately treated as medical services, is EPSDT. EPSDT is a program calling for early and periodic screening and diagnosis and treatment of children. It is an aspect of Medicaid. See *supra*, § 17. Total payments under Title IV–A will be reduced by 1% if a state fails to advise AFDC families annually of the program, and provide for services where requested. 45 CFR 205.146(c). The state must arrange for providers and assist recipients in obtaining their services.

In 1969 Congress amended one of the five requirements of Medicaid to, in effect, require each participating state to furnish a sixth basic service: early and periodic screening and diagnosis (EPSDT) of individuals who are eligible under the state plan and are under the age of 21 to "ascertain their physical or mental defects, and such health care, treatment, and other measures to correct or ameliorate defects and chronic conditions discovered thereby, as may be provided in regulations of the Secretary." 42 U.S.C. § 1396a (a)(4)(B).

The terms screening, diagnosis, and treatment are defined as follows: Screening is the use of procedures to sort out apparently well persons from those who have a disease or abnormality and to identify those in need of more definitive study of their physical or mental problems. Diagnosis is the determination of the nature or cause of physical or mental disease or abnormality through the combined use of health histories, physical, developmental and psychological examinations, and laboratory tests and x-rays. Although, in some instances, a presumptive diagnosis may be made at the time of screening, it will usually be necessary to refer the patient to an appropriate practitioner or medical facility for definitive evaluation. Treatment means physician's or dentist's services, hospital services, and all other Medicaid services to prevent, correct or ameliorate disease or abnormalities detected by screening and diagnostic procedures.

The components of the program include identifying which children need services and informing all families of the availability of services. The HEW manual further requires that officials encourage use of EPSDT. The officials must locate sufficient providers to meet demand, using existing providers of services whenever possible. Under HEW requirements, the local authorities must also conduct follow-up to determine whether people requesting services actually use them and whether those receiving services are benefited thereby. Finally, transportation and other services must be made available when needed.

EPSDT has been the subject of extensive litigation. In Stanton v. Bond, 504 F.2d 1246 (7th

Cir. 1974) cert. den. 420 U.S. 984 (1975), the District Court granted an injunction requiring local welfare officials to implement EPSDT. Only minimal implementation had been undertaken. Contracts had not been arranged with providers; follow-up had not been undertaken and the other requirements noted above were ignored. The court held, without more, that the plaintiffs were entitled to judgment as a matter of law.

In contrast, in Woodruff v. Lavine, 417 F.Supp. 824 (S.D.N.Y.1976), EPSDT was being conducted through welfare officials of the City of New York, but only ten to fourteen percent of the eligible population had enrolled. The plaintiffs maintained that this evidenced the inadequacy of the program. Plaintiffs' experts testified that the program could be deemed successful only if 80 to 85 percent enrolled, which would constitute some 750,000 people. The court held the City was adequately seeking to identify children in need of EPSDT through computer checking and person-to-person identification. Outreach was adequate, through various mailings and through semiannual recertification of AFDC eligibility. The number and capacity of providers was not sufficient for the entire eligible population, but the court held that it was sufficient for the segment of the population which was likely to use the services. The City was undertaking follow-up on requests for services and for services rendered.

All social services, as with EPSDT, are in some sense an "outreach" effort. To the extent that they seek to enhance or enlarge a program, again as with EPSDT or the requirement of notification with Food Stamps, they are clearly desirable. It is only when social services are addressed to the presumed causes or cures of poverty, as with family planning and sterilization, that they become objectionable. Both family planning and sterilization represent an intrusion upon privacy. Moreover, they are dangerous precisely in proportion to their appearance of voluntariness. As conditions—implied or explicit—upon welfare, social services can rarely be volitional.

§ 19. Social Insurance: Retirement and Disability

The term "welfare" is ordinarily used to describe programs having three characteristics: benefits are in the form of cash grants, with amounts determined by "need", with eligibility also being determined by need, not prior contributions. The paradigm of such programs is Aid to Families of Dependent Children (AFDC). In contrast are programs of social insurance, such as OASDI (commonly referred to as "social security"), workmen's compensation and unemployment compensation. With insurance programs, benefits and eligibility are largely determined by past earnings and paid regardless of need. Yet increasingly these programs depart from insurance or pension models: benefits are not limited to amounts paid, beneficiaries are expanded beyond the wage earner and the programs require increased subsidization from general tax revenues. This is best illustrated by retirement insurance benefits under OASDI.

The "insurance" nature of OASDI is largely illusory. Although benefits are related to earnings, there is at best only a rough relationship. Benefits are adjusted to keep pace with cost of living increases regardless of the recipient's contributions. Further, at least half of all contributions are by employers. And certain aspects of the retirement benefits are not tied to earnings, as with survivor's benefits. The latter are awarded even though no additional assessment or "premium" was charged the wage earner for the increased actuarial cost of covering the dependents, no matter how many. Finally, benefits may be lost or reduced if the retired worker continues to receive earnings. None of these features would be found in the kind of annuity program which could properly be termed "insurance". See Tenbrock and Matson, *The Disabled and the Law of Welfare*, 54 Calif.L.Rev. 809 (1966).

Although the distinction between public assistance and social insurance retains vitality, it is of unclear significance constitutionally. In Flemming v. Nestor, 363 U.S. 603 (1960), a deported worker was denied retirement benefits he had "earned" under OASDI. The Supreme Court upheld this, saying that the benefits were not "contractual", as they would be with private pensions, and could be withdrawn. Justice Black dissented vigorously, arguing that this was a "taking" of property. In his view, social insurance benefits could not be reduced, unlike welfare or public assistance benefits. Yet the majority view prevails today, with the result that individual entitlement under social insurance is no more constitutionally protected than the right to benefits under public assistance programs such as AFDC. See supra, § 8.

The distinction between social insurance and public assistance was urged by Justice Marshall, dissenting in Richardson v. Belcher, 404 U.S. 78 (1971). There, Congress provided that disability benefits under the Social Security Act could be offset by benefits received under state workmen's compensation programs. The disability program was a form of social insurance, since workers were required to contribute and were entitled to benefits regardless of need. Still, the majority upheld imposition of this "offset." Justice Marshall commented:

"Whatever might be said about the characterization of welfare assistance as 'property', surely a worker who is forced to pay a social security tax on his earnings has a clearly cognizable contract interest in the benefits that justify the tax. The characterization of this interest as 'noncontractual' in Flemming v. Nestor, is, in my view, incorrect. The analogy to an annuity or insurance contract, rejected there, seems apt. Of course, as the court says, Congress may 'fix the levels of benefits under the Act or the conditions upon which they may be paid'. But once Congress has fixed that level and those conditions, and a worker has contributed his tax in accord with the law, may Congress unilaterally modify the benefits in a way that defeats the expectations of beneficiaries and prospective beneficiaries?" (citations omitted) 404 U.S. at 96, FN. 10.

This view of Justice Marshall, as with that of Justice Black, has not prevailed in later decisions.

While the distinction between social insurance and public assistance programs is unclear and becoming less clear with time, the distinction retains some important theoretical consequences. Thus, in Rastetter v. Wienberger, 379 F.Supp. 170 (D.Ariz.1974), aff'd. 419 U.S. 1098 (1975), the court upheld exclusion of chiropractors from Medicare reimbursement. In part, the chiropractors placed their claim on equal protection grounds because they were eligible for reimbursement under Medicaid. However, the Court pointed out that Medicaid is a broad program of public assist-

ance. Medicare, in contrast, is a program of social insurance which undertakes only sharply restricted medical risks and with limited funding.
Hence, the claim of entitlement was *less* under
Medicare than under Medicaid, a program of public assistance.

Similarly, a distinction between public assistance and social insurance was involved in Geduldig v. Aiello, 417 U.S. 484 (1974). There, California had excluded maternity benefits from its
workmen's compensation disability program. Although this involved discrimination peculiarly relating to women, the Supreme Court upheld the
exclusion of maternity benefits. It did so on the
ground that maternity is an objective condition
and that legislation concerning it was not necessarily invidious or unreasonable. But the Court
also emphasized that the disability coverage was
in addition to existing programs and was funded
solely by employee contributions and that benefits were tied closely to contributions. Thus, the
program reflected certain of the qualities of social insurance and was unlike general public assistance or traditional welfare programs.

Ironically, then, social insurance benefits may
be granted *less* constitutional protection than
public assistance benefits, despite the popular
conception that social insurance is "earned."
More often, however, no distinction is drawn in
constitutional analysis. The distinction remains

important primarily in the ways social insurance programs operate in determining eligibility and setting benefits. Generally speaking, insurance must be earned by past contributions. Once this is done, benefits are paid regardless of need. This pattern is in sharp contrast to public assistance, such as AFDC, and strongly favors the person who qualifies for social insurance. The most significant of such programs is OASDI, paying retirement, survivors, disability and hospital ("Medicare") benefits.

Old age retirement survivors and disability insurance (OASDI) was first created by the old age retirement provisions of the Social Security Act, later supplemented to include survivors and disability benefits. 42 U.S.C. §§ 401–429. Contribution and supervision are provided through payroll regulation by the Internal Revenue Service. 26 U.S.C. §§ 1401–1403, 3101–26. Virtually all workers are covered, including agricultural and domestic employees and those who are self-employed, see 42 U.S.C. § 410(a) and (f), unlike unemployment compensation. Provisions for disability, survivors and dependents were added in 1939 and subsequent years; disability was not covered until 1956.

The growth in social insurance programs is underscored by the number of workers covered. In 1939, the total labor force included some 55,000,000 workers. Of these, less than half, some 27,000,000, were covered by public retirement programs. Thirty years later, as indicated the 1977 Social Security Bulletin, the labor force had increased to 84,000,000, a growth of some 60%. Of these 74,000,000 were covered by public retirement programs, over 90% of the work force. By 1975, the work force totalled 94,900,000 laborers, with coverage extended to 81,000,000. Many of these were also covered by other social insurance programs, such as unemployment insurance, workmen's compensation, and temporary disability insurance.

Over 90% of the people reaching age 65 are eligible for OASDI and 85% of those now over 65 receive such benefits. Still, many are not covered because of chronic unemployment or receive minimum benefits because of poor earnings while employed. Benefits often are at or below the poverty level, despite automatic cost-of-living increases mandated in 1972. In 1975 the average OAI payment was $2,465 for retired workers at a time when the federally-defined poverty level was $2,600. As a result, many OAI recipients also qualify for old age assistance under SSI; indeed, some 70% of those receiving old age assistance also receive OAI. And those under age 72 lose even these limited benefits if they receive income from employment, under excess earnings provisions of § 403(b) of the Act. See generally, 1975 Annual Statistical Supplement, Social Security Bulletin, pages 65–161.

OASDI is modeled after private insurance, but is not wholly self-funding. During the early years, contributions far exceeded payments. But by 1960, some ten billion dollars were paid in against expenditures of nearly eleven billion. Increased retirements and expanded benefits have continued. During the 1970's, there has been a net increase to reserves, however, due to increased payroll deductions. Despite payments of some fifty-five billion, reserves had doubled to forty-six billion by 1974. It is estimated that these reserves will begin diminishing in the late 1970's to about twenty-five billion dollars in 1980 under current provisions and that by the year 2000 payroll deductions will have to be 15% for the system to remain solvent.

The Social Security Act of 1935 covered employees in non-agricultural industry and commerce only. Since 1935, coverage has been extended to additional employment, so that today the old-age, survivors, disability, and health insurance program approaches universal coverage. During a typical week, more than 9 out of 10 persons who work in paid employment or self-employment are covered or eligible for coverage under the program, compared with less than 6 out of 10 when the program began in 1937. Except for special provisions applicable only to a few kinds of work, coverage is on a compulsory basis. Unlike some of the social security systems of other countries, OASDI program covers all kinds of workers whether they are wage earners, salaried, self-employed, farmhands or farm operators, including workers with high earnings. 20 CFR 404 et seq.

The majority of workers excluded from OASDI coverage fall into three major categories: (1) those covered under federal civil-service retirement systems, (2) household workers and farm workers who do not earn enough or work long enough to meet certain minimum requirements (workers in industry and commerce are covered regardless of regularity of employment or amount of earnings), and (3) persons with very low net earnings from self-employment (generally less than $400 a year).

To qualify for cash benefit payments and dependent or survivor benefits, a worker must have demonstrated attachment to the labor force by a specified amount of work in covered employment or self-employment. The amount of covered work required is, generally speaking, related to how long a person could be expected to have worked under the program. In the long run, a person must have worked at least 10 years in covered jobs to qualify for retirement benefits. The period of time a person must have spent in covered work to be insured for benefits is measured in "quarters of coverage." A person paid $50 or more in covered nonfarm wages in a calendar quarter is credited with a quarter of coverage. A person paid $100 or more of covered farm wages in a year is credited with a quarter of coverage for each full $100 of such wages ($400 or more of such wages result in four quarters of coverage).

For most types of benefits, the worker must be "fully insured." In general, a fully-insured person is one who has at least as many quarters of coverage (acquired at any time after 1936) as the number of years elapsing between age 21 and 62 or date of death or disability, whichever occurs first. A worker with 40 quarters of coverage is fully insured for life and needs no further employment to qualify for retirement or survivor benefits. A minimum of six quarters of coverage is required except that workers who reached retirement age or died before 1957 may acquire a "transitional insured status" with three to five quarters of coverage and receive special payments.

If a worker dies before acquiring a fully insured status, survivor benefits may be paid to the surviving spouse with children if the worker was "currently insured." An individual is currently insured with six quarters of coverage within the 13-calendar-quarter period ending with the quarter in which he died. To be insured for disability benefits, a worker must be fully insured and must meet a test of substantial recent covered work. The latter involves having worked in covered employment for at least 5 of the 10 years before the onset of disability. Somewhat more liberal insured status requirements apply to workers who are disabled before age 31 or who are blind.

Retirement benefits may be reduced to a beneficiary who has substantial earnings from work, depending on the amount of the annual earnings. This provision, which is generally called the retirement test, is included in the law to assure that monthly benefits will be paid to those who have substantially retired. This supports the basic purpose of monthly benefits under the program to replace some of the earnings from work that are lost by a worker who retires in old age, becomes disabled, or dies. The retirement test has been liberalized several times by the Congress to keep pace with higher earning levels and increased benefits. At present a beneficiary whose earnings do not exceed $2,100 a year can receive benefits for all twelve months of the year. For earnings above $4,000, one dollar in benefits is withheld for each two of earnings. Benefits are payable, though, regardless of annual earnings, for any month in which the beneficiary earns $334 or less in wages and does not render substantial services in self-employment. Benefits are also payable to beneficiaries beginning with the month when they reach age 72 regardless of their earnings.

OASDI benefits are available to a surviving spouse and children of a wage earner. The spouse receives survivor's benefits if caring for children or if over age 62, as well as a lump sum death payment. The marriage must have taken place at least nine months prior to death, Weinberger v. Salfi, 422 U.S. 749 (1975). In Weinberger v. Wiesenfeld, 420 U.S. 636 (1975), the Supreme Court held that such benefits may not be denied a surviving husband. Such discrimination had been rationalized on the ground that husbands were unlikely to stay home to care for children. But this is not true in all cases and, in any event, such legislation denies to the deceased woman the right to provide benefits for her family. See supra, § 12 and infra, § 24.

Retirement benefits under Social Security vary widely and have increased over time. But some examples at 1976 rates may be stated approximately as follows. A worker who retired at 65 and who earned $1,000 per year would receive $100 per month; $3,000 per year, $225; $6,000 per year, $350; and $10,000 per year, $475. Spouses would receive $50, $110, $170 and $235 for the wage earner indicated. Survivor's benefits would be approximately twice that of the spouse, unless there were dependent children, in which case the maximum family payment would be approximately equal to the combined retirement benefits of the worker and spousal allowances (e. g., at

$1000 per year earnings, $160.)   Precise amounts
vary with the number of children.

After 1974, all monthly benefits (except the
special minimum) have been tied to the cost of
living, as measured by the Consumer Price Index
of the Bureau of Labor Statistics, and are increased (but not more than once a year) by the
same percentage that the index increases if it ris-
es 3 percent or more from the time of last adjustment in benefits.   The increase in benefits is automatic unless Congress has enacted an *ad hoc*
general increase or one becomes effective in the
calendar year before the automatic increase
would otherwise go into effect.

The contribution and benefit base—the maximum amount of a worker's annual earnings on
which he pays contributions and that is creditable
for benefits—will also be subject to future automatic increases.   These increases can go into effect only in a year in which beneftis are automatically increased.   The base increases will assure
that the program continues to provide benefit protection which does not erode as wage levels increase and will help to finance the automatic increases in benefits to reflect increasing prices.

The monthly benefit for dependents and survivors is calculated as a percentage of the insured
person's primary insurance amount (see table 3).
Total family benefits are limited by a fixed maximum amount varying between 150 percent and

188 percent of the worker's primary insurance amount, as appears in a table in the law. The family maximum in 1977 ranges from $171.50 per month to $878.50 per month, the later being payable to a family of three or more on the basis of average monthly earnings of $825. Average earnings this high are possible in 1977 where the worker was relatively young at death.

An extensive system of hearings is established for reviewing claims under OASDI. In part because of this, the Supreme Court in Mathews v. Eldridge, 424 U.S. 319 (1976), held that there was no constitutional right to a hearing *prior* to termination of disability benefits, unlike AFDC benefits, because of the extensive termination process already provided. These include a preliminary state inquiry of the recipient and medical personnel, a notification of probable termination to the recipient with an opportunity to comment, *de novo* review by the Social Security Administration of the proposed decision and continued benefits for two months after the final date of termination, with retroactive reinstatement if the decision is reversed. This lengthy process is deficient in some respects, such as confrontation of witnesses, but it is far superior to that in most welfare programs. See supra, § 13 and infra, § 33.

Disability is a condition which, like old age, is covered under both insurance and assistance programs of the federal government. For those who have worked and qualify for OASDI, there are insurance benefits keyed to past earnings. Others who are disabled from employment qualify for assistance under SSI. The proof of "disability" requirements are essentially the same for both OASDI and SSI. Compare 42 U.S.C. §§ 423(d) and 1382c(a)(3). Until the advent of SSI, Aid to the Disabled was subject to varying state standards. Now that the definitions are essentially similar, disabled workers receiving OASDI may also qualify for SSI. Disability is defined as inability to engage "in any substantial gainful activity," by reason of any "medically determinable physical or mental impairment," expected to last beyond twelve months, and which precludes "any kind of substantial gainful work." See 42 U.S.C. § 1382c(a)(3).

In making a finding concerning disability, the court must find inability to engage in "any substantial gainful activity." This governing standard is difficult to meet. There are four elements of proof. These include medical findings, physician diagnosis, subjective testimony concerning pain and immobility and the claimant's capabilities as evidenced by age, education and work history. DePaepe v. Richardson, 464 F.2d 92 (5th Cir. 1972). Courts tend to uphold the HEW finding of no disability, since only "substantial evidence" is required. See Gentile v. Finch, 423 F.2d 244 (3rd Cir. 1970). However, a demanding scrutiny may be found in some cases, such as Stewart v. Cohen, 309 F.Supp. 949 (E.D. N.Y.1970), particularly where the administrative evidence was speculative; for example, as to whether there might be some job somewhere that the claimant could perform. And experience over the past few years indicates that nearly 50% of decisions finding no disability are ultimately reversed.

Disability payments under OASDI are keyed to the system of quarters needed for retirement benefits. If a wage-earner is disabled before age 24, credit for one and one half years is needed. At age 31 or later, credit for at least half of the preceeding ten years is needed. Payments are available to the spouse and dependents, much as with survivor's benefits under OASDI.

In addition to OASDI, the other major programs of social insurance are unemployment compensation and workmen's compensation. Unemployment compensation involves substantial federal funding and regulation, although it is primarily state-administered, and like other state/federal programs was created by the Social Security Act. It operates through an unemployment tax on employers, returned to states having unemployment programs. See 26 U.S.C. §§ 3301–3311, 42 U.S.C. §§ 501–504, 20 CFR 601.1 et seq. Eligibility and levels of benefits vary widely from state to state. All, however, require substantial past employment and involuntary unemployment for eligibility. This latter requirement has generated considerable litigation concerning strikers. See infra, § 28.

Workmen's compensation is designed to provide an employee with a method of relief from industrial accidents which is both expeditious and unconcerned with the question of fault. The various state programs provide cash benefits and medical care when a worker is injured in connection with his job, and monetary payments to his survivors if he is killed on the job. Unlike unemployment insurance programs, each of the fifty states and Puerto Rico has its own unique Workmen's Compensation program, independent of any federal legislation or administrative responsibility.

No state's laws cover all jobs. Among the most frequent exemptions are domestic service, agricultural employment, and casual labor. However, twenty-seven programs now have some coverage of agricultural workers and eleven programs have some coverage of domestic workers. Many laws also exempt employees of non-profit, charitable, or religious institutions. Some states limit coverage to workers in hazardous occupations, variously defined. Many of these limitations, in varying degrees, also apply to unemployment compensation statutes.

The usual condition for entitlement for workmen's compensation is that the injury or death "arises out of and in the course of employment." Most programs exclude injuries due to the employee's intoxication, willful misconduct, or gross negligence. Although at first virtually limited to injuries or diseases directly traceable to industrial accidents, the scope of the laws has broadened over the years to cover occupational diseases as well.

The benefits provided include periodic cash payments and medical services to the worker during a period of disablement, and death and funeral payments to the worker's survivors. The cash benefits for temporary total disability, permanent total disability, permanent partial disability, and death of a breadwinner are usually calculated as a percentage of weekly earnings at the time of accident or death, most commonly 60, 65 or 66⅔ percent. In some states, the percentage varies with the worker's marital status and the number of dependent children, especially in case of death. All the laws, however, place dollar maximums on the weekly amounts payable to a disabled worker or to survivors, so that many beneficiaries, particularly higher paid workers, do not receive the amount indicated by these percentages. Particularly in a period of rising wages, the lag in enacting statutory increases in the weekly benefit ceiling has undercut the objective of giving an injured worker a benefit equal to a stated percentage of his wage.

This review of the social insurance programs is admittedly superficial. Detailed development of benefits and entitlement is best sought by reviewing the constantly changing regulations and statutes. The overview in this section is intended only to indicate generally the contours of these programs as a counterpoint to the public assistance, cash-grant programs, the subject of the next section.

§ 20. Public Assistance: SSI and AFDC

General Assistance to adults has long been a component of the American welfare scheme. With the adoption of the Social Security Act in the 1930's four categories of aid serving the "worthy poor" became federally-funded. These "categorical" programs included three for adults, Old Age Assistance, Aid to the Blind and Aid to the Permanently and Totally Disabled, and one for children, Aid to Families of Dependent Children (AFDC). Each was state-administered, although largely (70% to 90%) federally-funded, and had multiple layers of legislation and regulations, often generating state-federal conflict. This was—and remains—particularly true of AFDC, the most politically controversial of the categorical programs. See supra, §§ 1–2.

As a result, the adult programs—but not AFDC—were "federalized" by Congress, which created the Supplemental Security Income program, on October 30, 1973, effective January 1, 1974. 42 U.S.C. § 1381 et seq. This became Title XVI of the Social Security Act, the basic provisions of which appear at 42 U.S.C. §§ 301, 1201, and 1351. The Department of Health, Education and Welfare has issued implementing regulations at 20 and 45 CFR. Essentially, SSI means that administration and funding of the adult programs are under the aegis of HEW, with certain optional arrangements which may be effected with the states. The administration of AFDC remains with the states. Perhaps it should be noted here that needy individuals who do not qualify for *any* of the categorical programs may receive General Assistance, which is funded and administered solely by state or local agencies. See supra, § 7.

Eligibility for SSI depends upon being blind, disabled or aged. 42 U.S.C. § 1382. The most difficult definition relates to disability, which must be "by reason of any medically determinable physical or mental impairment" expected to last beyond twelve months or lead to death, and which precludes not only prior employment but also "any other kind of substantial gainful work which exists in the national economy, regardless of whether such work exists in the immediate area." 42 U.S.C. § 1382c(a)(3). Blindness is evidenced by corrected vision of less than 20/200 or having a limited visual field of less than 20 degrees. 42 U.S.C. § 1382c(a)(2). There are certain other exclusions for people in institutions or who are addicted to drugs.

SSI originally provided a guaranteed annual income of $1752 for individuals or $2628 for couples. 42 U.S.C. § 1382(b). These levels of assistance were substantially below most definitions of "poverty", but were augmented by other programs, such as Food Stamps and Medicaid, generally available to the poor. In addition there are other programs designed specifically for the categories represented, such as retirement benefits for the elderly or disability payments for the disabled, although these may act to reduce payments under SSI. The total result is that those qualifying for SSI are—in the main—lifted above the poverty level. This remains true, despite the increasing cost of living, because SSI payment levels have been—and doubtless will continue to be—increased. In 1977, maximum payments were $2,-136.60 for a single person and $3200.40 for a couple, amounts which might be supplemented by state payments.

Qualified people must meet a financial test. SSI initially provided that income may not exceed $1752 for an individual or $2628 for a couple; resources could not exceed $1500 or $2250, respectively. 42 U.S.C. § 1382(a). As with the level of benefits these figures have been increased. Income has the effect of reducing SSI benefits. As with other programs, such as AFDC, Food Stamps and Medicaid, the terms "income" and "resources" exclude certain items and require careful calculation. Among these disregards with income are the earned income and tuition grants of a student and a portion of the unearned and earned income of adults with special provisions if the adult is blind or disabled. 42 U.S.C. § 1382a(b). State assistance based on need may also be excluded, pursuant to agreements between HEW and the states for optional state supplementation.

Resources receive similar specialized definition under SSI. 42 U.S.C. § 1382b. The Act provides for the exclusion of the recipient's home, household goods and other resources or belongings "essential to the means of self-support" in such amounts as HEW might prescribe. Insurance is valued at cash surrender value and excluded from consideration if face value is less than $1500. With these exclusions, it is possible for people to qualify for SSI and yet retain assets or property essential to a decent mode of living.

Initially, all SSI recipients were to be ineligible for Food Stamps. This was then changed to make SSI recipients eligible for Food Stamps if their SSI benefits were less than they would have previously received, totalling the old categorical assistance and the bonus value of the food stamps. This shifting treatment by Congress generated rather extensive, complex litigation, see Irizarry v. Weinberger, 381 F.Supp. 1146 (S. D.N.Y.1974) and California Legislative Council of Older Americans v. Weinberger, 375 F.Supp. 216

(E.D.Calif.1974), but has meant that the vast majority of SSI recipients are also eligible for Food Stamps. Their continuing eligibility must be recomputed, however. 45 CFR 205.25.

The Act also included rather complex provision for Medicaid. A state may choose to have HEW determine eligibility for Medicaid, which would otherwise be state-administered. 42 U.S.C. § 1383c. Further, a state may be required to extend Medicaid coverage to SSI recipients if the state is also required to supplement that person's SSI benefits. Mandatory supplementation is necessary for those states where SSI levels are lower than the benefits the state had been paying prior to SSI under the state's programs of aid to the aged, blind and disabled. This mandatory supplementation insures that SSI recipients will not get less than they did prior to SSI.

In addition to mandatory supplementation, supplementary state payments are optional for any state which wishes to augment the assistance of citizens receiving SSI. 42 U.S.C. § 1382e. Such payments are mandatory only in those states whose pre-existing categorical assistance was *higher* than SSI levels. Those states *must* augment SSI to bring the recipient who were on the rolls up to the level he or she would have received in December of 1973. States can arrange to have HEW administer the supplemental payments along with SSI, with a substantial administrative saving, an option chosen by a majority of states. As to new welfare recipients, supplementation is optional.

The advent of SSI was accompanied by considerable confusion. Additional legislation was necessary as problems arose between 1972 and 1975. Administrative problems have continued beyond that time. Extensive litigation was generated by the various provisions concerning Medicaid, Food Stamps and supplementary payments as states sought to maneuver for economic advantage in the transition. While many of these problems have been resolved with time, administration of SSI remains troubled by the complexity of a national bureaucracy and the coordination with varying state and federal supplementary programs.

Improper denials of benefits have generated extensive litigation concerning SSI. Unlike judicial review of state welfare decisions, federal denials must be first reviewed through an extensive administrative process. See Mathews v. Eldridge, 424 U.S. 319 (1976), discussed supra § 13 and infra § 33. Only after exhausting all administrative remedies may a litigant sue in federal court. 42 U.S.C. § 405(g). These processes may be bypassed if the claimant's challenge is to the constitutionality of a governing federal statute or regulation. See Weinberger v. Salfi, 422 U.S. 749 (1975) and § 37, infra. But in most instances, any challenge will simply be that HEW fact-finding was erroneous. For such cases, exhaustion of administrative remedies is a time-consuming and arduous requirement.

SSI encompasses only the "adult" programs created by the Social Security Act in 1935. The fourth categorical program, Aid to Families with Dependent Children, remains as it was originally, subject to state administration although largely federally funded. This discrimination is consonant with the position of AFDC over the decades. It has consistently been under-funded, controversial and plagued by political attacks flowing from local political responses to the dramatic increases of illegitimate children, non-supporting fathers and unwed mothers receiving AFDC. This has led to various limitations and multiple conditions on eligibility and procedures calculated to impose moral conditions upon those receiving or applying for AFDC. Racism, at least in the South, has also been a factor in state legislation concerning AFDC. See infra, § 31.

The *criteria* of eligibility, however, are established by federal statutes. Under the Supremacy Clause, any state choosing to participate in AFDC must abide by the federal standards of eligibility. In Townsend v. Swank, 404 U.S. 282 (1971), the Supreme Court held that a state could not deny AFDC to students attending college while granting such assistance to students attending vocational schools. The reason was that the definition provisions of AFDC in the federal statutes drew no such distinction. Thus, the state in that case was imposing an *additional* standard of eligibility beyond that authorized by Congress. As such, it was invalid. *Townsend* drew upon the earlier Supreme Court decision in King v. Smith, 392 U.S. 309 (1968), invalidating Alabama's wholesale denial of AFDC to mothers having sexual relations —however transient—with men not their spouses. There, too, the Court held the state regulations, by imposing additional criteria of eligibility, violated the supremacy of the Social Security Act. See supra, § 3.

Aid to Families with Dependent Children (AFDC) has consumed an increasing proportion of the total categorical assistance budget over the years. In 1936 AFDC totalled approximately $50,000,000, compared with $12,000,000 for the blind and $155,000,000 for the aged. By 1950, the figure for AFDC had increased tend fold, as had that for the aged, while aid to the blind had increased only four fold. In that year, the first for Aid to the Disabled, APTD totalled some $8,000,000. By 1960 AFDC had nearly doubled to $994,000,000, while assistance to the aged had increased by only $170,000,000, or some 10%. By 1970, AFDC involved nearly $5,000,000,000, approximately three times the amount of assistance to the aged.

AFDC is created by Title IV of the Social Security Act "for the purpose of encouraging the care of dependent children in their own homes or in the homes of relatives .   .   . to help maintain and strengthen family life and to help such parents or relatives to attain or retain capability for the maximum self-support and personal independence." 42 U.S.C. § 601. It includes aid to the child, a caretaker relative and any other essential member of the household. 42 U.S.C. § 606.

The term "dependent child" is defined by the Social Security Act, 42 U.S.C. § 606(a), as a "needy child" who is either a student or under age 18 and "has been deprived of parental support or care by reason of the death, continued absence from the home, or physical or mental incapacity of a parent." The child must, further, be living in the home of a relative. AFDC, under 42 U.S.C. § 608, may also be extended to a child in a foster home pursuant to a judicial determination.

In Youakim v. Miller, 425 U.S. 231 (1976), the Supreme Court considered provisions of the Social Security Act extending AFDC to children in the home of foster parents (AFDC-FC). This was an expansion of the original bounds of AFDC, which had been limited to children in the care of their natural parents. Illinois, however, had refused AFDC-FC to children in the care of siblings. This meant that the children were entitled to lower benefits, since AFDC-FC paid higher benefits in order to induce provision of care by foster parents. The assumption was that natural relatives would be motivated by the normal instincts of caring for their children.

The Department of Health, Education and Welfare filed a memorandum opposing the Illinois regulation as being inconsistent with the Social Security Act. The Supreme Court remanded and the district court held the Illinois provision to be invalid. There was nothing in the AFDC-FC definitional sections to exclude relatives. Additionally, the 1961 amendments to help foster children did not distinguish among them in terms of whether they were cared for by relatives or by unrelated caretakers. Youakim v. Miller, 431 F. Supp. 40 (D.Ill.1976).

A needy child to qualify for AFDC must be "deprived" of support "by reason" of the death or absence or incapacity of a parent. This applies whether or not the parent was the breadwinner and whether or not the parents were married. 45 CFR 233.90(c). "Absence" exists if it interrupts the parent's "functioning as a provider of maintenance, physical care or guidance for the child" and the duration precludes "counting on the parent's function in planning for the present support or care of the child." If so, the reasons for the absence and its length are immaterial. A state may choose to provide AFDC for children of unemployed fathers who work less than 100 hours per month and are not on strike or have not refused work without good cause. 42 U.S.C. § 607; 45 CFR 233.100.

AFDC requires that the child be "needy and deprived," due to the death or continued absence of *a* parent. 42 U.S.C. § 606. If both parents are present, although unable to provide support, the family will not qualify for AFDC. However, if one parent is in fact continuously absent, the reason is irrelevant. Thus, in Stoddard v. Fisher, 330 F.Supp. 566 (D.Me.1971); the court invalidated a Maine statute granting benefits where an absent father had been drafted, but not where he volunteered for the Army. This was held to be in conflict with the Social Security Act, which only requires the parent to be absent.

Eligibility for AFDC requires that a parent be absent from the home. This absence must be "continued." For AFDC purposes, federal regulations at 45 CFR 233.90(c)(1) state that the definition of continued absence includes absence where its nature is such as "either to interrupt or to terminate the parents functioning as a provider of maintenance, physical care, or guidance for the child, and the known or indefinite duration of the absence precludes counting on the parents performance of his function in planning for the present support or care of the child." Several states have attempted to prescribe a minimum number of days which must pass before an absence will qualify under the federal regulation. Sixty and ninety day periods have been found invalid. See Linnane v. Betit, 331 F.Supp. 868 (D. Vt.1971); Doe v. Hursh, 337 F.Supp. 614 (D. Minn.1970). However, in Smith v. Huecker, 531 F.2d 1355 (6th Cir. 1976) the Court upheld a thirty day period as being an appropriate measure of the parent's continued absence from the home in "*voluntary* absence cases."

The program of AFDC reaches "children." A definitional problem has arisen as to the meaning of that term. It has been argued on behalf of a number of pregnant women that the term "child" should be interpreted to include *unborn* children. This argument was accepted by several lower courts on the basis that AFDC was intended to assist "needy and dependent" children including those who were "deprived." This could include children for whom, prior to birth, a program of pre-natal care would be consistent with the benign objectives of AFDC. Further, HEW had interpreted the Social Security Act since 1941 to allow AFDC funds to be made available to pregnant women. Congress had never rejected this interpretation and had, in fact, rejected amendments which would have excluded unborn children.

In Burns v. Alcala, 420 U.S. 575 (1975), the Supreme Court rejected this analysis. It held that the lower courts had employed an inappropriate standard of interpretation, favoring inclusion unless exclusion was clear. Rather, the Supreme Court said, the rule of interpretation should be the normal one: that entitlement existed only where Congressional intent was clear and specific. That being true, unborn children did not qualify since their inclusion was, at best, ambiguous in Congressional history. Further, the Social Security Act's references to children in other contexts implied children "in being," not those as yet unborn. And the purpose of AFDC, to support children in the home rather than elsewhere, implied that financial assistance would be appropriate only where the child had already been born.

In Burns v. Alcala, the Supreme Court specifically avoided passing on any constitutional issues posed by the exclusion of unborn children from AFDC. It remanded to the district court for consideration of those issues. That court rejected the constitutional claims and was sustained by the Court of Appeals in Burns v. Alcala, 545 F.2d 1101 (8th Cir. 1976). In the Court of Appeals, the pregnant women argued that they were being denied equal protection. A woman who had no children but who was pregnant for the first time would be denied AFDC. In contrast, a woman who already had children and was again pregnant would be granted AFDC.

The Court of Appeals rejected this argument. It found that no fundamental rights were involved, since the discrimination would not affect interests in privacy or procreation. Therefore, only a rational basis was required to sustain the discrimination. That rational basis was found in the Congressional purposes underlying AFDC, which were to support children, not women. Further, the Court noted, the state and Congress both provide pre-natal and maternity care programs other than AFDC. Thus, the impact of any discrimination was attenuated at best.

Other eligibility aspects of AFDC are dealt with separately infra, §§ 23–28. These relate primarily to standards of financial need which—unlike SSI—are left for state determination. States have attempted, in varying ways, to convert financial standards into moral conditions by imputing assets or income to AFDC recipients because of their relationship to men or because of their presumed capacity to work. This mode of "deeming" assets is better treated separately, as an aspect of determining need, and so will not be discussed here. However, one further dimension of AFDC eligibility does warrant attention at this point: the requirement of the absent parent.

The AFDC requirement that a parent be absent from the home has long been controversial. Its purpose, as the Supreme Court noted in King v. Smith, 392 U.S. 309 (1968), is to encourage fathers to work and to provide assistance only when the "breadwinner" is absent. But commentators have argued that it also encourages fathers to leave home or not to return in order to assure continued assistance. To this extent, AFDC is a disincentive to family unity but has been held constitutional. See Henry v. Betit, 323 F.Supp. 418 (D.Alaska 1971). In response, in 1961 Congress created AFDC-UF, an optional program for states to support families where *both* parents are present and unemployed. 42 U.S.C. § 607(a).

For the first time, by the optional AFDC-UF program, Congress has dealt with the issue of eligibility of an unemployed, yet perhaps employable, adult. Several contrasting requirements of eligibility were imposed. A strong connection with the work force was required, so that benefits would be available under 42 U.S.C. § 607(b)(1)(C) only if the child's father had not been employed for at least thirty days, had not "without good cause" declined employment and had six or more quarters of work in any thirteen calendar quarters or was qualified to receive unemployment compensation within one year prior to application for aid. These provisions assured that AFDC-UF would be only a temporary or limited program, reaching those whose connection with the work force was substantial and whose separation was such that a family experienced a substantial loss of income.

A state which chooses to participate may define the eligibility of applicants within the limits prescribed by Congress. In Philbrook v. Glodgett, 421 U.S. 707 (1975), the plaintiffs challenged Vermont's definition because it denied AFDC-UF to a family in which the unemployed father was *eligible* to receive—but not receiving—unemployment compensation. The Court held that this interpretation conflicted with the Social Security Act, which in 1968 had been amended by Congress so that *actual* receipt of unemployment compensation, not mere eligibility, was required. 42 U.S.C. § 607(b)(2)(C). The state argued that such a reading was contrary to the general principle of considering all income which might be *available* to a family. But while mere availability was relevant in determining whether there was a connection to the work force, under § 607(b)(1)(C), the Court held that actual *receipt* was required under § 607(b)(2)(C).

The result of the holding in Philbrook v. Glodgett was that a recipient might decline unemployment compensation in order to qualify for higher benefits under AFDC-UF. This option has been foreclosed by subsequent Congressional amendments to the program. As a consequence, eligibility under AFDC-UF not only requires a substantial connection to the work force but also requires that one not be eligible for unemployment compensation. The impact of this is to narrow significantly the number of people eligible, since most people with a "substantial connection to the work force" will qualify for unemployment compensation. Only a few will not so qualify, and only those few will be eligible for AFDC-UF.

The requirement in 42 U.S.C. § 607(b), that the father be unemployed, also specified that he must not have refused an offer of employment without good cause. A number of states interpreted this to exclude strikers, an interpretation permitted by HEW regulations. 45 CFR 233.-100(a)(1). The Supreme Court upheld this view in Batterton v. Francis, 432 U.S. 416 (1977), reversing decisions by lower courts. The Court's reasoning was that Congress had specifically instructed HEW to promulgate regulations on the subject, implying an intent to permit state latitude and that HEW had so acted. Further, the discrimination against strikers was a rational choice which would further policies concerning labor disputes. See infra, § 28.

AFDC-UF is an attempt to meet a major deficiency in the definitional provisions of AFDC. Another deficiency concerns non-recurring emergency needs. As with AFDC-UF, Congress has created an optional program, Emergency Assistance, which states may choose to offer in connection with other federally-funded programs. "Emergency Assistance" is defined by the Social Security Act, 42 U.S.C. § 606(e)(1) to mean aid not exceeding thirty days in any twelve-month period, to a child who qualifies for AFDC. The aid may be "money payments, payments in-kind, or such other payments as the state agency may specify." A child qualifies who:

> " . . . is without available resources (and) the payments, care, or services involved are necessary to avoid destitution of such child or to provide living arrangements . . ."

Eligibility for Emergency Assistance is not limited to AFDC recipients. Nor is it limited to those receiving public assistance of other forms. Rather, Emergency Assistance under § 606(e) is available for anyone under age 21 who is faced with "destitution". The statute does require that the needy child be living with relatives specified in 42 U.S.C. § 606(a). In addition to destitution, the funds may be available to provide living arrangements in a home. The need may not have arisen because the child or relatives refused without good cause to accept training or employment. Emergency Assistance thus reaches a broad group of people normally relegated to General Assistance (see supra, § 7) as well as those receiving AFDC.

As with other programs supported by federal funds, a cooperating state must comply with federal requirements. In Mandley v. Trainor, 523 F.2d 415 (7th Cir. 1975), the State of Illinois chose to participate in the Emergency Assistance program. However, it limited eligibility to those who were receiving AFDC, and provided that Emergency Assistance would be available only for certain specified needs, such as rent due to prevent eviction or monies necessary to restore utility service or other urgent items of basic need, such as moving costs. The court held that the state provisions were void. The Supreme Court reversed, *sub nom.* Quern v. Mandley, 46 L.W. 4594 (1978), on the ground that Congress had intended to leave latitude to the states, but the Court remanded for further proceedings, thereby leaving unresolved the full range of that latitude. Problems of state non-conformity thus left open, see supra, §§ 3–5, are substantial.

Emergency Assistance was also involved in the case of Lynch v. Philbrook, 550 F.2d 793 (2d Cir. 1977). The plaintiffs there were denied Emergency Assistance by the Vermont Department of Welfare. One of the plaintiffs had emergency needs because her welfare check had been stolen. Another had to replace a broken refrigerator. The State Department of Welfare had denied benefits because an AFDC recipient would be eligible for Emergency Assistance only when necessitated by one of four factors: death of a spouse or child, eviction, a disaster such as that involving flood or fire, or "an emergency medical need." A family *not* receiving AFDC was not limited to these causes. The Court rejected the distinction. It held that Emergency Assistance, although optional with the states, requires the states to abide by federal definition requirements and that Congressional intent was to assist all children, whether or not their families were receiving AFDC. Although Vermont was complying with this mandate, it was extending only reduced benefits to AFDC families.

Emergency Assistance limitations were similarly held invalid in Bacon v. Toia, 437 F.Supp. 1371 (S.D.N.Y.1977), where New York automatically denied Emergency Assistance payments in the form of cash to families eligible to receive AFDC and in all cases of "loss, theft or mismanagement of a public assistance grant" and in all cases when the Emergency Assistance was sought to replace or duplicate a "recurring public assistance grant." In *Bacon* each of the plaintiffs had been denied Emergency Assistance although their AFDC or items purchased with AFDC had been stolen or lost. The court held that the denial of cash assistance to AFDC recipients was contrary to the purpose of § 606(e), which was designed to cover, at a minimum, all AFDC recipients. The court similarly invalidated the automatic denial where the emergency circumstances resulted from loss or theft of the public assistance grant on the ground that this was an invalid restriction as to the type of emergency for which assistance was provided under § 606(e). The court did not, however, comment on the denial of emergency assistance in cases of mismanagement.

Another aspect of the New York limitations on Emergency Assistance was involved in Davis v. Smith, 431 F.Supp. 1206 (S.D.N.Y.1977). There, the challenge was to the New York practice of denying emergency assistance where the recipient was facing a termination of utility service. The state afforded advances on subsequent payments, from which the advance would be recouped, denying emergency assistance. The court held that this violated 42 U.S.C. § 606(e), funding Emergency Assistance without regard to the source of the emergency. The status of the opinions in *Davis, Lynch* and Bacon v. Toia is unclear in the light of the remand in Quern v. Mandley, and important issues concerning state/federal relations in AFDC and Emergency Assistance therefore remain unresolved.

This brief review of SSI and AFDC is intended only as an introduction to the basic elements of the programs. Particularly with respect to AFDC, an extensive body of constitutional law has developed concerning additional criteria of eligibility. These relate not only to financial need but also to issues concerning residency, illegitimacy, sex and morality. Because such concepts are not limited to SSI or AFDC, but relate broadly to many programs affecting the poor—including social insurance, Food Stamps and Medicaid—they are treated separately in the next sections.

IV. ELIGIBILITY

§ 21. Residency and Alienage

Historically, welfare has been viewed as a local matter. The Elizabethan Poor Laws incorporated the principle of settlement and limited a community's liability to supporting only the poor who properly belonged there. Others could be forced to return to their place of settlement. And much welfare litigation in the United States during the 1800's was between communities seeking to shift the cost of supporting the poor among themselves according to the principle of settlement. In City of New York v. Miln, 36 U.S. 102 (1837), the Supreme Court upheld New York City's ban on poor immigrants, saying that a community could regulate and exclude the poor like any other plague or pestilence. See supra, §§ 1–2, 7.

These tenets of the Elizabethan Poor Laws ran counter to fundamental policies which emerged during the 1930's. The legislative policy reflected in the Social Security Act was that poverty and public assistance were national concerns. At least for the poor included in the categories of assistance created by the Social Security Act, local assistance was no longer the primary source of welfare. Although benefits might vary from one state to another, the basic entitlement to categorical assistance under the Social Security Act became a matter of national right. This was in direct response to the nationwide economic chaos created by the Great Depression of the 1930's, which generated a national crisis of poverty transcending state bounds.

In Edwards v. California, 314 U.S. 160 (1941), the Supreme Court invalidated California's law punishing anyone who assisted a person without employment coming from another state. The Court noted that the localizing principles of the Elizabethan Poor Laws no longer comported with the reality of a national poverty problem. California could not zone out the poor or zone in its wealth. See supra, § 2.

Despite the holding of *Edwards,* the majority of states imposed "residency" requirements of a durational nature, requiring that a person be in a state for at least a year before qualifying for welfare. In AFDC, this was given some support by the Social Security Act, which banned such requirements only if they exceeded a year's duration. 42 U.S.C. § 602(b). The validity of durational residency requirements came before the United States Supreme Court in Shapiro v. Thompson, 394 U.S. 618 (1969). Several of the plaintiffs had moved to states in order to live with relatives and, upon arrival, found that public assistance was necessary. One of the plaintiffs had been a patient at St. Elizabeth's Hospital in the District of Columbia since 1941 and, upon her release, had applied for public assistance. Another had been a long time resident of Pennsylvania and had moved to South Carolina to care for a relative and then returned to Pennsylvania, where she applied for public assistance. Each of the plaintiffs had been denied welfare under a durational residency requirement of one year.

The Court held that this denied equal protection of the laws under the Fourteenth Amendment. Justice Brennan, writing for the majority, noted that durational residency requirements or waiting periods created two classes of otherwise identical individuals. It was necessary, therefore, for a state to justify the discrimination. The Court began by noting that the most obvious justification was to avoid supporting people from other parts of the country. The history of that justification flowed from the Elizabethan Poor Laws and, in fact, the means chosen were precisely tailored to the objective. But the Court held that exclusion of those who travel interstate was a constitutionally impermissible objective, since it penalized the constitutionally protected right to travel.

Another justification was to deter those who had come specifically to obtain higher welfare benefits. As to this, the Court noted that the means was *not* precisely tailored to the objective. In effect, the one year waiting period irrebuttably presumed that *all* had come for the higher welfare benefits. In fact, this was not true. In any event, moving interstate to improve one's position was a constitutionally protected exercise of the right to travel. A person could move for improved welfare benefits just as he or she might seek improved schools or parks.

The Court also rejected the claimed justification that states wished to reward their citizens for past contributions to the welfare of the state. For example, long-term residents oftentimes have paid taxes or contributed to the political life of a state. Residency requirements, it was argued, rewarded them. The Court rejected this rationale because, in fact, residency requirements might work to the detriment of some long-term residents who had left for a short time. Further, this rationale would limit public services to those who had paid taxes. As with schools and parks, this was impermissible with welfare.

The states asserted that budget predictability was enhanced by residency requirements. In fact, however, budget planning was not undertaken and was not feasible as to in-state residents for the same reasons that it was not feasible as to out-of-state residents. Nor was a waiting period necessary administratively to establish residence. Other more detailed criteria were available for that purpose, in the Court's view. This was equally true of the states' desire to avoid fraud. Other means could serve far better than a one-year waiting period. As to fraud, such a durational requirement was overly broad, since many of the people who would be penalized by it would not be engaged in fraud.

Significantly, the court in Shapiro v. Thompson subjected the durational residency requirements to a searching, *strict* scrutiny far beyond that traditionally undertaken in equal protection cases. The reason was that the discrimination affected a *fundamental* right: that of travel. Consequently, the states were required—and failed— to assert a *compelling* state interest. This would have to meet a four part test: that the objectives were not constitutionally impermissible, that the legislation was not over or under inclusive, that there were no alternatives and that the asserted objectives were, in fact, pursued and implemented. This "strict scrutiny" test is discussed supra, § 11, and as is noted there, its continuing vitality is limited. See also, § 12 supra.

Justice Harlan's dissenting criticisms of the strict scrutiny test in Shapiro v. Thompson have proven to be well taken. The requirement of a compelling state interest to justify discrimination founded upon suspect criteria has proven difficult to apply. The issue of what constitutes suspect criteria remains unclear. Sex and illegitimacy, for example, have been most troublesome. Age also poses problems. See infra, §§ 22–24. In these instances legislation discriminates against people on factors beyond their control, as with race, but it is at least arguable that, unlike racial discrimination, these factors may have some consequences or aspects which may reasonably be reached by legislation.

Similar questions remain with respect to defining "fundamental" rights. The Supreme Court held in Shapiro v. Thompson that the right to travel qualifies. But in Wyman v. James, 400 U. S. 309 (1971) the Supreme Court held that a welfare recipient could be required to submit to home visits as a condition of receiving public assistance, even though the plaintiff maintained that this was an abrogation of her rights under the Fourth Amendment. Similarly, in Maher v. Roe, 432 U.S. 464 (1977)., the Supreme Court held that a state might deny funds for elective abortions, while providing funds for therapeutic abortions and full-term delivery, despite the plaintiffs' argument that this penalized the right of privacy which had been held in Roe v. Wade, 410 U.S. 113 (1973) to include the right to obtain an abortion. These and other dimensions of the *Shapiro* strict scrutiny test are discussed supra, §§ 9–12 and will not be further explored here. The remaining discussion in this section will be directed towards the continuing vitality of residency requirements.

Waiting periods for residency purposes were invalidated in *Shapiro* because of their impact upon the right to travel. The recipients had argued that the right to travel was infringed but argued at the same time that no state need fear an influx of travelers seeking higher benefits. The dissent noted this inconsistency: if few wanted to travel, how could it be said the right was infringed? Essentially, the question raised was whether a burden *in fact* was required to be shown in challenging a residency requirement. In Memorial Hospital v. Maricopa County, 415 U.S. 250 (1974), the Supreme Court addressed this question by noting that the right to travel might be jeopardized either by deterring its exercise or by putting a price or penalty on it. Either way, such a condition was impermissible, absent a compelling state interest. And in Dunn v. Blumstein, 405 U.S. 330 (1972), invalidating a residency requirement for voting, the Court stated that requiring a showing of deterrence in fact was a "fundamental misunderstanding of the law" and that:

> "Shapiro did not rest upon a finding that denial of welfare actually deterred travel. Nor have other 'right to travel' cases in this court always relied on the presence of actual deterrence. In Shapiro we explicitly stated that the compelling state interest test would be triggered by 'any classification which serves to penalize the . . . right to travel.'" 405 U.S. at 339–340.

A legitimate waiting period to *establish* residency might have been permissible, as the Court suggested in Dunn v. Blumstein, concerning the right to vote, or in Vlandis v. Kline, 412 U.S. 441 (1973), concerning non-resident university tuition rates. But one year was an unnecessarily long presumption of non-residency, since—in that period of time—people usually do decide to become residents and election or college officials are easily able to enroll them. In *Vlandis*, the Court invalidated the waiting period on the basis that it irrebuttably presumed that a person was not a resident for a full year. Since this was inaccurate, factually, the Supreme Court held the waiting period requirement denied due process.

Significantly, in *Vlandis* the Court commented that education is unlike welfare in the sense of not involving the basic necessities of life. Hence, greater latitude would be available to a state in limiting benefits to residents. Similarly, in Sosna v. Iowa, 419 U.S. 393 (1975), the Supreme Court upheld Iowa's law restricting divorces to people who had been residents for one year. The majority emphasized that divorce is a matter of peculiarly local law, as evidenced by the practice until the early 1800's of requiring separate legislative action on each divorce. This local emphasis may be said, too, of welfare. But the Court distinguished Shapiro v. Thompson on the ground that the asserted justification there had been fiscal; in *Sosna,* the justification was the state's overriding interest in marriage, family and divorce.

The implications of *Sosna* for welfare are unclear, but the case does represent a clear holding that one year waiting periods are permissible as a requisite for residency. The context in *Sosna*, of course, was divorce, which involves controversial matters of social policy. Arguably, welfare is quite different since it involves matters of economic necessity for the recipients, has largely been nationalized by the Social Security Act, and the remaining local interests are chiefly financial or administrative. But *Sosna* and *Shapiro* do leave open questions of whether one year waiting periods could be imposed on purely local programs, such as General Assistance. There, the *Sosna* rationale of "locality" would seem strongest, invoking the vestiges of the Elizabethan Poor Laws. Similarly, waiting periods remain a possibility with in-kind programs, such as housing, which are in short supply. See supra, §§ 1–3, 7.

Some guidance is provided by the Supreme Court decision in Memorial Hospital v. Maricopa County, 415 U.S. 250 (1974). There, Arizona required that a person be a resident for at least one year in order to qualify for services in a county public hospital. The plaintiff had moved to Maricopa County from New Mexico and, one month later, suffered a respiratory attack. The County refused medical services.

The issue in Memorial Hospital was significantly different from that in *Shapiro*. *Shapiro* had involved simply cash grant assistance. *Memorial Hospital* involved, in contrast, assistance related to capital expenditures to develop in-kind, limited physical facilities. Justice Rehnquist argued in dissent that such programs lacked the flexibility of cash grant assistance. Further, because they were locally generated there was a legitimate interest in giving preference to local residents who might look to the programs they had supported for the services created. Finally, Justice Rehnquist noted that Arizona did create an exception to the waiting period for Emergency Assistance. Hence, the imposition was less than that in Shapiro v. Thompson.

The Court specifically rejected these rationales, which had only been marginally involved in *Shapiro*. The Court rejected the argument that a county program should be limited to county residents as an inducement to them to support the program. This "contributory rationale" was overly broad and the benefits were not tailored to the contributions. In addition, a political motivation to encourage residents to pay taxes was constitutionally impermissible since "a State may not employ an invidious discrimination to sustain the political viability of its programs." 415 U.S. at 256. The Court drew no distinction between the cash grant program involved in *Shapiro* and the in-kind program in *Memorial Hospital*; for both, a one-year durational residency requirement was invalid.

Shapiro left open the question of whether *legitimate* residency requirements may be imposed. In *Memorial Hospital*, the majority noted that such requirements are permissible, although they would impede movement to some extent.

It is the right to settle, not the right of movement, which was protected by the Constitution. Thus, a state might legitimately limit public assistance to those who are bona fide residents. Defining this, however, might be troublesome. Residence usually implies physical presence for a minimum period of time. This may be different from domicile, which implies an intent to remain permanently. Whether a state could also require that latter intent as a condition of eligibility for public assistance is therefore a difficult question. It would seem that a state could at least require physical presence coupled with intent to remain or with actual presence for a minimum period of time, somewhere between thirty and ninety days. Such requirements are permissible for administrative processing of applications to vote. Administrative needs might justify such a time period in qualifying a person to receive welfare, since some time would be necessary to conduct an investigation to detect fraud.

The trend of development from *Shapiro* through *Memorial Hospital* to *Sosna* suggests certain considerations concerning durational residency requirements. First, the threshold issue concerning their validity turns upon the nature of the individual right asserted. The right to travel is clearly constitutionally mandated, but employment and divorce are of less obvious footing. Secondly, the extent to which the right is infringed may vary with the facts of a particular case. The right to travel was denied in a final sense by the residency requirements in *Shapiro*. But in *Sosna*, there was no *final* denial since after one year the plaintiff would become eligible to seek a divorce. Thirdly, the state rationale to justify the durational waiting period may become stronger as one moves from strictly budgetary or financial considerations towards policy or value judgments, which, at bottom, were what distinguished *Sosna*. Their consideration may not, however, preserve the county waiting periods which are characteristic of the General Assistance, despite its history of being of traditionally local concern.

In Hawk v. Fenner, 396 F.Supp. 1 (D.S.D. 1975), the court held that a state may constitutionally impose upon applicants a waiting period or residency requirement based upon the following "compelling state interests":

> "(1) A legitimate need to establish bona fide good faith residence of the applicant in the state and in the county, (2) a valid interest in preventing fraud by the applicant, whether a newcomer or a long-time resident and

(3) an effective safeguard against the hazard of double payments by two jurisdictions." 396 F.Supp. at 8.

The court further relied on Shapiro v. Thompson for the proposition that "the constitutional right to travel includes not only interstate but intrastate travel as well". 396 F.Supp. at 4. See also King v. New Rochelle Housing Authority, 442 F. 2d 646, 647 (2nd Cir. 1971) and Cole v. Housing Authority of Newport, 435 F.2d 807, 809 (1st Cir. 1970).

Residency requirements do, in fact, operate now in some areas of public assistance. States need not provide benefits to transients. The thirty day delay often following AFDC applications before benefits begin tends to assure that only residents will qualify. Some major programs, such as workmen's compensation or unemployment compensation, by definition are limited to those who have contributed in the past and who will usually be residents. Housing programs, by maintaining waiting lists in order of application, tend to favor residents. While some programs of general or emergency assistance do reach transients, experience indicates that they often must rely upon private charities.

Residency requirements are also frequently mandated as conditions of employment by state or municipal agencies. In McCarthy v. Philadelphia Civil Service Commission, 424 U.S. 645

(1976), the Supreme Court upheld residency requirements against a challenge that they denied equal protection of the laws. There may be a number of reasons for such rules. Among these are the belief that local residents are more likely to understand local problems and the expectation that taxes and expenditures of employees residing in a municipality will contribute to the support of that municipality. See Cook County College Teachers Union v. Taylor, 432 F.Supp. 270 (N.D. Ill.1977).

A distinction has been drawn in the employment area between initial residency requirements and those relating to continuing residency. In Mogle v. Sevier County School District, 540 F.2d 478, 483 (8th Cir. 1976) the Court upheld a school board's requirement that a teacher move into and live in the school board's geographical area. It noted that durational residency requirements were reviewed in *Shapiro, Dunn,* and *Memorial Hospital* under the compelling state interest test, but concluded that "continuing residency requirements" are instead subjected to the less stringent standard generally applied in equal protection cases. The Court referred to McCarthy v. Philadelphia Civil Service Commission, supra, as differentiating "between a requirement of continuing residency and a requirement of prior residency of a given duration." Further, the Court concluded that imposing a residency requirement for employees did not create a presumption that they were incompetent if they lived outside the affected geographic area. Rather, the requirements simply reflected a local legislative judgment that local residency would enhance effectiveness of employees.

To some extent, the controversy concerning residency requirements has become a moot issue. Although *Shapiro* suggests some ways for maintaining or instituting such requirements, those avenues are not administratively feasible. Further, HEW has promulgated regulations barring any residency requirement which denies benefits to anyone who is an actual resident, although not meeting a fixed requirement of a particular waiting period. Also, the developments in other areas of public assistance have been significant. The federally funded program of Emergency Assistance under 42 U.S.C. § 606(e) of the Social Security Act reduces the importance of residency, as does the nationalization, under SSI, of the adult categories of aid to the aged, blind and disabled. Finally, the slow development and spread of increasingly adequate levels of benefits among many states has reduced the likelihood of mass migrations—if it ever existed—for better benefits.

Residence requirements, however, continue to be a subject of litigation. In Gautier-Torres v. Mathews, 426 F.Supp. 1106 (D.P.R.1977), a recipient of disability benefits under SSI challenged the provision which limited benefits to people living in the 50 states or the District of Columbia. The plaintiff had been a resident of Connecticut when he qualified for disability payments, but the payments were discontinued when he moved to Puerto Rico. The court sustained his challenge. It held that Congress might legitimately deny SSI benefits to residents of Puerto Rico but, in this case, the plaintiff had been a resident of the United States and terminating his assistance would be a penalty on his right to travel. No compelling state interest had been shown, as required by *Shapiro*. But, cf., Flemming v. Nestor, discussed supra, §§ 1, 8 & 10.

Another recent decision concerning residence and alienage is Nyquist v. Mauclet, 432 U.S. 1 (1977). There, the State of New York provided financial assistance to students in the form of scholarships, tuition grants and loans. Aliens were excluded, however, unless they were intending to apply for citizenship. The two plaintiffs had no such intent although they had been residents of New York for a number of years. The Supreme Court invalidated the New York legislation. It noted that alienage is a suspect criterion and that legislation concerning it required a compelling state interest. The Court found no such interest. The most obvious objective of the legislation was to conserve state funds, but this may not be done at the expense of constitutional rights.   A secondary objective would be to encourage citizenship, but the Court held this was an impermissible objective, since immigration and naturalization are matters of pre-eminently federal concern.

The decision in *Nyquist* related to discrimination against aliens, a legislative concern of long standing, particularly in property and employment legislation.   In welfare cases, it seems clear that a state may not deny assistance to an otherwise eligible person because he or she is an alien. In Graham v. Richardson, 403 U.S. 365 (1971), the Supreme Court invalidated Arizona's requirement that an alien wait fifteen years before qualifying for welfare.   The Court relied upon *Shapiro* but also, as in *Nyquist*, held that the Arizona law affected immigration and naturalization in a way which collided with the supremacy of federal control over aliens.   See supra, § 3.

In summary, *Shapiro* would leave states free to impose limited genuine residency requirements. But these could not be defined in terms of time periods beyond those reasonably necessary to determine eligibility, perhaps thirty to sixty days. The time would have to be roughly comparable to that imposed in determining eligibility for in-state residents.   And this would be true of both state and local programs.   The Elizabethan Poor Law concept of local welfare for local residents has little, if any, remaining vitality.

§ 22. Illegitimacy

Illegitimacy is rarely a factor in welfare for determining either the level of benefits or eligibility for assistance. Indeed, AFDC provides assistance to thousands of children born out of wedlock. Denying assistance to such children would be imposing a condition of eligibility over which they have no control, with the only possible rationale being that of "punishing" or deterring their parents' sexual relations.

In King v. Smith, 392 U.S. 309 (1968), such a rationale was rejected. There, the Alabama welfare department promulgated "man-in-the-house" rules and terminated AFDC to mothers having illicit sexual relations. The Supreme Court held this violated the Social Security Act and that punishing the children for parental misconduct was impermissible. Alabama was obligated to continue assistance, although it could arrange an alternative placement of children if the existing home was unfit. The Court's holding was, however, based on statutory—not constitutional— grounds. See supra, § 3 and infra, § 25.

In New Jersey Welfare Rights v. Cahill, 411 U. S. 619 (1973), the United States Supreme Court upheld a constitutional challenge to New Jersey's state-funded program of General Assistance to families "which consist of a household composed of two adults of the opposite sex ceremonially married to each other who have at least one minor child . . . of both, the natural child of one and adopted by the other, or a child adopted by both . . . " The program was thus limited to people who were married and had legitimate children. It excluded those who were involved in an extra-legal relationship. It also excluded illegitimate children and those who bore them and declined to legitimize them. The federal district court had upheld the stattuory scheme on the ground that it was designed "to establish, protect and strengthen family life." 349 F.Supp. 491, 496 (N.J.1972).

The Supreme Court rejected the New Jersey scheme. It referred to earlier cases which had invalidated discrimination against children who were illegitimate: Weber v. Aetna Casualty & Surety Co., 406 U.S. 164 (1972); Levy v. Louisiana, 391 U.S. 68 (1968); and Gomez v. Perez, 409 U.S. 535 (1973). In a *per curiam* opinion, the court said:

> "Those decisions compel the conclusion that appellants' claim of the denial of equal protection must be sustained, for there can be no doubt that the benefits extended under the challenged program are as indispensable to the health and well being of illegitimate children as to those who are legitimate." 411 U.S. at 621.

Significantly, in New Jersey Welfare Rights v. Cahill, the Supreme Court did not refer to King v.

Smith. That case had held that a state could not
terminate assistance to children where the parents were engaged in sexual misconduct. However, King v. Smith had rested its holding on specific provisions of the Social Security Act. To
have relied upon King v. Smith in *Cahill* would
have elevated those statutory provisions to a constitutional level. The consequence would have
been, to some extent, to prohibit a state from
seeking to discourage immorality and encourage
ceremonial marriage as a constitutional matter.
These objectives remain open to the states but,
after the decision in *Cahill*, the means and alternatives available for achieving the objectives are
far from clear.

Justice Rehnquist dissented in New Jersey W.
R. O. v. Cahill on the ground that the New Jersey
legislation did not discriminate between children,
as such, but instead provided grants to classes of
"families as units." Whatever denial of benefits
the classification made was imposed "equally on
the parents as well as the children." Justice
Rehnquist argued:

> "It does not seem to me irrational in esta-
> blishing such a special program to condition
> the receipt of such grants on the sort of cer-
> emonial marriage that could quite reasonably
> be found to be an essential ingredient of the
> family unit that the New Jersey legislature
> is trying to protect from dissolution due to

the economic vicissitudes of modern life. The Constitution does not require that special financial assistance designed by the legislature to help poor families be extended to 'communes' as well." 411 U.S. at 622.

Illegitimacy is not, then, a proper basis for denying welfare, which—after all—is intended to help the "needy" without regard to circumstances of birth. But illegitimacy has been upheld as a factor in social insurance. To some extent, this may be because social insurance is akin to privately purchased pension programs normally supporting those in the worker's immediate family, as to whom there is a legal obligation of support. See supra, § 19. Thus in Mathews v. Lucas, 427 U.S. 495 (1976), the Supreme Court upheld a requirement of the Social Security Act that survivors be "dependents" of a deceased wage-earner, and that *proof* of dependency be required only of children who are illegitimate. The children were unable to offer the necessary proof and claimed that such discrimination was unconstitutional. The Supreme Court upheld the Act, on the basis that illegitimacy—unlike race—is not a "suspect criterion" requiring extraordinary constitutional protection and that the rebuttable presumption was rationally related to the probability of dependency at death. The Court thus declined to invoke the "strict scrutiny" approach of Shapiro v. Thompson, preferring to require only the minimal rationality required by traditional equal protection analysis under Dandridge v. Williams. See supra, §§ 10–12.

The Court commented in *Lucas* that:

"[T]he legal status of illegitimacy, however defined, is, like race or national origin, a characteristic determined by causes not within the control of the illegitimate individual, and it bears no relation to an individual's ability to participate and contribute to society." 427 U.S. at 505.

Still, the Court observed that while classifications based upon such criteria may be irrational, all such classifications are not "inherently untenable." Moreover:

". . . . while the law has long placed the illegitimate child in an inferior position relative to the legitimate in certain circumstances, particularly in regard to obligations of support or other aspects of family law . . . perhaps in part because the roots of the discrimination rest in the conduct of the parents rather than the child, and perhaps in part because illegitimacy does not carry an obvious badge, as race or sex do, this discrimination against illegitimates has never approached the severity or pervasiveness of the legal and political discrimination against women and Negroes." 427 U.S. at 505–506.

The Court therefore adhered to its earlier views, that discrimination between individuals on the basis of their legitimacy does not "command extraordinary protection from the majoritarian political process . . . which our most exacting scrutiny would entail". 427 U.S. at 506.

However, these excerpts from *Labine* and *Lucas* must be considered against the background and holding in the Supreme Court decision in Weber v. Aetna Casualty and Surety Company, 406 U.S. 164 (1972). There, illegitimate children sued to recover benefits under Louisiana's workmen's compensation laws, seeking to be placed "on an equal footing" with dependent legitimate children. The Court upheld the claim, on the authority of Levy v. Louisiana, 391 U.S. 68 (1968), in which a Louisiana statute barring an illegitimate child from recovering for the wrongful death of a mother had been invalidated. The Court had said in *Levy:*

> "Legitimacy or illegitimacy of birth has no relation to the nature of the wrong allegedly inflicted upon the mother. These children, though illegitimate, were dependent on her; she cared for them and nurtured them; they were indeed hers in the biological and the spiritual sense; in her death they suffered wrong in the sense that any dependent would." 391 U.S. at 72.

Thus *Weber* and *Levy* clearly indicate that some forms of discrimination against illegitimates are invalid, although—in the light of *Lucas*—not all.

In *Weber*, it seems that the Court was employing a "middle-range" style of equal protection analysis. It did not specifically denominate illegitimacy as a "suspect criterion" under the *Shapiro* framework for strict scrutiny analysis. Rather, the Court referred to traditional equal protection cases, such as Williamson v. Lee Optical Corp., but then imposed a stricter standard, phrased as follows:

> "Though the latitude given state economic and social regulation is necessarily broad, when state statutory classifications approach sensitive and fundamental personal rights, this court exercises a *stricter scrutiny* (emphasis supplied)."

The Court then added:

> "The essential inquiry in all the foregoing cases is, however, inevitably a dual one: what legitimate state interest does the classification promote? What fundamental personal rights might the classification endanger?" 406 U.S. at 172–173.

As Justice Rehnquist observed in dissent, this phraseology was neither the traditional equal protection standard nor the strict scrutiny standard of Shapiro v. Thompson. Justice Rehnquist commented:

> "The Court in today's opinion, recognizing that two different standards have been applied in equal protection cases, apparently formulates a hybrid standard which is the basis of decision here." 406 U.S. at 181.

Thus the status of illegitimacy remains unclear after *Lucas* and *Weber*. It does not qualify as a "suspect criterion" invoking the "strict scrutiny" of Shapiro v. Thompson; yet it does qualify as warranting more than minimal, traditional scrutiny. In the illegitimacy cases, it would seem, the Supreme Court has created a third, "hybrid" standard of equal protection analysis. See supra, §§ 10–12.

One further decision perhaps should be noted. In Norton v. Mathews, 427 U.S. 524 (1976), the plaintiff challenged denial of death benefits under the Social Security Act to illegitimate children. The Act provided that a legitimate child automatically qualified as "dependent." But an illegitimate child would be required to show proof. The hearing examiner found that the claimant was in fact the son of the deceased wage earner, but held that benefits should be denied because he was not living with his father at the time of the father's death. The District Court held that this was valid. 364 F.Supp. 1117 (D.Conn.1973). Although it said that there was no constitutional right to social welfare and that "strict scrutiny does not apply to welfare legislation," nevertheless it commented that "it would appear this case calls for the application of the new rational basis approach. Weber v. Aetna Casualty Co. . . . ." 364 F.Supp. at 1122.

Under the appropriate standard, the court found that the Social Security Act provision was valid. It distinguished Gomez v. Perez, 409 U.S. 535 (1973) where Texas law had denied any obligation of support between a father and an illegitimate child on the basis that there Texas law had denied all entitlement, whereas the provisions in Norton v. Mathews simply required that illegitimates *prove* entitlement. The court's conclusion was that "plaintiff's problem—and the underlying reason for his failure to qualify—is that the child's insurance benefits provisions of the Social Security Act were never intended to cover Gregory Norton or the class he represents." 364 F.Supp. at 1129.

The decision in *Norton* was vacated and remanded by the Supreme Court for reconsideration in the light of Jimenez v. Weinberger, 417 U.S. 628 (1974). In *Jimenez*, illegitimate children who were born after their father became disabled were denied benefits under the Social Security Act, although benefits were available to their older illegitimate sister who had been born prior to the onset of the father's disability. The Supreme Court invalidated the discrimination. On remand in *Norton*, the District Court held that unlike the plaintiffs in *Jimenez*, "Norton was denied benefits because, in fact, he never was dependent and because Congress never intended to aid Norton's class of nondependents." 390 F. Supp. 1084, 1088 (D.Md.1975). This subsequent decision was affirmed by the Supreme Court on the strength of Mathews v. Lucas, supra.

After the Supreme Court decisions in *Jimenez*, *Weber* and *Levy*, it would appear that legislation which denies benefits solely because of illegitimacy would violate the Constitution. However, given *Lucas* and *Norton*, illegitimacy may be a basis for imposing burdens of proof where the *fact* of illegitimacy permits an inference concerning *other* facts which themselves may be the basis for denying benefits. Thus, in Mathews v. Lucas, it was the fact of dependency which determined whether benefits should be accorded; the fact of illegitimacy was deemed sufficiently related to dependency to require that an illegitimate child prove dependency. In contrast, in the field of sex discrimination, the fact of sex does not permit an inference of dependency; hence, a burden of proof concerning dependency cannot be imposed on women where it is not equally imposed upon men. See infra, § 24.

The result is that illegitimacy may pose an obstacle in obtaining benefits. But it will be chiefly a problem of procedure and operate primarily in programs of social insurance, not public assistance. And even in social insurance, imposing a barrier on illegitimates requires more of a justification than is traditionally required in equal protection analysis, although less than that required in a context warranting "strict scrutiny."

§ 23. Age

Discrimination on the basis of age is commonplace in a wide spectrum of public assistance programs. Entire programs, such as housing for the elderly or Aid to Families with Dependent Children, are directed towards segments of the population defined by age. Even within programs reaching the general population, certain aspects may be keyed to age. This is true, for example, with OASDI, the program of social insurance commonly known as "Social Security," where attaining age 65 may entitle one to retirement benefits or attaining age 18 may terminate one's survivor's benefits.

In these areas, the legislatures make broad judgments about the scope of benefits and risks. Conflicting judgments may often arise, however, and may be subject to judicial scrutiny. Thus, in Martinez v. Trainor, 556 F.2d 818 (7th Cir. 1977), a district court judgment was upheld invalidating an Illinois provision which denied AFDC to mothers who were under the age of 21. The district court rested its opinion upon the conflict between this provision and the provisions of

the Social Security Act, which did not limit the
age of eligible mothers. In Lund v. Affleck, 388
F.Supp. 137 (R.I.1975), the district court similarly invalidated a Rhode Island provision that limited AFDC to mothers or caretaker relatives above
the age of 18. Although the grandmother of a
child might apply, the court rejected this as being
in conflict with the Social Security Act, since

> "the thrust of the policy is to pressure minor
> mothers to live in the household of a related
> adult who in the Department's view would be
> a more responsible and emotionally stable
> person. Such position finds no support in
> the statute nor can it be logically analogized
> from controlling decisional law." 388 F.
> Supp. at 141.

Most often, age discrimination challenges have
been based on the ground that the discrimination
involves federal funds but is not authorized by
the Social Security Act. See Townsend v. Swank,
404 U.S. 282 (1971), supra § 3. But a challenge
may also be based on constitutional grounds.
Such a challenge lies in those cases where age is
used to discriminate among potential beneficiaries who are otherwise identical. Most often, age
is used as a rough gauge of self-sufficiency, so
that the very young and very old may properly
be distinguished from the rest of the population.
But when lines are drawn on the basis of age
among the very young or among the very old, the

rationale becomes harder to find. This arbitrariness then becomes the basis of a challenge under the Equal Protection Clause. Two examples will illustrate this.

In Burns v. Alcala, 420 U.S. 575 (1975), the plaintiffs challenged denial of AFDC to pregnant women on the basis that it discriminated, *inter alia,* against the unborn child. Unborn children, the argument went, were surely as needy and "dependent" as other children who *were* receiving AFDC. Several lower courts had sustained this argument on the basis that Congress, in defining "child", had intended to include those as yet unborn, Carver v. Hooker, 501 F.2d 1244 (1st Cir. 1974), and at least one court had held that denial of benefits would constitute a denial of equal protection. The Supreme Court rejected the statutory argument and remanded the Constitutional argument, which was ultimately rejected in the lower court. But the Supreme Court has yet to rule on this issue. See supra, § 20.

Another case, Mazer v. Weinberger 385 F.Supp. 1321 (E.D.Pa.1974), involved a challenge by the elderly to those provisions of Social Security old age insurance which limit a recipient's right to earn income until he or she is 72. The plaintiffs argued that this chilled their "right to work" and favored those recipients below 72 who could receive unlimited income through investments, without any justification in public policy. The court rejected the argument.

Significantly, in these cases, the courts required only minimum rationality to justify the age discrimination. As with sex and illegitimacy, courts have not applied a strict scrutiny to age discrimination and, as a consequence, are usually able to sustain the legislation under challenge. Yet this may be changing. Increasing public awareness of the problems and potential of the young and old may generate a change in judicial and legislative attitudes. That this is already happening is evidenced by recent Congressional legislation banning age discrimination in employment. Congressional concern for the elderly is also manifested by its federalization of Aid to the Aged through SSI and by its continuing expansion of Old Age Insurance.

The Supreme Court's developing concern for age discrimination is evidenced by In re Gault, 387 U.S. 1 (1967), holding that juveniles charged with crimes may not be denied constitutional guarantees, such as counsel and cross examination, simply because they are processed in Juvenile Court. Similarly, in Stanton v. Stanton, 421 U.S. 7 (1975) and Craig v. Boren, 429 U.S. 190 (1976), the Supreme Court invalidated state legislation discriminating between boys and girls as to age of maturity and the age at which beer might be purchased. These latter cases, as with

Alcala, raise age discrimination in a context which also involves other important interests, such as sex discrimination or the right to procreate, and it is therefore difficult to isolate the degree of importance attached by the Court to age discrimination *per se*.

Age discrimination was explicitly dealt with by the Supreme Court in Massachusetts Board of Retirement v. Murgia, 427 U.S. 307 (1976), where the Court upheld a Massachusetts law requiring state police officers to retire at age 50. The plaintiff had argued that the statute denied equal protection of the laws and was subject to strict scrutiny under Shapiro v. Thompson on the ground that it involved a "suspect criterion." The Court rejected this. Further, the Court added that the right to governmental employment *per se* is not "fundamental." In the light of this, the Court upheld the statute on the ground that it rationally furthered legitimate purposes of the state in assuring "physical preparedness of its uniformed police." There had been no showing that the statute had the effect of "excluding from service so few officers who are in fact unqualified as to render age 50 a criterion wholly unrelated to the objective of the statute." The Court added:

> "While the treatment of the aged in this nation has not been wholly free of discrimination, such persons, unlike say, those who

have been discriminated against on the basis of race or national origin, have not experienced a 'history of purposeful unequal treatment' or been subjected to unique disabilities on the basis of stereotyped characteristics not truly indicative of their abilities." 427 U.S. at 313.

Age discrimination has been upheld in other employment contexts than those where physical fitness, as with police, is a prerequisite. In Klain v. Pennsylvania State University, 434 F.Supp. 571 (M.D.Pa.1977), the court held that mandatory retirement at age 65 for faculty members did not violate the Constitution. It reached this result although the plaintiff had offered ample proof of competence. The Court commented:

"It is sufficient that the mandatory retirement policy serves to make future personnel needs somewhat predictable, creates employment and promotion opportunities for younger employees, helps to allocate personnel to areas of need, and presents a recognized policy of retirement which treats each employee impartially and which affords him sufficient notice to enable him to prepare for retirement. The fact that the policy may in certain instances result in seemingly harsh decisions, oblivious to individual capabilities, needs and demands, does not alter the fact that all employees are treated equally and fairly." 434 F.Supp. at 579.

Perhaps future treatment of age discrimination in welfare programs is best suggested by Morales v. Minter, 393 F.Supp. 88 (D.Mass.1975). Massachusetts denied General Relief, which was wholly state-funded, to the young (under 18) and the old (over 65) alike. The original rationale had been that these groups were eligible for federally funded programs, such as AFDC and SSI. This, however, was untrue as to many under 18 and those over 65 who usually had to wait a few months after applying for SSI before actually receiving SSI benefits. The court declared that the exclusions were therefore irrational and created false presumptions, violating both the due process and equal protection guarantees of the Constitution.

It may be that courts will view age discrimination differently depending upon the context. Discrimination against juveniles, as in *Gault*, is oftentimes invidious while discrimination against the elderly may simply represent program or benefit limitations rather than the deprivation of rights. Too, discrimination against the elderly will often not involve other important dimensions, such as sex classifications or procreation, which subject discrimination against the young to rigorous scrutiny.

§ 24. Sex

Sex discrimination is a pervasive dimension of the American welfare system. That system historically has made certain simplistic assumptions concerning sex roles: men work and women rear children. Thus unemployment compensation and AFDC-UF are directed towards men; AFDC and survivors benefits are directed towards women. Workmen's compensation did not contemplate maternity coverage; AFDC did not contemplate a man in the house. This discrimination is suspect not only because these stereotypes are outdated but also because they imply a relative inferiority in the role assigned to women. Nowhere is this better illustrated than in the levels of income and benefits available to men and women.

Table 11 of the 1975 Annual Statistical Supplement, Social Security Bulletin, reflects trends in poverty among families by sex, age and work experience of the head of the family. Perhaps the most significant trend is that concerning female-headed families. In 1959 they constituted 23% of all poor families. *By 1975 they represented* 44.6%. Thus, nearly half of poor families are headed by women. Since the majority of families in the United States are headed by men, with female-headed families being in the minority, this means that a female-headed family has a substantially greater likelihood of being poor.

Yet the levels of benefits available to women are measurably less than those available to men. The reason is that men typically qualify for SSI, workmen's compensation or unemployment compensation. Women are disproportionately dependent upon AFDC, which historically has been funded at a lesser percentage of need than other welfare categories. See 1975 Annual Statistical Supplement, supra. The inferior status of women imposed by relegating them to a disfavored program of welfare is further extended to those women who qualify for social insurance through employment.

The number of recipients of monthly benefits under OASDI is reflected in Table 54 of the Annual Statistical Supplement. In 1975, there were thirteen million workers receiving retirement benefits. Of these seven million were women. The average benefit for men was $225 per month, for women $181 per month. 1,750,000 workers were receiving disability payments. Of these, some 600,000 were women. The average benefits were $240 per month for men, $185 per month for women. Survivors benefits, averaging $195 per month, were paid to 3,600,000 widows and nearly 500,000 families with children and a widowed mother.

OASDI mirrors the job market and therefore discriminates against women. Over the past decade, the earnings of women have typically been 60% of male earnings. Those women receive lower benefits upon retirement. It is also true, of course, that many women are never employed outside the home and therefore receive benefits only as survivors or dependents of male wage earners. There are, in addition, limitations on how old a woman must be, or how long married, in order to qualify for dependent or survivor benefits and these limitations operate in a manner discriminatory against women. See Weinberger v. Salfi, 422 U.S. 749 (1975). Significantly, women often can receive higher benefits as dependents than through their own records of earnings, creating a disincentive to employment.

Sex discrimination in the welfare area is nowhere more apparent than in legislation involving childbirth and pregnancy. The Supreme Court has held that childbirth expenses may be excluded from state-supported programs of disability insurance, Geduldig v. Aiello, 417 U.S. 484 (1974), as well as from privately funded programs for employees, General Electric v. Gilbert, 429 U.S. 125 (1977). In addition, the Supreme Court has upheld state Medicaid legislation which funded only childbirth expenses and therapeutic abortions while denying benefits for elective abortions. Beal v. Doe, 432 U.S. 438 (1977), Maher v. Roe, 432 U.S. 464 (1977). In these cases, the exclusions concerned only those medical expenses peculiarly important to women. The exclusion was upheld in *Geduldig* on the basis that the program was contributory and of limited scope financially and maternity benefits would have increased the cost to participants by approximately one third. The exclusion in *Maher* was upheld on essentially public policy grounds permitting states to choose funding live births rather than abortions. See supra, § 17. Whatever the rationale, the impact of discrimination in the medical benefits field is peculiarly felt by women.

Sex as a basis for social legislation has received increasingly rigorous scrutiny, however, by the courts. *Geduldig* and *Gilbert* arguably dealt with secondary aspects of sex; *Beal* and *Maher* dealt with obligations affirmatively to assist women. These are distinguishable from cases where statutes categorically or invidiously discriminate against women by denying them benefits. In such cases, courts have had little difficulty in finding denials of equal protection or due process of laws. For example, invidious discrimination against women was invalidated in Reed v. Reed, 404 U.S. 71 (1971). There, women were disfavored for consideration to administer estates. The Supreme Court held that this was sex discrimination of an invidious sort and without rational justification. Similar discrimination against men was invalidated in Stanley v. Illinois, 405 U.S. 645 (1972), where state law disqualified unmarried men from consideration as guardians of their own children. In both cases, the Supreme Court voided the exclusions as creating irrebuttable presumptions of incompetency not founded upon fact. See supra, § 12.

But none of these cases dealt with welfare. Frontiero v. Richardson, 411 U.S. 677 (1973) approached the welfare area. There, the armed services provided allowances for dependents of men. A service woman would receive an allowance only if she could demonstrate that her dependent male spouse required at least half of her income for his support. This further requirement, discriminating against women, was held to be invalid on the authority of the earlier decisions in *Reed* and *Stanley*.

Frontiero is particularly significant because it raised the question of whether sex discrimination against women involved a "suspect criterion" under the test of Shapiro v. Thompson. See supra, § 11. If so, the strict scrutiny requirement of *Shapiro* would operate and only a compelling state interest could justify discrimination. Only a plurality of the Court held that sex was a suspect criterion, and that issue remains open. Sex, like other suspect criteria such as race, is a condition of birth. There is no way to control it. But, unlike race, sex does have important physiological consequences. Only women can become pregnant and bear children. It is this feature of sex that has attracted legislative attention in the welfare area.

A case illustrating this is Geduldig v. Aiello, supra. The plaintiffs challenged a California disability insurance program which did not pay maternity benefits. The State of California maintained it simply insured against disability risks covered by the program and that the exclusion of this particular disability, maternity, was reasonable because the program involved was in addition to other programs and was tied closely to funding through employee deductions. The Court upheld the exclusion of maternity benefits. It said:

> "There is no evidence in the record that the selection of risks insured by the program worked to discriminate against any definable group or class in terms of the aggregate risk protection deprived by that group or class from the program. There is no risk from which men are protected and women are not. Likewise, there is no risk from which women are protected and men are not." 417 U.S. at 496–497.

The Court in *Geduldig*, at footnote 20, distinguished *Reed* and *Frontiero* on the ground that pregnancy is an objective condition and may be the subject of legislation so long as there is no discriminatory intent. Thus, realistically viewed, the Court holding in *Geduldig* was that any sex discrimination was secondary, although present. It may well have been that a different result would follow if women had been altogether excluded from the program. As it was, the Court emphasized that although women contributed only 28 percent of the total contributions to the program, they received 38 percent of the benefits.

417 U.S. at fn. 21. The Court also emphasized that the program in *Geduldig* was contributory, with benefits closely tied to earnings, unlike public assistance.

Perhaps only two cases have been decided by the Supreme Court concerning sex discrimination in a conventional welfare context. The first of these, Weinberger v. Wiesenfeld, 420 U.S. 636 (1975), invalidated a provision in OASDI which granted survivors benefits to a widow caring for children but denied them to a widower who was left to care for his children. The Court analogized this to the *Frontiero* case, saying that the legislation assumed that a woman would be dependent but that a man would not. While this is sometimes true, the Court said:

> " . . . such a gender-based generalization cannot suffice to justify the denigration of the efforts of women who do work and whose earnings do contribute significantly to their families' support." 420 U.S. at 645.

This focus by the Court was thus on the right of the deceased female wage-earner to provide support for her surviving male spouse. This discrimination, the Court said, " . . . deprives women of protection for their families which men receive as a result of their employment." 420 U. S. at 645.

The holding in *Wiesenfeld* invalidated legislation not because it related to sex but because it made certain assumptions about sex. Factual assumptions may deny due process if they infringe upon important rights or sensitive areas. See supra, § 12. Thus in Cleveland Board of Education v. LaFleur, 414 U.S. 632 (1974), the Supreme Court held that a city could not impose a rigid maternity leave policy which, in effect, presumed all women teachers to be incompetent by the third month of pregnancy. So also, the traditional sex stereotypes of women as dependent and not as wage earners were rejected in *Frontiero* and *Wiesenfeld*.

Significantly, there were no dissents in *Wiesenfeld*. However, four justices dissented in the later case of Califano v. Goldfarb, 430 U.S. 199 (1977). In *Goldfarb*, the legislation being challenged was again that providing for survivors benefits under OASDI. Survivors benefits were available to a male only if he was receiving one half of his support from the deceased female wage earner. There was no such requirement for a female survivor. As in *Wiesenfeld*, the court invalidated this provision on the ground that it discriminated against female wage earners. The focus was thus on the deceased wage earner and not on the survivors. As to the latter, of course, the discrimination favored women.

The Court observed that it may well be true that surviving men are less needy more often than surviving women. However, such arguments had been advanced in *Wiesenfeld* and rejected as involving " . . . old notions . . . such as assumptions as to dependency . . . that are more consistent with the role-typing society has long imposed . . . than with contemporary reality . . ." 430 U.S. at 207. In any event, Congress had chosen not present need but past dependency as a basis for disqualifying men. Hence there was no rational basis for the discrimination and it was invidious as to the deceased female wage earners.

The dissenting Justices argued that sex discrimination in welfare contexts should be treated differently from that in other areas, such as those involved in Stanley v. Illinois or Reed v. Reed, supra. Welfare, they argued, necessarily involves piecemeal extension of coverage and benefits. Further, because of the large numbers of people and dollars involved, it is necessary to balance administrative convenience and the desire to treat people individually. Such considerations would justify an assumption that men can support themselves better, more often and are less needy than women. Moreover, the dissents emphasized that the interests involved in OASDI are non-contractual benefits; hence, the deceased wage earner had a lesser interest in them.

The decisions in *Wiesenfeld* and *Goldfarb* represent a substantial rejection of sex discrimination in the welfare context. They are puzzling however, in their rationale. They do not represent a view that sex is a "suspect criterion" in the sense of Shapiro v. Thompson, imposing strict scrutiny on the governmental interests advanced as supporting a legislation challenge. Nevertheless, in the two cases the Court did *in fact* impose strict scrutiny. The legislation was held to be over-inclusive, under-inclusive and defective because better alternatives were available. These are the reasons usually advanced under a strict scrutiny test for invalidating legislation. Yet, the equal protection strict scrutiny analysis of Shapiro v. Thompson was not triggered, simply because the Court refused to hold that sex is a suspect criterion.

Also, particularly in *Goldfarb,* the Court looked at the real motivations and rationale of Congress. It ascribed to Congress "old notions" that are "more consistent with the role-typing society has long imposed . . . than with contemporary reality." Justice Stevens concurred specially on the ground that administrative convenience might be a legitimate basis for excluding men from survivor's benefits but *in fact* that was not the real reason. Rather, Stevens emphasized that the real reason was use of a traditional way of thinking about women as dependent and about men as non-dependent. Similarly, in *Wiesenfeld,* the majority emphasized that the legislation discriminating against women wage earners providing for male survivors was based upon old fashioned assumptions to the effect that women are *not* wage earners and male survivors do *not* care for their children.

This examination into the precise motives of Congress goes far beyond the analysis permitted by traditional equal protection and due process cases. See supra, § 10. Indeed, it is in addition to the analysis customarily found even in strict scrutiny cases. See supra, § 11. So viewed, *Wiesenfeld* and *Goldfarb* can be seen to have involved a most demanding form of strict scrutiny without having answered the perplexing question of whether sex is a suspect criterion within the meaning of Shapiro v. Thompson. In this sense, a middle range theory of equal protection may be seen to have evolved for treating sex discrimination, akin to that involved with age and illegitimacy. Craig v. Boren, 429 U.S. 190 (1976). See Weber v. Aetna Casualty & Surety Co., 406 U.S. 164 (1972), discussed supra, § 22.

Any analysis of sex discrimination in welfare encounters three significant obstacles. The first has already been noted and was involved in *Geduldig, Gilbert* and *Maher*: pregnancy is a condition peculiar to women yet of independent social significance and legislation concerning maternity is often—tenuously—defended as therefore not invidious. Two other factors should be noted, however. First, the status of being a woman has historically been the subject of well-intentioned, albeit misguided, discrimination. And, secondly, much welfare legislation insures the *dependence* of women not because it *assumes* them to be dependent but because it needs them to be dependent in order to care for young children.

Historically much of sex discrimination in social legislation was intended to protect women. This was the case with laws limiting their employment, upheld in Goesaert v. Cleary, 335 U.S. 464 (1948). Present federal legislation may bar such distinctions. But in areas beyond such legislation, it is not clear what the Constitution permits. For example, in Kahn v. Shevin, 416 U.S. 351 (1974), Florida legislation was upheld although it allowed tax preferences for widows, but not widowers. The Court specifically noted that sex was an offensive criterion for equal protection purposes only when discrimination was invidious. But the dissents accurately observed that the issue was not the propriety of affording benefits to women; it was the propriety of denying benefits to men. While they might often need assistance less, the statute raised this probability to an absolute rule.

Affirmative discrimination also received tacit approval in Weinberger v. Wiesenfeld, supra. There the Court invalidated a portion of the Social Security Act denying survivors benefits to men and limiting them to widows. In so doing, the Court distinguished *Kahn*, on the specific ground that the discrimination there *favored* women. In contrast, in *Wiesenfeld*, the discrimination denied to the working woman the right to create survivors benefits for her husband. Thus *benign* discrimination may be constitutionally permissible. But what is "benign" is hardly clear: in earlier times it meant excluding women from certain forms of employment. And in *Wiesenfeld*, it meant creating a statutory preference for widows which was held to deny fairness to working women.

There is a basic tension and internal conflict in seeking to analyze welfare problems in terms of sex discrimination. In contexts such as employment, sex discrimination operates upon only one person, either by inclusion or exclusion. If a man is hired, a woman is not; the reverse is also true. However, in a welfare context the discrimination may also affect the *dependents* of the primary figure and, oftentimes, the dependents are intended as the primary beneficiary of the program. In Weinberger v. Wiesenfeld and Califano v. Goldfarb, surviving males were being denied benefits available to surviving females. In a sense, this was discrimination in favor of women. As such, it might be analyzed in an approving manner as in the Supreme Court decision in Kahn v. Shevin. But it also represented discrimination *against* women, by its impact upon the deceased female wage earners who were being denied the opportunity to generate benefits for their dependents.

It is the welfare system's concern with *dependency* which makes sex a difficult concept for analytical purposes. If welfare is to relieve dependency it must, by reason of pervasive sexual role patterns and discrimination in our society, be directed chiefly towards women. This is reflected in the definitional sections of the categorical assistance programs adopted in the 1930's through the Social Security Act. In those programs, as well as in the social insurance programs, Congress contemplated a male wage earner. Survivors and widow's benefits were directed towards women and often were legislative afterthoughts. This is best reflected by the AFDC program, directed towards dependent children whose *father* had become absent. In the 1960's, Congress provided that AFDC might be available to a family where both parents were present, but only if the *father* had recently become unemployed.

Thus many welfare programs involve a curious form of sex discrimination. They are directed towards relieving dependency, a condition peculiar to women either because of their dependency on men or because of their roles as homemakers or both. But to the extent that benefits are conferred upon *only* those who are dependent, dependency is *pro tanto* reinforced and perhaps institutionalized. Incentives for women wage earners are not found in the welfare system. Because of pervasive sex discrimination in private enterprise, opportunities of economic independence are lacking in employment. To the extent that this remains true in the future, there is little reward for women who work, and the continuance of welfare benefits for dependent women tends to support economic sex discrimination rather than force an end to it.

This raises, in an indirect fashion, the role of welfare work programs in sex discrimination. They are characteristically attached to AFDC, which primarily affects women. This, in itself, is a form of sex discrimination. Yet if the programs succeed in ending dependence upon welfare, the discrimination may be benign. An evaluation of these programs is undertaken infra, § 28.

§ 25. Moral Fitness and Men in the House

Welfare programs have long been concerned with "fitness". The "worthy poor" were the first beneficiaries of public assistance under the Elizabethan Poor Laws. They continued to be the beneficiaries under the Social Security Act, which provided categorical assistance on behalf of the aged, the blind, the disabled, and dependent children. The last category has involved elaborate legislative efforts directed towards sexual misconduct which might produce dependent children, and has generated most of the controversy concerning morality in welfare.

Under the Social Security Act, a number of states attempted to regulate the sexual conduct of AFDC mothers. So-called "suitable home" provisions were imposed, terminating AFDC if the AFDC mother was found to be having sexual relations with a man. Suitable home provisions came under attack during the 1940's. The criticisms were that they forced destitute mothers into increased immorality as a means of earning money and that they were habitually used to disguise systematic racial discrimination. Moreover, they punished impoverished children on the basis of their mother's behavior, while inconsistently permitting them to remain in the alleged unsuitable homes. In 1945 the predecessor of HEW produced a state letter arguing against suitable home provisions. Fifteen states abolished these provisions during the next decade.

In 1960 Louisiana enacted legislation specifying that any home in which an illegitimate child had been born subsequent to the receipt of public assistance would be considered "unsuitable." During the summer, 23,000 children were dropped from Louisiana's AFDC roles. The Secretary of HEW issued what became known as the "Flemming Ruling" providing in essence that:

> "A state plan . . . may not impose an
> eligibility condition that would deny assist-

ance with respect to a needy child on the basis that the home conditions in which the child lives are unsuitable, while the child continues to reside in the home."

Congress approved the Flemming Ruling. 42 U.S.C. § 604(b). Congress also provided that AFDC could be paid on behalf of children placed in foster homes or child care institutions. 42 U.S.C. § 608. State plans are now required to provide for a rehabilitative program of improving and correcting unsuitable homes. 42 U.S.C. § 602(a).

The propriety of suitable home requirements was litigated in King v. Smith, 392 U.S. 309 (1968). There, Alabama had denied assistance to an AFDC mother who was visited periodically by a man who himself had nine children and who contributed nothing to the financial well being of the AFDC recipient's home. Nevertheless, Alabama terminated assistance. The adoption of the regulation under which Alabama acted led to a reduction in AFDC rolls of some 20%, terminating assistance to 16,000 children.

The Supreme Court held that this conflicted with the Social Security Act. Alabama argued that the termination of assistance would tend to discourage immorality and to treat married and unmarried households alike. The Court held that discouraging immorality could not, consistent with the Social Security Act, be achieved at the expense of the children. And the male visitor could not be treated like a ceremonial married husband, since he was not obligated under Alabama law to support the children of the woman he was visiting. In treating him as a "parent" under the Social Security Act, Alabama was misconstruing Congressional intent, which had contemplated a "breadwinner," not an occasional visitor to the home. The conflict was resolved in favor of the federal government, under the Supremacy Clause. See supra, § 3.

The Court in King v. Smith, after summarizing the history reflected above, commented that:

> "In sum, Congress has determined that immorality and illegitimacy should be dealt with through rehabilitative measures rather than measures that punish dependent children and that protection of such children is the paramount goal of AFDC . . . it is simply inconceivable, as HEW has recognized, that Alabama is free to discourage immorality and illegitimacy by the device of absolute disqualification of needy children." 392 U.S. at 325–326.

The Court noted that Alabama's argument based on immorality at one time would have been "quite relevant." It observed:

> "A significant characteristic of public welfare programs during the last half of the 19th Century in this country was their pref-

erence for the "worthy" poor. Some poor persons were thought worthy of public assistance, and others were thought unworthy because of their supposed incapacity for "moral regeneration" . . . this worthy concept characterized the mothers' pension welfare programs which were the precursors of AFDC . . . [which] were customarily restricted to widows who were considered morally fit." 392 U.S. at 320–321.

Alabama argued that the substitute father regulation was justified as a means of treating married couples and unmarried couples alike:

"[S]ince in Alabama the needy children of needy couples are not eligible for AFDC aid so long as their father is in the home, it is only fair that children of a mother who cohabits with a man not her husband and not their father be treated similarly." 392 U.S. at 327.

The Court rejected this argument. It noted that the man who was "cohabiting" had no legal obligation of support. Thus, he was in quite a different position from the lawfully married husband. The Court reviewed Congressional history behind the Social Security Act and concluded that Congress intended to terminate assistance only when there was a "breadwinner" in the home. This would be a man who was either contributing to the support of the home or legally obligated to do

so. The Court noted that this interpretation of
parent, to mean the person legally obligated to
support the children, was consistent with other
provisions of the Social Security Act requiring
mothers to report the identity of the absent parent and requiring states to locate any parent
against whom a support petition had been filed.

King v. Smith was decided on statutory
grounds. Justice Douglas, concurring, would
have decided the case on constitutional grounds
and found a denial of equal protection of the
law. However, under traditional equal protection analysis, a state could legitimately seek to
discourage immorality and to encourage ceremonially married relationships. With these objectives conceded, the state would be free to choose
any means it desired. It is, therefore, not clear
that man-in-the-house rules, such as those employed by Alabama, would fail under a constitutional analysis. Perhaps the most significant argument would be that a state could not seek to
advance its interests in discouraging parental immorality at the expense of children who have little or no control over parental misconduct.

In King v. Smith, the Court held that Alabama's
regulation conflicted with Congressional policy which favored rehabilitation as a means of
dealing with illegitimacy. It also permitted terminating assistance only where the "man in the
house" had a legal obligation of support. In a

sense, Alabama had been presuming the presence of income or assets which, *in fact,* were not there. In that sense, although the Court did not so rule, the legislation was void as constituting a presumption contrary to fact and violating the Due Process Clause, see supra, § 12. But on another level, Alabama was simply making a moral judgment and creating inducements toward moral behavior. So viewed, as an inducement to future conduct, the Alabama legislation might well survive an equal protection challenge, despite Justice Douglas' concurring opinion. Significantly, the case was decided on statutory grounds, avoiding these conceptual difficulties.

Following King v. Smith, the Department of Health, Education and Welfare adopted a regulation governing men in the house. 45 CFR 233.-90(a). That regulation provided that a state could consider only the income of a natural or adoptive parent or of a step-parent:

> ". . . who is ceremonially married to a child's natural or adoptive parent and is legally obligated to support the child under state law of general applicability which requires stepparents to support stepchildren to the same extent that natural or adoptive parents are required to support their children."

The regulation further provided that the inclusion in the family or the presence in the home of a "substitute parent" or "man in the house" or any other individual would not be an acceptable basis for a finding of ineligibility or "for assuming the availability of income by the state". Finally, the regulation mandated that in considering income or resources for financial eligibility:

> "[O]nly such net income as is actually available for current use on a regular basis will be considered and the income only of the parent described in the first sentence of this paragraph will be considered available for children in the household in absence of proof of actual contributions."

The validity of this regulation was tested in Lewis v. Martin, 397 U.S. 552 (1970). There, California had provided that the income of a man assuming the role of spouse ("MARS") would be considered in computing AFDC benefits whether or not that income was actually used or available. The MARS was defined as a male who regularly made his place of abode with the woman receiving the AFDC benefits and who appeared or held himself out to be regularly assuming the role of spouse. California maintained that the HEW regulation was unauthorized and invalid.

The Supreme Court held otherwise. It repeated the finding from King v. Smith that Congress had intended AFDC to be paid if a parent were absent. By "parent" Congress meant a breadwinner. The presence of a MARS did not meet that definition. The Court said that King v. Smith had

". . . held only that a legal obligation
to support was a necessary condition for
qualification as a "parent"; it did not also
suggest that it would always be a sufficient
condition." 397 U.S. at 559.

Therefore, California could assume that income
would be available only as to a natural or adoptive parent. It could not make such assumptions
with respect to a non-adopting step-father. Nor
could it make any assumption concerning the income of a MARS "whatever the nature of his obligation to support." However, of course, the
state was free to count as income any actual contributions by any person.

Although Lewis v. Martin upheld the HEW
regulation counting income of natural parents, it
is clear that income may not be counted unless it
is "actually available." An absent parent who
chooses not to support children cannot thereby reduce benefits. See, e. g., Buchanan v. Essex
County Welfare Board, 272 A.2d 768 (N.J.Super.
1971). The court there invalidated a county
practice of reducing benefits by the amount of
court-ordered support payments. In each instance, the reality was that the support payments
were not being made. The court held that this
violated the provisions of the HEW regulation to
the effect that only income which was *actually*
available for current use on a *regular* basis" may
be counted.

One of the questions left open by King v. Smith was whether a stepfather might be deemed liable for the support of an AFDC family, thereby rendering them ineligible. In Lewis v. Martin, the brief of HEW described a state statute which might satisfy its regulation. Such a statute would impose a duty of support which could be enforced by court order even after the parent had deserted or abandoned the household, regardless of whether the children might receive AFDC payments. It would not suffice, for example, to require that a man living in an AFDC household assume an obligation of support by the fact alone of the household's welfare eligibility. Thus, in one case a step-parent obligation limited to children under 18 was held to be incompatible with the federal regulations since it did not even create a legal obligation co-extensive with the child's welfare eligibility. Bunting v. Juras, 502 P.2d 607 (Or.1972).

In Archibald v. Whaland, 555 F.2d 1061 (1st Cir. 1977), the Court of Appeals considered whether a New Hampshire statute qualified. The statute provided that there was a general obligation on the part of every person "whose income or other resources are more than sufficient to provide for his or her reasonable subsistence compatible with decency of health" to support a spouse or child, including a natural, adopted or step-child. The district court had held that the New Hampshire statute did not qualify as being of "general applicability" because the obligation arose only when the spouse or child was "in need." Further, the step-children were not protected "to the same extent" as natural children because they were excluded from the coverage of state general domestic relations laws as well as those relating to criminal liability.

The Court of Appeals disagreed. The limitation of the statute creating step-parent liability to cases where the child was "in need" did not prevent the statute from being one of general applicability. The Court of Appeals said:

> "We think that the requirement of "general applicability" focuses on arbitrary limitations which make it clear that the duty of support is defined not in terms of the step-parent relationship, but primarily in terms of welfare eligibility." 555 F.2d at 1065.

The Court then went on to consider whether the step-parent obligation was of "the same extent" as that of natural parents and concluded that it was. The unavailability of criminal sanctions, the Court of Appeals held, was irrelevant. It was the civil liability statute which created the legal obligations, which were enforceable. While there might be some difference in statutes concerning support payments in divorce contexts, the Court held that this was a relatively minor difference between the natural parent and step-parent obligations and that the parity of obligation need only be "approximate," not precise.

The issue, under the HEW regulations, is no longer one of moral concerns, as in King v. Smith, but of economic concerns: may a state in some way account for the presence of a noncontributing person in a household? In United States Department of Agriculture v. Moreno, 413 U.S. 528 (1973), the Supreme Court invalidated a federal statute that would have denied Food Stamps to households which included unrelated members. The Court's reasoning was that this was a conclusive presumption that the unrelated persons were contributing to the household and that the household was not needy. See supra, § 12. The Court also noted that the legislation was politically motivated.

A somewhat different approach was invalidated in Van Lare v. Hurley, 421 U.S. 338 (1975). There, the State of New York reduced the shelter allowance in AFDC if a "lodger" was living in the AFDC household. The lodger need not be a person obligated to make support payments or contributions and there was no requirement that the state welfare department determine whether such payments were, in fact, being made. Rather, the total payment to the household for shelter allowances was simply reduced *pro rata*.

The State's rationale in Van Lare v. Hurley was that the legislation did not create an additional condition of eligibility, unlike King v. Smith, because it did not bar *all* relief to a home. See supra, § 3. Further, the legislation did not impute income to the home. Rather, the legislation simply involved a finding that benefits should be reduced, where a home had an additional member, because the additional presence indicated that benefits were excessive, at least in the sense that the shelter allowance was purchasing space which was not needed. Further, the State argued that the focus should not be on the eligibility of the AFDC recipient but on the lodger, who was receiving benefits although ineligible.

The Court rejected these arguments on the ground that the State's policy was to reinstate benefits if the lodger moved out or to allow the lodger to remain with the home receiving reduced benefits. Either way, the state would be paying additional benefits contrary to its own arguments. Reduction of benefits to prevent lodgers from getting welfare would be at the expense of the children. The Court commented that " . . . States may not seek to accomplish policies aimed at lodgers by depriving needy children of benefits". 421 U.S. at 348. It seemed clear to the Court that the "lodger" rules were just another effort to control privacy and associations, in much the same manner as the legislation involved in King v. Smith and *Moreno*.

The man-in-the-house or step-father rules held invalid in King v. Smith and Lewis v. Martin have continuing vitality. In Van Lare v. Hurley, they appeared in the guise of a "lodger" rule. In Boucher v. Minter, 349 F.Supp. 1240 (D.Mass. 1972), they appeared in the guise of a redefinition of the AFDC "unit." The Commonwealth of Massachusetts had a four-category system of allocating benefits. The highest benefits were paid to those in group one, an AFDC unit which bore all of the expenses of living together. Group four, in contrast, was an AFDC family which did not pay rent or fuel expenses. Massachusetts, by regulation, provided that a family with a step-father would be treated as falling within group four.

The court invalidated this approach. It noted that step-parents were not required to support step-children under Massachusetts law. Thus the case was akin to King v. Smith and Lewis v. Martin. The state's rationale was to distinguish those cases on the basis that, by remarriage, the mother was creating two separate family units: one involving the mother and step-father, who provided the home; the other involving the mother and children, who did not need to have the state provide a home. The court rejected this reasoning on the basis that the original AFDC unit involving the mother and children remained, in fact, intact. Further, the grouping in category four impermissibly presumed that the father was providing shelter support, contrary to the constitutional guarantees of due process. The court did however note that the Commonwealth could re-classify families with step-parents as falling into group two, where expenses are shared.

In Houston Welfare Rights Organization v. Vowell, 555 F.2d 1219 (5th Cir. 1977) the Court of Appeals considered a Texas policy of budgeting only a *pro rata* share of shelter and utility expenses when a non-AFDC recipient shares a recipient's residence. The Court held that this was invalid on the same grounds as the New York policy invalidated in Van Lare v. Hurley. The state argued that it was not presuming income to the recipient. Rather, it was only finding that the recipient's standard of need was reduced because the nonrecipient would pay his or her own way. This, with economies of scale and group living, would reduce the needs of the recipient. The Court held that these arguments were foreclosed by Van Lare v. Hurley and, further, that they involved an impermissible presumption that the non-recipient lodgers had income, which might well be contrary to fact.

After King v. Smith, it seems clear that the moralistic values reflected in the man-in-the-house legislation of Alabama must be pursued, if at all, by some means other than terminating welfare benefits. Termination of benefits was common as late as the 1950's, but is incompatible with the Social Security Act as Congress has developed it over the past 40 years. But the Su-

preme Court has never said that a state is foreclosed from conditioning programs to encourage
morality.   Indeed, it has recently held that states
need not provide funds for abortions, precisely
because of the moral issues posed.   The primary
constitutional impediment to state legislation has
arisen when the impact would be felt by children,
not the parents whose conduct was offensive.   In
such a context, denial of benefits is discriminatory and irrational as to the children.

An example of this is provided by New Jersey Welfare Rights Organization v. Cahill, 411
U.S. 619 (1973), in which the State of New Jersey limited its General Assistance program to
couples who were ceremonially married.   Since
the program was not federally funded, the limitation did not run afoul of the statutory limitations
on eligibility involved in King v. Smith.   The
State justified the eligibility requirement on the
ground that it encouraged marriage and family
stability.   The Supreme Court held that the limitation was invalid.   It referred to earlier cases
which had invalidated discrimination against children who were illegitimate.   See, supra, § 22.
Weber v. Aetna Casualty & Surety Co., 406 U.S.
164 (1972);   Levy v. Louisiana, 391 U.S. 68
(1968);   Gomez v. Perez, 409 U.S. 535 (1973).

Cahill is significant because it deals with the
right of a state to address immorality through
discouraging the bearing of illegitimate children,

and by encouraging ceremonial marriage. In a sense, this involves discrimination against children for reasons beyond their control. In *Cahill* the Supreme Court was rejecting the proposition that children could be punished for parental misconduct, and doing so on a constitutional basis. But the Court was also confronting the essential dilemma involved in assisting those who are "dependent": in order to encourage conformity with legitimate state objectives, it may be necessary to terminate the assistance of caretaker relatives. The discrimination thus resulting is not so much a result of intent to punish or of discrimination against the dependent recipients as it is an effort to encourage future behavior by the caretakers.

The end result is that a state may be concerned with encouraging morality through its welfare program but it may not punish immorality by terminating benefits unless alternative arrangements are made for the children. Reductions in benefits are not permissible for moralizing purposes, only for economic purposes and then only where income is actually or realistically available. Thus the step-father, MARS and lodger cases lead naturally to a consideration of what assets and income may be counted in determining financial eligibility, the subject of the next Section.

§ 26. Financial Eligibility: Assets

Financial need is the primary test of eligibility for welfare programs. This is true of the cash grant programs, such as SSI and AFDC or General Assistance, as well as the in-kind programs, such as Food Stamps and Medicaid. It is not true of social insurance. Programs such as OASDI workmen's compensation and unemployment compensation pay benefits largely without regard to need. There are some exceptions, as for example with the limitation on earned income for recipients of retirement benefits under OASDI but, generally speaking, social insurance is treated much as any privately purchased annuity. Public assistance, in contrast, is available only for those who establish financial need.

Income definitions usually involve a two-stage process. The first involves what is counted as income. Earned income is counted in virtually all programs. However, even this obvious source of income is disregarded in certain programs such as SSI, where earned income is necessary for self-support of the blind or in Food Stamps where the earnings are by a child under the age of 18 who is a student. Similarly, in AFDC there is a disregard of the first $30 of earned income each month, plus one-third of the remainder. Thus, even in dealing with the most obvious form of income, public assistance programs make policy judgments designed to encourage certain persons or certain activities by benefiting them selectively.

In addition to income considerations, eligibility also is affected by resources. Most programs allow an applicant to retain *some* resources. Typically, a recipient of public assistance will qualify although he or she has some equity in a home, possesses furnishings or has personal belongings such as an automobile or working tools. SSI for example permits a couple to retain $2,250.00 in personal belongings and permits a single person to retain $1,500.00. The retention of assets represents a concession to applicants which leads to an allocation of public resources and which may also lead to inequities, since persons without assets may, *pro tanto*, lose public funding which might otherwise be available. A somewhat different aspect of inequality arises by allowing the retention of certain assets, such as working tools, but not of others, such as life insurance in excess of a specific amount.

The Social Security Act initially did not speak in terms of assets of applicants. In 1939, Congress required that states consider all "available" assets of a person before determining eligibility for categorical assistance. 42 U.S.C. § 602(a)(7). This was a limitation on state discretion and latitude. However, it left to the states broad latitude in determining which assets and how much might be retained. This has been removed with respect to SSI, which now prescribes the assets retention levels noted above. 42 U.S.C. § 1382b. But states continue to prescribe retention levels for AFDC and for those programs which are wholly state-funded.

Provisions typical of state statutes were involved in Charleston v. Wohlgemuth, 332 F. Supp. 1175 (E.D.Pa.1971), aff'd 405 U.S. 970 (1972). Pennsylvania required that a person assign real estate prior to receiving public assistance, although the assignment would remain dormant while the person occupied the realty. An assignment was also required of personalty. This was effective immediately and included goods and chattels such as automobiles, alimony and support order payments; life insurance and OASDI or retirement benefits; sick benefits and personal damage claims and awards. The assignments of the personalty operated only to the limit of the amount of public assistance paid.

Plaintiffs challenged this provision on the ground that it constituted an additional condition of eligibility, contrary to the Social Security Act. The court rejected this argument. It noted that such provisions had been approved by HEW in state plans for the preceding 25 years. The plaintiffs also maintained that the failure to execute such assignments would result in denial of benefits to the children, thereby punishing them for parental misconduct. The court rejected this argument on the strength of Wyman v. James, 400 U.S. 309 (1971), where the Supreme Court had held that benefits could be denied because parents had refused to allow home visits. See supra, § 9 and infra, § 34.

The list of assets in Charleston v. Wohlgemuth is typical of many state statutes. See, also, Snell v. Wyman, 281 F.Supp. 853 (S.D.N.Y.1968), aff'd 393 U.S. 323 (1969). Yet the items included are significantly different from each other. For example, personal injury claims may include compensation for out-of-pocket expenses, for future loss of earnings or personal advancement or for pain and suffering. Life insurance, in contrast, may represent creation of an asset of benefit to another person. Privately purchased retirement benefits represent a corpus which most people view as "earned." Forcing assignments of such benefits may impose quite different consequences in loss of dignity and psychological or economic independence.

State latitude for determining assets retention has therefore been somewhat curbed. HEW has established maximum limits which an applicant may retain and still be eligible. In 1965, the maximum dollar value was $800. In 1975, HEW proposed a change in its maximum limits. The new regulation would have allowed an AFDC family of four to retain up to $2,500 in assets in addition to a home in a reasonable amount to be established by a state agency, an automobile not to exceed $1,200 in value and personal property necessary for independence or employment. These regulations were challenged in NWRO v. Mathews, 533 F.2d 637 (D.C.Cir. 1976) on the ground that HEW had no authority to publish such regulations and that, in any event, the regulations actually published were contrary to statute. The Court held that HEW had authority to promulgate regulations concerning assets pursuant to 42 U.S.C. § 1302, which provides that HEW may:

> ". . . make and publish such rules and regulations, not inconsistent with this chapter, as may be necessary to the efficient administration of (its) functions . . ."

The Court noted that Congress had been consistently curbing state latitude. In 1939 it required states to consider all available assets in determining eligibility. Since 1955, HEW had set maximum figures and Congress had not rejected them. More recently, Congress had added income disregards binding on the states in computing eligibility for AFDC.

The Court nevertheless found the regulations defective on two grounds. First, the proposed regulations did not deduct any encumbrances against the property in determining the value. Rather, the regulations simply considered the market value of the property without deducting amounts owed. This was contrary to the policy of the Social Security Act of considering only "available" assets. Secondly, the Court also held that the specific dollar figures were invalid. There was no factual basis for them, and absent some factual basis, either in the notice of proposed rule making or in the preface to the final rules, there was no basis for the Court to determine under the Administrative Procedure Act whether the regulations were arbitrary. The status of the new regulations is—at this time—still unclear.

In considering available assets to determine financial eligibility, valuation must be realistic. In Wilczynski v. Harder, 323 F.Supp. 509 (D.Conn. 1974), the district court invalidated a Connecticut Medicaid policy which valued life insurance policies at their face value rather than their cash surrender value. The court held that this policy conflicted with federal statutory requirements. It commented:

> "Reasonable evaluation of available assets in the context of eligibility for public assistance must have reference to evaluation for purposes of meeting those present needs for which assistance would otherwise be provided . . . any other measurement of value, e. g., the future value to a recipient's estate of a life insurance policy, is irrelevant to whether a recipient can meet out of his

own assets his present subsistence needs."
323 F.Supp. at 517.

In addition to realistic evaluation, assets—like
income—must be actually available. Thus in
Kaisa v. Chang, 396 F.Supp. 375 (D.Hawaii
1975), the district court considered a Hawaii provision that required AFDC recipients to forfeit
their income tax refunds or suffer reduction in
assistance. The court held that this was improper. The requirement that income be available
"on a regular basis" was not satisfied by tax refunds which, although actually available, were
provided only on an *irregular* basis. It is significant, however, that in one of the cases cited by
the court it had been held that tax refunds could
be treated as an asset, like personal property.
Thus, while income tax refunds may not affect eligibility in income terms, they may have bearing
on eligibility as it is affected by limitations on retention of assets.

In considering assets, a number of states have
attempted to deal with the problem of fraudulent
transfers. Such transfers would arise when property is transferred for less than its value with the
purpose of qualifying the transferor for public assistance. If valid, the transfer would deny to the
state the right to reimbursement through acquisition of the property. Often the property is transferred to a relative or a friend and may remain
available to the transferor. Provisions barring

fraudulent transfers may be valid if they do not *presume* fraudulent intent from the mere fact of a prior transfer. See infra, §§ 34–36.

A typical provision dealing with fraudulent transfers was that involved in Owens v. Roberts, 377 F.Supp. 45 (M.D.Fla.1974). There, Florida had provided by statute that an applicant for public assistance who had transferred property within the two prior years was required to show that it was not for the purpose of establishing eligibility. An administrative regulation had further provided that if the transfer was for less than market value the person was *automatically* disqualified. One of the plaintiffs had sold a home for $1,000 in order to pay her husband's funeral expenses; another had sold business equipment for $200 on directions of her physician. In both instances, the property was worth approximately three times the amount for which it sold.

The court invalidated both the statute and the regulation. The regulation was invalid because it created an irrebuttable presumption of fraud simply because property had been transferred for less than market value. While prevention of fraud was conceded to be a fair objective of the state, the court held that such a presumption did not serve the objective. In fact, the transfer for less than full value might be precipitated by simple ineptitude or necessity.

The court further held that the statute itself was void. Although, in its terms, it provided for

only a *rebuttable* presumption the court held that
this was irrational. The mere transfer of property within two years prior to application did not
suggest a purpose of qualifying for welfare. Indeed, the opposite might be true: the person
might be attempting to avoid welfare. Further,
the rebuttable nature of the presumption was not
helpful:

> ".   .   . since those persons to whom the
> presumption is directed are typically the
> least capable socially, intellectually, economi-
> cally and physically to employ the means to
> rebut the presumption." 377 F.Supp. at 53.

In addition to these constitutional grounds, the
court also found grounds in the Social Security
Act for invalidating these provisions as constituting an additional condition of eligibility.

A similar result obtained in Buckner v. Maher,
424 F.Supp. 366 (D.Conn.1976). There Connecticut had denied eligibility for AFDC if a person
had transferred property within seven years prior
to application "without reasonable compensation
or for the purpose of qualifying for an award."
The State did not claim that there was any fraud
involved in the cases of the two plaintiffs. Nor
was there a claim that the transfers had been for
the purpose of qualifying for public assistance.
The court found that there was no authority for
the presumption created, in fact, and for:

> ".   .   . an elderly Medicaid applicant suf-
> fering from senility who has been cajoled

out of his assets or actually defrauded, the presumption can be a cruel and irrational one." 424 F.Supp. at 373.

The assets requirements in most public assistance programs may well be destructive of individual initiative. They have a considerable leveling influence, reducing most people to approximately the same level of capital retention or acquisition. For a person late in life, this is a bitter and ironic ending. It may well be, as HEW argued in NWRO v. Mathews, that assets limitations are designed to discourage buying on credit, to prevent accumulation of luxury items and to cut welfare costs. However, it is equally true that one of the purposes of the AFDC program as stated in 42 U.S.C. § 601 is to "help maintain and strengthen family life and to help such parents or relatives to attain or retain capability for maximum self-support and personal independence". The tension, then, is between the political and social need to "level" people receiving public assistance, on the one hand, and the importance of enabling such persons to retain the fruits of life-long industry or to acquire the assets necessary to seek life-long independence.

§ 27. Financial Eligibility: Income

All programs of public assistance pay benefits only to those in "need", unlike social insurance. This involves a means or financial eligibility test.

Essentially, the test concerns all sources of income. While it may focus primarily on earned income, a financial eligibility test may also include investment income or—more often—other governmental benefits. For example, a person receiving social insurance for disability under OASDI may find those benefits disqualifying him or her for public assistance or—another variant —the social insurance benefits may themselves be reduced. Thus financial eligibility for one program is often affected by receipt of other benefits, such as SSI or OASDI, unless statutes creating such benefits (as with Food Stamps) specifically provide otherwise.

The interrelationship of public assistance programs is complex, in part because there are several levels of government involved but also in part because there are competing demands upon a limited pool of resources. Thus what the federal government may deem important may be disregarded or discounted by a state. Further, in a scheme of cooperative federalism the federal government must choose between mandating or shifting expenses to the states on the one hand and leaving latitude to the states on the other. Complicating all of this is a third dimension, caused by the creation of specific programs on an *ad hoc* basis to deal with limited objectives, such as medical care, nutrition, fuel or housing. These limited programs do not fit well with each other or with the more comprehensive cash grant programs.

Thus, an important issue emerges as to when varying forms of public assistance will be treated as income. Any program, whether it is general or categorical assistance or, more narrowly, nutrition or medical assistance, involves a financial eligibility standard. If benefits are counted as income, then assistance is reduced by benefits which may have been intended to enhance a person's status, an intention which would be neutralized if other benefits are reduced. On the other hand, if governmental benefits are disregarded or discounted then eligibility will be enhanced and additional benefits paid, possibly duplicating the benefits which were disregarded and creating a drain on limited resources which might be better allocated to applicants who have no other benefits.

In Richardson v. Belcher, 404 U.S. 78 (1971), the United States Supreme Court considered whether reduction of OASDI benefits because a recipient was also receiving workmen's compensation might deny equal protection of the laws. The Court held that Congress could rationally find that reducing OASDI benefits would avoid duplication with workmen's compensation programs. This would encourage continued funding of those programs. It would also provide an incentive to the worker to return to the job. These objectives were legitimate and the Court therefore upheld the legislation, concluding that it was not part of its responsibility "to consider whether the legitimate purposes of Congress might have been better served by applying the same offset to recipients of private insurance or to judge for ourselves whether the apprehensions of Congress were justified by the facts." 404 U.S. at 84.

In dissent in Richardson v. Belcher, Justice Douglas found a denial of equal protection of the laws because similar reductions were not applied to persons receiving private insurance payments or public insurance payments under the Veteran's Administration program, Civil Service Retirement Act or Railroad Retirement Act. Persons receiving duplicate payments under such supplementary programs exceeded those receiving duplicate payments under workmen's compensation. Justice Marshall argued in dissent that it was further irrational to deny benefits to a person who was receiving workmen's compensation on the mistaken assumption that doing so would "discourage the erosion of workmen's compensation," when there was no evidence that indeed that objective would be obtained. "If anything," Justice Marshall argued, "the states are encouraged to cut back on their programs," by the majority's holding. 404 U.S. at 94.

The usual approach is to "set off" benefits against income. This was the approach in Richardson v. Belcher. Occasionally, however, categorical exclusion may be provided. Thus, in Philbrook v. Glodgett, 421 U.S. 707 (1975), the Supreme Court upheld a provision of the Social Security Act in which the family receiving unemployment compensation would be ineligible for AFDC–UF. The unemployment compensation benefits were less than would be received under AFDC–UF; nevertheless, the receipt of the benefits had been made a basis for denying *all* AFDC eligibility by Congress. It was not the income but the *source* of the income which was critical.

More often, receipt of benefits does not disqualify a person from other programs; rather, there is simply an offset and the other benefits are reduced. In Philbrook v. Glodgett, receipt of unemployment compensation automatically disqualified men, but not women, from AFDC. 42 U.S.C. § 607(b)(2)(C). Thus, where an AFDC mother is receiving unemployment compensation there is no disqualification from also receiving AFDC. AFDC may be reduced, however, since unemployment compensation constitutes income. See Finch v. Weinberger, 407 F.Supp. 34 (N.D.Ga. 1975). In *Finch*, the court upheld reduction of AFDC by the receipt of unemployment compensation and rejected the AFDC recipient's arguments that portions of the unemployment compensation should be disregarded as is done with earned income. The court held that the earned income disregard does not apply to unemployment compensation, citing 45 CFR 233.20(a)(6), which provides that "earned income" shall not include benefits accruing as compensation for lack of employment.

Another example of offsets is in the Food Stamps program. In Patrick v. Tennessee Department of Public Welfare, 386 F.Supp. 944 (E. D.Tenn.1974), plaintiffs challenged a provision under the Food Stamps regulation which reduced benefits because of rent supplements under HUD programs. The Secretary of Agriculture defined income as including public assistance, General Assistance "or other assistance programs based on need." Benefits were excluded, however, if they were "not in money." The court rejected the argument that this definition was wholly within the discretion of the Department of Agriculture, finding that review was possible under the Administrative Procedure Act. However, it then upheld the provisions on the basis that "income" under the statute could include governmental benefits.

Again, in Knebel v. Hein, 429 U.S. 288 (1977), the Supreme Court upheld a regulation of the Department of Agriculture which counted as "income" a transportation allowance which a Food Stamp recipient received from the State of Iowa to defray the cost of commuting to a nurses training program. There was, the Court noted, a standard 10% allowance within the calculation of income for Food Stamps purposes as an offset for expenses. And the Court noted that there was rationality to the regulation being challenged since "disparate treatment of trainees and wage earners could be criticized as unfairly discriminating against the worker." Although transportation allowances were not available for the purchase of food, working families got no allowance at all.

Essentially, then, income may include governmental benefits, unless there is a specific statutory exclusion. There are many such exemptions. For example, although Food Stamp eligibility may consider other programs, the latter are themselves precluded from counting Food Stamps as "income." In Dupler v. City of Portland, 421 F.Supp. 1314 (D.Me.1976), the court held that General Assistance could not be reduced by receipt of Food Stamps benefits. 7 U.S.C. § 2019(d) specifically forbade reducing "welfare grants or other similar aid." The Congressional purpose of Food Stamps, the court held, was to meet previously unmet needs. If General Assistance could be reduced, Food Stamps would simply be paid in lieu of other benefits and the net result would be a shifting of burdens from local or existing programs to the Food Stamps program, without any enhancement of the position of recipients.

As another example, in Johnson v. Harder, 383 F.Supp. 174 (D.Conn.1974), aff'd 512 F.2d 1188, the plaintiffs challenged a Connecticut regulation which reduced AFDC when a child in the family was eligible for survivors benefits under OASDI.

The court held that this was inconsistent with HEW regulations requiring that survivors benefits be used on behalf of the child for whom they were intended. Thus, any excess was to be set aside for the future needs of the child and could not be allocated by state mandate for the use of the other children. As to them, AFDC must provide the source of support.

In addition to these exemptions as to governmental benefits, calculating income may be affected by specific prohibitions as to other kinds of income. Mandatory "disregards" relate primarily to employment, to encourage people to seek work. Akin to the disregards are requirements that certain work-related expenses be deducted before calculating eligibility. These requirements are of particular significance in AFDC but exist as well in other programs, such as SSI and Medicaid.

With respect to earned income, states are required to disregard the first $30 of each month's earnings plus one-third of the remaining balance in determining the benefits (but not the eligibility) of AFDC applicants. 42 U.S.C. § 602(a)(8). Income is also disregarded when earned by students. In SSI, recipients are permitted to retain $20 in personal income per month. Unlike work-related deductions, the income disregard is not tailored to individual cases. Rather, it is a categorical exclusion keyed to a flat dollar amount plus a fraction of the remaining earnings, regardless of the earnings or needs of the individual recipient. And the income disregard applies in addition to work-related expenses which must be deducted *after* the disregard is applied.

Calculation of income disregards can be complex. In Richman v. Juras, 393 F.Supp. 349 (D. Or.1975), Oregon had treated student loans and scholarships as income for AFDC purposes. The plaintiff had a federal loan, a federal scholarship and a state scholarship, the total of which exceeded her educational expenses by some $1,200. The plaintiff relied upon two separate income disregards under federal programs. The first, 45 CFR 233.20(a)(4)(ii), requires a state to disregard any federal grant or loan for educational purposes. The second, 42 U.S.C. § 1382a(b)(7) requires a state to disregard any grants, whether state or federal, which pay tuition. The court upheld the state's action, finding that the state had disregarded the federal grant to the extent of applying it against the plaintiff's educational expenses. The state grant could be counted, since it was not necessary for tuition, which had been paid by the federal grant. Hence, the disregard requirements had been satisfied, yet governmental benefits were still being counted as "income" to reduce AFDC.

Again, in Friedman v. Berger, 547 F.2d 724 (2d Cir. 1976), the Court considered the income disregards provided under Medicaid to SSI recipients. Institutionalized Medicaid recipients were to be permitted to retain $20 in a personal income disregard, in addition to the basic $25 per month which all SSI recipients could retain. However, New York State permitted retention of only $28 per month, not the total $45. In effect, the state was "recapturing" the disregard. The Court nevertheless upheld this practice. Although SSI provided, 42 U.S.C. § 1396a(a)(14), that a state could not impose "deduction, cost sharing or similar charge" on SSI recipients, the court said that there was no showing Congress intended to prohibit the "spenddown" of disregarded income to cover the cost of institutionalized care. Since the state-supported institutions provided the care needed for the SSI recipients, the Court held it was permissible for the state to limit recipients to retaining only $28 per month. By so doing, the state would be encouraged to provide such care.

Perhaps the most significant limitation in calculating income for eligibility is that it must be actually available. This is a regulatory requirement in most federal programs. See 45 CFR 233.20(a)(3). It is also an aspect of due process, since otherwise a welfare agency would be disqualifying a person on a presumption contrary to fact, the reason that man-in-the-house and "lodger" regulations are void. See supra, §§ 12 & 25. Ordinarily, availability is not a difficult concept where income is earned by the person being considered for eligibility.

Even earned income sometimes may not qualify, however. Particularly for the poor, in a credit-oriented society, income may be pledged before it is received. As such, it is not realistically available for present or current needs. In Powell v. Austin, 423 F.Supp. 533 (D.Va.1976), 427 F. Supp. 749 (1977), the court considered a suit by AFDC recipients challenging a Virginia regulation which counted wages as income although the wages were withheld by an employer pursuant to a creditor's garnishment. The state position, endorsed by HEW, was that garnished wages should still be considered "available" and not disregarded. Otherwise, welfare would "encourage parents . . . to rely on the government, not themselves, as the guarantors of their installment debts." Although initially unpersuaded, the court ultimately accepted the government's reasoning on the basis that garnished wages are available:

> ". . . in the sense that they provide actual, not assumed, benefits to the recipients in the form of extinguishing part of an outstanding debt." 427 F.Supp. at 751.

The requirement that income be realistically available must be interpreted in the light of the experience of the poor, who often are living from week to week and have no capital reserves to sustain them. This is typically and dramatically represented by the litigation involved in Gutierrez v. Butz, 415 F.Supp. 827 (D.D.C.1976).

There, the Department of Agriculture published a regulation which provided that:

> "Monthly income means all income which is received or *anticipated* to be received during the month." 7 C.F.R. § 271.3(c)(1).

This meant that a person's eligibility for Food Stamps was not determined by the amount of income or cash on hand at the beginning of the month. Rather, it was determined by the amount of income *anticipated* during that month. The discriminatory impact of this on farmworker households was argued as follows by the plaintiffs:

> "Farmworker households who are destitute at the commencement of the work season have no income available from past employment, but are denied food stamps or required to pay an unrealistically high amount for stamps during the initial one to four week period in which income is anticipated but not yet received." 415 F.Supp. 830.

The court invalidated the regulation. It noted that considering "anticipated" income might be legitimate with employees who had stable employment leading to regular income. But farmworkers do not so qualify. They are frequently migrant, traveling from place to place. This means that while they have weeks of high income, they also have weeks when no income at all is earned. Moreover, it means that there are weeks of ineligibility and administrative delay in each community to which the migrants travel. And such delay is recurrent as the travel continues. Hence, the Department of Agriculture regulation was peculiarly discriminatory in its treatment of farmworkers.

In determining whether income is "available," ordinarily only the applicant's income—and not that of others—is considered. Generally, eligibility is determined on an individual basis. This is true with most programs, such as SSI and Medicaid. Two exceptions are Food Stamps and AFDC. In these programs, the entire "household" must qualify and benefits are determined by the total income of the household. In such instances, income of others may not be attributed or imputed or "deemed" available when—realistically—it is not. See supra, §§ 12 & 25. It is also true that needs of some—such as lodgers—living in a household need not be considered in payment of benefits.

One of the problems with group or "corporate" eligibility is defining the unit. This is important not only to determine whether the unit is one possessing the characteristics which the welfare program is designed to address, but also to determine what income is available through members of the unit to the corporate entity as a means of ascertaining financial eligibility. For example, if there is a lodger or an unrelated male in the house or even a ceremonially married step-father, that person's income may be included only to the extent of *actual* contributions unless there is a state law making the step-father fully responsible for the step-children. See supra, § 25. It is improper for a state to presume that the presence of a person in the home means excessive benefits or additional income are being paid. See 42 U.S.C. § 602(a) (7).

In determining income and eligibility, at least for AFDC purposes, a household may be considered as a unit. All of its income is, in general, available to each member. However, there are exceptions. For example, in Gilliard v. Craig, 331 F.Supp. 587 (D.N.C.1974). AFDC benefits were held to have been wrongfully reduced to the plaintiff family where support payments were made for the benefit of one child and were attributed generally to the entire household. The court held that the single child should be deemed ineligible for AFDC and his inclusion in the family's AFDC budget violated the Social Security Act. Further, the federal requirement that all income available "to the family" be considered did not require appropriating to the family income belonging to a single member. Accord: Johnson v. Harder, supra.

In considering the income of a household, courts have been reluctant to "deem" that income of one member will be available for the needs of others. In Burns v. Vowell, 424 F.Supp. 1135 (S. D.Texas, 1976), the court considered a reduction in Medicaid benefits from $537 to $153 where the state presumed that any income of a spouse beyond the SSI standard was available to pay for the nursing home care of the other spouse. The plaintiff husband established, in fact, that his expenses exceeded the amount allowed by SSI and that his income was unavailable to support his wife. The court looked to the federal statute, 42 U.S.C. § 1396a(a)(17) which provided that a state shall take into account only such income as is available to an applicant without considering the financial responsibility of any individual unless such individual is a spouse. The implementing HEW regulations, 42 CFR 448.3(b), however, provided that "only such income and resources as are actually available will be considered and that income and resources will be reasonably evaluated." The court held that the Texas practice violated the statute and the regulation. It held, additionally, that the Texas relative responsibility statute could operate to obligate the noninstitutionalized spouse, but only to the extent of permitting a demand for reasonable payment. See also Franssen v. Juras, 406 F.Supp. 1375 (D.Or. 1975).

The requirement that only "available" income be considered in determining eligibility means not only that the beneficiary must receive the income but that it be available for support. An implication of this is that only net income be considered. Expenses for employment should be deducted.

While this may not be constitutionally mandated, the Social Security Act, 42 U.S.C. § 602(a)(7) provides that in determining net income "any expenses reasonably attributable to the earning" of income are deducted from gross income. In AFDC if the amount left is less than the predetermined statewide standard of need, the applicant is eligible for AFDC. 45 CFR 233.20(a)(3)(ii)(A). This is consistent with the general federal policy of considering only assets or income which are *actually* available in determining financial eligibility.

In Shea v. Vialpando, 416 U.S. 251 (1974), the Supreme Court considered a Colorado provision which allowed thirty dollars per month as work-related expenses to be deducted from income in determining eligibility. From this figure, a person could deduct child care expenses. The Supreme Court held this was invalid under 42 U.S. C. § 602(a)(7), which required that *actual* work-related expenses be "take[n] into consideration" under AFDC. The plaintiff's actual expenses were in excess of $100 per month, for the purchase of an automobile and for travel to and from work. The "averaging" approach reflected in a flat allowance did not allow for individualized consideration of expenses, as mandated by the statute. The Court did not, however, hold that such an approach would be constitutionally impermissible; it was invalid only because it conflicted with a specific statutory provision.

The requirement that work expenses shall be deducted before determining income for eligibility is resolved by the Social Security Act in federally-funded programs. However, that Act does not apply to programs which are wholly state funded. In Roundtree v. Berger, 420 F.Supp. 282 (E.D.N.Y.1976), recipients of New York State's Home Relief program challenged the provision of that program which allowed deduction of work expenses up to $80 per month. The plaintiffs incurred work expenses in excess of $80 and the excess was not deducted from their income. The court upheld the lesser benefits on the basis that the discrimination was not subject to "strict scrutiny" since it did not involve a fundamental right or suspect criteria, and therefore could be sustained so long as there was a rational relationship to a legitimate governmental interest. That interest, the court found, lay in "the legitimate desire on the part of the state to conserve limited public resources." 420 F.Supp. at 284. See supra, §§ 3, 7.

Work related expenses raise difficult questions. One obviously, relates to the definition of what will be considered "work-related." The most obvious of these would be transportation to and from the place of employment and purchase of necessary clothing or equipment. Related expenses raise somewhat different questions, however, as with purchases of lunch or dinners and arrangements for child care. And still further issues may be involved to the extent that work-related expenses involve capital acquisitions, such as those involved with tools and automobiles. In varying ways, most states consider some or all of these expenses as deductible from employment income for purposes of determining eligibility. The purpose, obviously, is to encourage labor by those who receive public assistance. That subject receives further amplification in the next section of this text.

§ 28.　Financial Eligibility:　Employment and WIN

Throughout the history of American welfare is a persistent theme emphasizing the primary place of earnings as a means of support with welfare as a means to relieve temporary unemployment or a substitute for those who cannot work. This theme has ancient roots. The Elizabethan Poor Laws emphasized the importance of labor. Journeymen laborers were not permitted to go from place to place to ply their trades without licenses to travel. Any person who was found unemployed could be returned to his place of settlement. Upon return, a person could be forced to work in public employment projects. Willful idleness was a crime.

Employability as a limitation in latter-day welfare assumes many forms. One is to deny public assistance to those who are employable. Another is to require cooperation in work programs or in seeking work as a condition for receiving public assistance. A third approach is to extend public assistance to a person while working, without loss of benefits. This may be achieved by disregarding some of the income generated in determining or counting income for eligibility purposes. Or it may be achieved by deducting work related expenses from income generated by employment so that only "net" income is counted for eligibility purposes. See supra, § 27.

Many programs deny welfare to people who leave employment to qualify for public assistance. In Lavine v. Milne, 424 U.S. 577 (1976), the Supreme Court upheld New York legislation which "deemed" that a person who applied for assistance within seventy-five days after voluntarily terminating employment or reducing earning capacity had done so for the purpose of qualifying for such assistance, in the absence of contrary evidence. The program at issue in Lavine v. Milne was the New York State Home Relief program. The plaintiffs conceded the validity of a work requirement as a condition of eligibility, but challenged the presumption.

The Supreme Court rejected the challenge on the ground that the statute only created a rebuttable presumption. It noted:

> "As with any other welfare scheme, New York home relief imposes a host of requirements; and as is the case when applying for

most governmental benefits, applicants for home relief bear the burden of showing their eligibility in all respects". 424 U.S. at 582–583.

The Court noted that the sole purpose of the provision being challenged was to indicate that, as with other eligibility requirements, the burden lay with the applicant rather than the state. The Court concluded that "the provision carries with it no procedural consequence; it shifts to the applicant neither the burden of going forward nor the burden of proof, for he appears to carry the burden from the outset." 424 U.S. at 584. See supra, §§ 12 & 22.

The decision in Lavine v. Milne related to General Assistance. However, New York imposed similar requirements with respect to AFDC. Although those were not at issue in Lavine v. Milne it would seem that the Court's reasoning would apply with respect to AFDC as well as to Home Relief. Under AFDC it is necessary that the children be "dependent". This means that their income or that of their household must be inadequate to support them. If a parent has left employment without good cause in order to obtain welfare, the household would not so qualify. It may be, however, that "good cause" within the context of AFDC might permit a mother to leave employment in order to care for her children. In a related context, under the AFDC–UF program, courts have upheld state payment of benefits to a home where the father left employment as part of a labor dispute and strike.

Eligibility of strikers for welfare is a relatively recent and controversial issue. At the time of the Elizabethan Poor Laws—and indeed until the 1930's—there was virtually no right to strike or to organize for labor disputes. With the passage of the National Labor Relations Act, those rights were created. But a striker could not qualify for welfare under the federal categorical assistance programs unless he or she were aged, blind, disabled or a child. Welfare entitlement of adult wage-earners became an issue only in unemployment compensation contexts or, in the late 1960's in those states which participated in the optional AFDC–UF program, extending AFDC to homes where *both* parents were present because the wage-earner had become unemployed. In AFDC–UF the question posed is whether that unemployment may be the result of a choice to strike.

In Batterton v. Francis, 432 U.S. 416 (1977), the Supreme Court considered the denial of AFDC–UF to strikers in Maryland. That State had adopted a policy of denying benefits to strikers, pursuant to an HEW regulation at 45 CFR § 233.100(a)(1) which provided that:

> "At the option of the state, such definition need not include a father whose unemploy-

ment results from participation in a labor
dispute or who is unemployed by reason of
conduct or circumstances which result or
would result in disqualification for unemployment compensation under the state's unemployment compensation law."

A lower court, in Francis v. Davidson, 379 F.
Supp. 78, 81 (D.Md.1974) had held that the regulation was invalid because the reason for unemployment was irrelevant to AFDC and the HEW
regulation involved an impermissible delegation
of authority to the states, making a uniform national standard impossible. The Supreme Court
held to the contrary.

It upheld the HEW regulation and the Maryland regulations adopted pursuant to it. It noted
that the legislation involved a unique delegation
by Congress to HEW for the prescribing of standards as to what constitutes "unemployment" for
purposes of AFDC–UF. The delegation was not
under the general rule-making authority of HEW.
Rather, it was incorporated directly in the
AFDC–UF statute and, therefore, the Court commented

"In a situation of this kind, Congress en-
trusts to the Secretary, rather than to the
courts, the primary responsibility for interpreting the statutory term. In exercising
that responsibility, the Secretary adopts regulations with legislative effect. A reviewing

court is not free to set aside those regulations simply because it would have interpreted the statute in a different manner." 432 U.S. at 425.

The Court noted that the amendments to the program were designed to lead towards a national standard of uniformity in determining what "unemployment" meant. But the Court concluded that the term might be defined by reference to the reasons creating the unemployment and that uniformity might be achieved, at least partially, by reference to state unemployment compensation statutes. This would mean that strikers could be deemed ineligible.

What is clear from the AFDC–UF program and from Batterton v. Francis is that a state may choose to provide AFDC–UF to a family where the parent is unemployed. And a state may choose to exclude those families where unemployment stems from a strike. Or a state may choose to *include* strikers. In Super Tire v. McCorkle, 550 F.2d 903 (3d Cir. 1977), plaintiffs challenged New Jersey's decision to pay welfare benefits to strikers. The Court upheld the payments. The statutory authority was clear under New Jersey statutes. The plaintiffs, however, argued that such payments conflicted with federal statutory policy under labor relations statutes governing collective bargaining. Their contention was that public assistance would distort the equality necessary for labor negotiations. Since the strikers would thereby be relieved of economic pressures, their willingness and ability to endure a lengthy strike would be enhanced to the detriment of the employer.

The Court was unpersuaded. It noted that earlier courts had upheld unemployment compensation payments to strikers. And it noted that the Supreme Court had found "no substantial federal question" in a similar challenge. It therefore upheld New Jersey's choice to provide public assistance to strikers.

In addition to disqualifying those who choose not to work, welfare programs have long included work requirements for those receiving assistance. This was true of the Elizabethan Poor Laws and it remains true of the categorical assistance programs created by Congress in 1935. However, it was not until 1967 that Congress amended the Social Security Act to require states to incorporate the Work Incentive Program (WIN) into their AFDC plans. 42 U.S.C. §§ 602(a)(19), 630–644. Every state AFDC plan must provide that certain "employable" individuals shall register for manpower services, training and employment under regulations promulgated by the Secretary of Labor. Supporting services to be provided by the state must include health, vocational rehabilitation, counselling, child care and others. Employment consists of work in the regular economy and participation in public service programs. 42 U.S.C. §§ 630–633.

The Social Security Act, 42 U.S.C. § 632, provides that the Secretary of Labor shall establish work incentive programs in each state. These shall include employment, on-the-job training, institutional and work experience training if likely to lead to regular employment and public service employment for individuals for whom a job in the regular economy cannot be found. The Secretary is to certify people for such programs unless there is "good cause" for exclusion. 42 U.S.C. § 633. Priority is to be given to unemployed fathers, mothers who volunteer, other mothers and pregnant women, dependent children and other relatives over age 16 and not in school. A statewide plan is to be developed, as well as individual work plans for each person referred.

The Social Security Act requires states to register all applicants as a condition of eligibility for "manpower services, training and employment." 42 U.S.C. § 602(a)(19). People are excluded if they are under 16 or in school fulltime, ill or incapacitated or "of advanced age," too remote from a work incentive project, required at home because of the illness or incapacity of a member of the household, or a parent or relative caring for a child under six. Training incentives are to be disregarded in determining income. Aid will be denied anyone refusing without good cause to register or accept work. 45 CFR 224.20.

Persons eligible for WIN are registered and referred to the appropriate WIN sponsor, 45 CFR

224.21, which may be a state or private agency. The sponsor may de-certify a person. Otherwise, the sponsor provides employment information and referral to the recipient, after an appraisal interview. The state is required to provide services to assist in employment, including child care and vocational rehabilitation. Provision is made for expenses and incentive payments during training. A hearing shall be afforded any recipient who disputes certification for WIN. 45 CFR 224.60.

Employment under WIN must be "within the scope of an individual's employability plan," 45 CFR 224.34, and must be within "the capability of the individual to perform the task on a regular basis." Total daily commuting may not exceed two hours, excluding transportation of children. Employment must meet federal and state standards and may not be discriminatory. Pay must meet applicable statutory minima; if no minimum is prescribed, then it must be no less than three-fourths of the minimum wage. No person may be required to break a strike or union rules.

Under these programs, public service employment may be provided by the Secretary of Labor under agreement with public or private agencies. 42 U.S.C. § 633(e). The Secretary may pay 100% of the cost in the first year, 75% in the second and 50% in the third. Wages must be at least the minimum applicable. Conditions of work must be reasonable and include appropriate workmen's compensation. 42 U.S.C. § 633(f). Incentive payments for training and institutional work may be paid, not exceeding $30 per month. Relocation assistance is available to those seeking it if wage rates would equal their full need under State standards. 42 U.S.C. § 637.

The elements and contours of work programs for welfare recipients are represented in typical fashion by the two programs challenged in Aguayo v. Richardson, 473 F.2d 1090 (2d Cir. 1973). There, HEW had approved experimental funding for two limited programs in the State of New York. One was known as Public Service Work Opportunities Project (PSWOP) and the other as Incentives for Independence (IFI). Under PSWOP semi-monthly interviews were to be scheduled for recipients with employment counsellors in order to develop an employment "Plan." Employment might be in a private sector job, public service employment or a job specially developed for PSWOP. The last option would become mandatory within thirty days if other employment could not be found. PSWOP employment might involve working for a state, city, town or village agency or school district. The work would be "of the sort which, because of budgetary problems or otherwise, would not be undertaken except for PSWOP." Workers would not displace those who would be otherwise employed.

No individual would be required to participate in PSWOP unless satisfactory child care arrangements were developed. They would not receive earnings over and above their welfare benefits. The number of hours to be worked would be determined by dividing the amount of the participant's grant by the hourly wage. The hourly rate would be the state minimum wage or that paid to employees for comparable work. There would be reimbursement for lunch and transportation or other work related expenses. Refusal of PSWOP employment would lead to denial of benefits.

The Incentives for Independence Program (IFI) had four components. There was a combination of public employment programs, including PSWOP and an Emergency Employment Act public service program for adults unable to find regular employment. In addition, there was an earnings exemption and a counseling program directed towards school youth and the parents of truant children. All non-working employable recipients were required to participate in counseling and report for job interviews. No recipient would be considered employable unless a satisfactory child care arrangement had been made. Unlike PSWOP, non-compliance in IFI districts was punished by a flat $66 per month reduction in assistance. And unlike PSWOP workers, employees could work full-time and be paid full wages.

They would also receive workmen's compensation, health insurance and other fringe benefits.

Criticisms of such programs are obvious. The plaintiffs in Aguayo v. Richardson maintained that the standards for selecting those who would be deemed "employable" were vague and permitted undue discretion and discrimination. Similar vagueness and lack of standards related to the selection of jobs and the creation of employment possibilities. The differentials between payments to the participants and those to regular employees were challenged. The plaintiffs maintained that child care and standards relating to child care were both inadequate. The conditions of labor and the quality of employment were poor. And, the plaintiffs maintained, the types of jobs to which welfare recipients would be assigned would not provide experience qualifying a welfare recipient for employment in the general economy. Furthermore, it was argued as being highly improbable that many jobs akin to those in PSWOP or IFI would be available in the economy.

While these criticisms of work incentive programs are widely applicable and have great merit, they have not persuaded any court to invalidate such programs. In *Aguayo*, the Court simply held that the programs were within the proper constitutional latitude of Congress and HEW. Under the Administrative Procedure Act, 5 U.S.C.

§ 701 et seq., and 42 U.S.C. § 1315, the Secretary could find such programs might "assist in promoting the objectives" of the Social Security Act. This deference to legislative/administrative latitude has characterized court treatment of both federal and state work programs, at least to the extent the latter complement and do not conflict with federal programs.

The extensive program of work requirements adopted by Congress in 1967, collectively known as WIN, requires cooperation by the states. The states, of course, may have their own work programs for locally funded welfare recipients. However, New York State has also imposed a program of work requirements, denominated Work Rules, on AFDC recipients. Under the New York Work Rules, a presumption was created that certain recipients of public assistance were employable, chiefly those who were not students, aged or needed full-time in their home. Persons who were deemed eligible were required to pick up their assistance checks in person every two weeks and to report for employment interviews. They were prohibited from declining suitable employment when available. The Work Rules also permitted the creation of public works projects in New York's social service districts. In these respects, the New York Work Rules were similar to those which had been imposed traditionally under state and locally funded welfare programs for decades.

The New York Work Rules were challenged in New York State v. Dublino, 413 U.S. 405 (1973). The plaintiffs maintained that the federal legislation setting up the federal WIN program precluded operation of the New York Work Rules, at least as to AFDC recipients, essentially on the ground that Congress had "pre-empted" the field. The Court rejected this argument. It quoted from Schwartz v. Texas, 344 U.S. 199, 202–203 (1952) as follows:

> "If Congress is authorized to act in a field, it should manifest its intention clearly. It will not be presumed that a federal statute was intended to supersede the exercise of the power of the state unless there is a clear manifestation of intention to do so. The exercise of federal supremacy is not lightly to be presumed." 413 U.S. at 413.

The Court noted that this approach had particular relevance to the field of welfare, where the operating principle of cooperative federalism left latitude to the states to determine standards of need and levels of benefits. Further, the Court noted, at the time of the creation of the Federal Work Incentive Program in 1967, twenty-one states already had initiated welfare work requirements as a condition of AFDC eligibility. No express intention was reflected in Congressional committee reports or in the statute to displace these programs.

Moreover, the Court found "persuasive affirmative reasons" for concluding that Congress did not intend to displace state programs. WIN itself was not intended to be comprehensive. Federal Work Incentive Programs were to be established only where the Secretary of Labor determined there was a "significant number of individuals" eligible for AFDC who might qualify for work programs. 42 U.S.C. § 632(a). In New York this meant that WIN was operating in only fourteen of New York's sixty-four social service districts. Even in those districts, the opportunities were limited. Although there were 150,000 WIN registrants, only 90,000 of them were eligible for placement and only 17,000 were referred for less than 10,000 positions. The Court noted that California's programs had similar experience, with over 122,000 employable AFDC recipients available for only 18,000 WIN slots.

In Woolfolk v. Brown, 393 F.Supp. 263 (E. D.Va.1975), the Federal District Court considered the compatibility of Virginia's work rules with the WIN provisions of the AFDC program. The plaintiffs maintained that the Virginia rules conflicted with 42 U.S.C. § 602(a)(19)(A) which provided that AFDC recipients were to register for manpower services under Department of Labor Regulations unless the person was so remote from a work incentive project that his or her effective participation was precluded. The plaintiffs' argument was that Virginia's work rules were applicable in localities not served by WIN, thus creating a blanket exemption from mandatory referral to WIN for residents of political subdivisions in which WIN was not operating, increasing the number of recipients required to register and participate in the state work program. The court held that the state work rule was void, since it did not require an individualized determination of remoteness and exemption from the federal WIN program but simply required everybody in certain designated areas to cooperate with the state work rules. Further, the court held that the state work rule was in conflict with Department of Labor Regulations which permit all persons who are exempt from WIN registration to register voluntarily.

The Court of Appeals reversed the lower court in Woolfolk v. Brown, 538 F.2d 598 (4th Cir. 1976). It held that a state could offer a work incentive program, as Virginia had done, in those counties where the federal WIN program was available. Moreover, residents in the non-WIN areas could be excluded from WIN. Otherwise, designation of a single county as having a WIN program would open that program to all residents in the state. The Court of Appeals thus disagreed with the district court and disagreed further in finding, contrary to the lower court, that there was no right for persons ineligible for WIN to register voluntarily. The course of litigation in *Woolfolk* illustrates the depth of commitment to work requirements on the part of the states and the difficulty of coordinating local programs with the already complex federal programs requiring tri-partite administration by the state, HEW and the Department of Labor.

The Work Incentive Program was enacted in 1967. Despite extensive amendments, experience has not been satisfactory. Criticisms have related to the method of assigning people; to the quality and conditions of work; and to the inadequacy of training. Basic problems of waste and confusion inhere in the tri-partite form of administration, involving HEW, the Labor Department and state welfare departments. Even more basic has been the confusion of competing goals: they include relieving welfare expenses, preparing welfare recipients for employment and providing working parents as role models in welfare families. WIN has sometimes been an economic tool, sometimes punitive and sometimes rehabilitative. See Comment, *The Failure of the Work Incentive Program*, 119 U.Pa.L.Rev. 485 (1971).

V. BENEFITS

§ 29. Computations, Flat Grants and Averaging

The Introduction provided certain statistical information concerning the numbers of dollars and people involved in the American welfare system. The earlier discussion in § 14, dealing with the definition of poverty provides a useful standard, if one were needed, to support the proposition that welfare benefits rarely exceed the poverty level. See generally, 1975 Annual Statistical Supplement, Social Security Bulletin. Only in the Food Stamp program is there a commitment to "adequacy." In other programs, such as General Assistance, Medicaid, SSI and AFDC, benefits usually equal only a percentage of need and may vary from state to state. This is particularly true of AFDC.

Historically, AFDC benefits have not met the needs of recipients. Moreover, AFDC has paid a lesser percentage of need than has been paid in other programs of categorical assistance, such as Aid to the Blind, Aid to the Disabled and Aid to the Aged. Congress addressed this problem in 1967 by amending the Social Security Act to provide that:

> "A state plan for aid and services to needy families with children must . . . (23) provide that by July 1, 1969, the amounts used by the state to determine the needs of individuals will have been adjusted to reflect

fully changes in living costs since such
amounts were established, and any maximums that the state imposes on the amount
of aid paid to families will have been proportionately adjusted . . ." 42 U.S.C. §
602(a)(23).

In Rosado v. Wyman, 397 U.S. 397 (1970), the
plaintiffs argued that this amendment required
the states to increase AFDC benefits to meet the
1969 cost of living of the AFDC family. This
would have represented a radical departure from
the principle of cooperative federalism, which
leaves amounts of AFDC benefits to the states.
The Supreme Court rejected the argument.

The Court held that with respect to welfare
payments, apart from any questions concerning
maximum limitations on maximum payments, the
section simply required a state to compute the
components of need accurately. This required a
state to "lay bare the extent to which their programs fall short of fulfilling actual needs." A
state was left free, after recomputing its standard
of need, to "pare down payment to accommodate
budgetary realities by reducing the percent of
benefits paid or switching to a percent reduction
system." The only impact on benefits, as such,
was with respect to "maximums," which the
Court noted had to be adjusted. Thereby, Congress was viewed as having introduced an incentive for the states to abandon a maximum grant
system, under which many states had fixed an up-

per limit on the amount of assistance to a household regardless of size. See infra, § 30.

Following Rosado v. Wyman most states adjusted their standard of need to the 1969 level. There has been no federal statutory requirement that they continue to adjust their standards of need to reflect current costs of living. Many states, in fact, do not do so. Thus, in many states the standard of need does not reflect current living costs and benefits are rendered further inadequate by representing only a percentage of the already inadequate standard of need. Since there is no constitutional "right" to welfare, states are free to pay inadequate benefits, no matter how computed. And most, after computing need, reduce benefits to a certain percentage thereof—a process known as "ratable reduction."

The principle of cooperative federalism under the Social Security Act thus leaves broad latitude to the states in computing need and benefits. Perhaps the largest area of discretion is in computing need, since this permits a state to determine what needs are to be included and at what valuation. Such mechanical choices, seemingly insignificant, have great impact. In Jefferson v. Hackney, 406 U.S. 535 (1972), the Supreme Court upheld the right of Texas to compute need, then reduce that need by a percentage (25%) to determine how much of need would be paid, and then to reduce those benefits by earned outside income. Each of these steps had considerable significance in reducing both the number of persons eligible for AFDC and the level of benefits for each. In fact, if the last two steps had been reversed—so that income was deducted from benefits *before* benefits were reduced—some 2,400 families would have then become eligible for AFDC.

The plaintiffs maintained that the method of calculation violated 42 U.S.C. § 602(a)(23), which required states to update their standards of need at least through 1969. They argued that Texas was obscuring the true standard of need by computing a person's needs and then reducing that by a percentage factor, from which outside income was then deducted before actual benefits could be determined. This method also, the plaintiffs argued, discouraged people from working. If the outside income were deducted first, then the percentage reduction applied to the remainder, there would be a higher standard of "need" remaining, and consequently higher benefits would be paid. With a family having $200 in need and $100 in outside income, the Texas system would pay only $50 in benefits. Deducting the outside income and then applying the 75% reduction factor would leave $75 in benefits.

The Court found, however, that the Texas method of calculation did not obscure actual need. Rather, actual need was computed and a ratable reduction system applied to determine the benefits which would be paid. This sequence had been explicitly permitted by Rosado v. Wyman. The plaintiffs argued that the intent of § 602(a)(23) had been to expand the number of people who were determined to be eligible. While the Court agreed this might be one of the *results* of that section, it nevertheless concluded that the section actually mandated only an up-dating of the standard of need, which Texas had done.

One dimension of the issue in Jefferson v. Hackney which deserves emphasis is the impact of the Texas method of calculating eligibility on the availability of collateral services, such as Medicaid or Family Planning. A method of computing benefits which would deny eligibility for AFDC might also deny eligibility for other services. Consequently, the dissent argued in *Jefferson* that Congress intended, particularly through § 602(a)(23), to broaden eligibility as much as possible. A restrictive method of calculation might mean far more than just the loss of a few dollars per month to a family; it might well mean the loss of vital services and benefits in programs where eligibility was keyed to eligibility in AFDC or some other cash grant program.

As interpreted by the United States Supreme Court in Rosado v. Wyman, § 602(a)(23) required the states only to update their standards of need to a realistic level as of 1969. After that, the states remained free to reduce benefits, although the standard of need may not be reduced below the 1969 level. This issue has remained of considerable importance as states have shifted from individualized determinations of need to a "flat grant" system. Under a flat grant system, a state allows a specific amount for particular needs, rather than paying the precise amount needed by an individual. Individualized determinations of need were the rule prior to 1969; they have become the exception since. Instead, many states have gone to a flat grant system based on the "average" needs of an "average" family.

In Rosado v. Wyman, the Supreme Court held that New York's conversion to a flat grant system was invalid. It had led to a forty million dollar decrease in welfare benefits. The Court held that this conflicted with § 602(a)(23). While a state remains free, under that section, to pay only a percentage of need, the Court held that a state was not free to reduce significantly the "needs" embraced. New York's flat grant system was invalid because it did not include allowances for items formerly covered by the so-called "special" grants.

The flat grant system may pose the risk of reduction in several ways. The items included in the flat grant oftentimes do not include items for which benefits may have previously been available. This is most often true of what was referred to as "special needs" categories. Items in the special need category were either routinely needed but of varying amounts, (such as transportation, furniture and medical care) or they were of catastrophic, non-recurring nature, (such as replacement of vehicles or appliances which had broken down or payment of extraordinary medical expenses). Omission of these by a flat grant system arguably violates 42 U.S.C. § 602(a)(23).

There are substantial difficulties in arriving at averages to provide a basis for flat grants. But the Supreme Court in Rosado v. Wyman made it clear that such averaging is permissible. And this remains true even though, to a considerable extent, averaging involves presumptions that, although obscured by the overall process of averaging, may be contrary to fact. The flat grant for a hypothetical family of four will, since it is based only on average needs, be insufficient for the needs of at least half of the target population. The presumption of adequacy is therefore false. In an appropriate case it may well be that averaging would be subject to a challenge under the due process clause for creating a presumption contrary to fact. See supra, § 12.

Another problem with averaging is to determine whether the average should reflect payments by a welfare department or actual expenses of welfare recipients. Averaging of the payments to welfare recipients is administratively easier, but would not reflect actual needs of those recipients. Such payments may in the past have been only a percentage of need and, with respect to particular needs or particular kinds of recipients, may have been disproportionately deficient. Examining the actual expenses of recipients would reveal more accurately the needs of average families. But the difficulty of determining how people in fact spend their money and for what necessities over a period of time is considerable.

On remand from the Supreme Court in *Rosado*, the district court addressed the issue of whether New York's flat grant system—based on average needs of an average family—had violated 42 U.S.C. § 602(a)(23) by omitting benefits previously paid. Although averaging was permitted, it could not exclude previously included items. 322 F.Supp. 1173 (E.D.N.Y.1970), aff'd 402 U.S. 991(1971). The issue on remand, then, was what constituted "fair averaging." The state attempted to establish that the items of special need eliminated in July, 1969 were "accounted for" in the new flat grant schedules. Since the new method and the old method were vastly different, no meaningful comparison could be made between the two need "schedules." It was therefore necessary to make comparisons between actual payments to similarly situated individuals. If the change had been less dramatic, a simple comparison between the old schedule and the new would have been sufficient. But a comparison could not be obtained from the schedules because the special need items had been individually tailored payments made upon individual application and verification.

The court considered whether, in the averaging process, certain budgetary techniques previously used should be reflected. It concluded, for example, that the previous policy of providing an additional payment where two adults were included in the family should be continued. The court ruled similarly with respect to handicap allowances and diaper services, although the latter apparently had previously been included as a special need by error. Laundry allowances, the court held could be excluded from averaging since they had been previously deleted. Perhaps the most difficult issue concerned the previous policy of replacing cash or checks which had been lost or stolen. The State maintained that this policy did not relate to assistance tailored to need, but simply represented a means of assisting a family to resolve a need previously met. The State did not consider that replacement monies were "assistance" in the sense of doubling the payments to a family or addressing a need twice as great as previously determined. But the court held that replacement checks were a special form of assistance and could not be averaged consistently with 42 U.S.C. § 602(a)(23).

Litigation concerning the adequacy of benefits has continued to focus on whether the averaging which underlies flat grants has violated § 602(a)(23) by eliminating former needs and benefits. Thus in Rhode Island Welfare Rights Organization v. Department of Social Services, 329 F.Supp. 860 (D.R.I.1971), plaintiffs challenged suspension of payments for items previously contained in the "special needs" category of AFDC assistance. Among these were transportation, housekeeping services, household equipment and furnishings, telephone, indebtedness, moving, burial and special medical supplies. The state had transferred these to a new category of "emergency assistance," subjecting the needs to more restrictive conditions on eligibility. The court held that § 602(a)(23) has been violated.

In Roselli v. Affleck, 373 F.Supp. 36 (D.R.I. 1974), the plaintiffs challenged Rhode Island's transition to a flat grant system on four grounds. It failed to compute independently the needs of units living in public and private housing, it presumed that non-recipients were able to contribute and did in fact contribute a pro-rated share to defray living expenses of AFDC recipients, it failed to average or survey actual rents and, finally, it failed to account for inflationary increases in rents from the date of the averaging of shelter costs in November, 1972 (when rent increases were tightly regulated by statute) to the time of implementation in November, 1973. Prior to converting to a flat grant system, Rhode Island had not stated a specific dollar amount for rent. Rather it established the "standard of need" and the amount of payment upon actual need, "subject only to the limitation of reasonableness." That is, it paid whatever was needed.

The court, therefore, found that the flat grant system, which did not pay actual housing needs, violated the federal statute. The State argued that it was only required to pay the same dollar amount that it was paying as of 1969. The court rejected this. The court did hold, however, that it was fair for the state to average both public and private housing in determining actual need. But while the court would not look to the components of the averaging, it did look to the end result, since averaging or merging of separate categories of people is not acceptable where a substantial distortion of the typical "standard of need" is created. The court concluded that if the number of AFDC recipients living in public housing equaled or exceeded those in private housing, there would, in fact, have been a broad distortion.

The impact of a decision such as Roselli v. Affleck is, in effect, to prevent flat grant averaging where the state previously paid actual need. The only alternative, then, for such a state is to continue individualized grants, at least as to rent, and then impose a ratable reduction upon the items previously budgeted at need. However, even this may constitute an impermissible reduction in the standard of need. If so, a state such as Rhode Island would be locked into a standard of need which pays actual expenses for rent.

The decisions in *Rosado, Rhode Island Welfare Rights* and *Roselli* indicate the continuing importance of § 602(a)(23). A state is prohibited by that section from reducing its standard of need. A flat grant averaging system inevitably does this. The course of litigation under § 602(a)(23) has been confusing because *Rosado* held that averaging is in fact permissible and so—to some degree—a state may, despite the previously discussed cases, reduce its standard of need if the averaging is "fair." Two cases, Johnson v. White and Houston Welfare Rights Organization v. Vowell, will illustrate the complexity of determining what is "fair."

In Johnson v. White, 353 F.Supp. 69 (D.Conn. 1972), the State of Connecticut proposed to convert virtually the entire AFDC program to a "flat grant" system with identical payments to every family within each size assistance unit. The court considered a challenge to this in terms of two elements: the adequacy of the standard of need as reflected in the new flat grant system and the statistical method of averaging employed by the state to reach that standard. The court noted that inevitably under an averaging system some would receive more and some less. In fact, nine thousand assistance units would receive lower payments, while about twenty thousand would receive higher payments, with a total additional cost of fifteen million dollars.

The plaintiffs maintained that the averaging had improperly grouped two different types of assistance units: those in which all members were eligible for assistance ("equal assistance units") and those in which welfare recipients lived with persons not eligible for AFDC. The plaintiffs showed that the average budgeted needs of equal assistance units are substantially higher than the average budgeted needs of unequal assistance units. By combining them, the result was a reduction of the average need of the equal assistance unit and an increase for the unequal assistance unit. The court nevertheless held that this was permissible under 42 U.S.C. § 602(a)(23) as interpreted in *Rosado,* which had permitted averaging the needs of two distinct populations, those who had received special needs and those who had not.

On the same authority, the court rejected the plaintiffs' argument that it was improper to average the needs of units which had special needs and those which did not. The court also rejected the plaintiffs' claim that it was improper to average the needs of assistance units of different sizes. The state had, with respect to assistance unit sizes ten through fifteen, averaged the budgeted needs for shelter, excess utilities, recurrent and non-recurrent needs. Consequently, the budget under the new flat grant system was the same for a family of ten as for a family of fifteen. The plaintiffs maintained that this obscured the standard of need for the larger families. The court found that includung these disparate size groups had not been a major factor in the averaging because of the small number of the larger groups. Hence, the averaging process was upheld.

The preceding challenges were based, as was true in *Rosado*, on the argument that distinct populations had been improperly grouped for averaging purposes. A somewhat different argument was also advanced in Johnson v. White: that the standard of need had been obscured, contrary to § 602(a)(23), by basing the flat grant on the previously budgeted needs for specific items, such as rent, rather than on the actual cost of the items. The plaintiffs' argument was that although limited amounts had been budgeted previously, in fact recipients had drawn upon other portions of grants in order to pay for needs which had been underbudgeted. The court nevertheless found that the flat grant standard was valid because a survey established that the previous rent allotments were adequate except in approximately two percent of the cases.

Flat grant averaging was challenged in Houston Welfare Rights Organization v. Vowell, 555 F.2d 1219 (5th Cir. 1977). The plaintiffs challenged Texas' practice of averaging amounts paid to AFDC households with actual shelter needs above the DPW ceilings at the ceiling amount, as well as averaging in AFDC households with no shelter expense at all. The ceilings had been updated to reflect the cost of living at 1969 levels, as required by 42 U.S.C. § 602(a)(23). But by including families who received actual shelter needs which were less than the ceiling without including any of those with needs which exceeded the ceiling, the state assured that in the averaging process no flat grant for shelter would exceed the previously existing ceiling. The Court held that this was consistent with the "fair pricing" and "fair averaging" requirements of Rosado v. Wyman, and did not obscure the standard of need as of 1969 levels.

It is difficult, if not impossible, to reconcile the cases dealing with flat grant averaging. They represent an inconsistent pattern of interpreting § 602(a)(23) and its requirement that states not conceal the standard of need by reducing the components of that standard. In concentrating on these cases, however, there is a danger of ignoring the basic reality that—despite § 602(a)(23)—a state is free to *pay* any percentage of benefits it chooses. Regardless of what must be in the standard of need to comply with § 602(a)(23), a state need only pay a *percentage* of that amount. Further, § 602(a)(23) is a limitation only as to AFDC. States may set benefits at any level they choose as to other programs, such as General Assistance. If this latitude is curbed at all it must be through special legislation—as with Medicaid—or constitutional limits on discrimination. See infra, § 31.

§ 30. Maximum Grants

The preceding Section developed the basic proposition that states and the federal government are free to set welfare benefits at whatever level they choose. The Constitution does not require any particular level of assistance. Congress can impose some limits on states, as in 42 U.S.C. § 602(a)(23), but it rarely has done so. The chief federal restraint on the states has limited the kinds of programs which may be funded with federal dollars, not the level of benefits. The only constitutional challenge to this principle of cooperative federalism has been in those instances where it could be argued that benefit levels were discriminatory, denying equal protection of the laws.

A well established means of limiting the benefits of welfare recipients is to impose maximum limitations on grants. Grants may involve benefits increased by each member in a household. However, typically a state will not increase benefits beyond a certain number of recipients. Thus the AFDC grant to a family with four children may increase if there is a fifth. However, if there are children beyond that, there may be no increment. This is, in some degree at least, a deterrent to increasing family size. However, a family which is already too large before it becomes dependent upon welfare has no choice other than to separate in order to form two welfare units. Otherwise, it faces a limitation on the benefits which may be received for each individual in the home.

In Dandridge v. Williams, 397 U.S. 471 (1970), the Supreme Court considered a challenge to the scheme of maximum grants. Most lower courts had invalidated them. The Supreme Court nevertheless upheld maximum grant limitations. It found that they were consistent with the Social Security Act, which mandates assistance to *families* with dependent children. Although the plaintiffs argued that the later children in the family received nothing, the Court reasoned that in fact the *family* still continued to receive benefits and simply shared them among a greater number of children. The Court also held that HEW had frequently approved state plans containing maximum grant limitations and that Congress itself, in 42 U.S.C. § 602(a)(23), had acknowledged the existence of maximum grants and required only that they be "proportionately adjusted," not abandoned. To uphold the legitimacy of maximum grant limitations would advance the state's power, under the Social Security Act, to set the level of benefits and the standard of need.

The plaintiffs in Dandridge v. Williams maintained that the maximum grant limitations violated the Equal Protection Clause. They argued that the limitations discriminated against large families, by allowing each member a lesser amount of assistance than if he or she had been in a smaller family. Similarly, they argued that the limitation of assistance to a lesser number of dependents in effect denied all assistance to dependents added subsequently to the family unit.

The Court found that there were rational objectives to be served by the maximum grant legislation. Such legislation encourages employment and avoids discrimination between welfare families and the families of working poor. When the maximum grants equal the minimum wage, a steadily employed head of household receives parity with the benefits paid to the non-working poor. While this might deny AFDC to welfare recipients who *could not* work, and while AFDC benefits would be paid to those in small families who *could* work, these imprecisions were not of concern to the Court.

The Court, in rejecting these arguments, held that the legislation should be tested under "traditional" concepts of equal protection, that a legislative classification needs only "some reasonable basis" and does not offend the Constitution simply because the classification "is not made with mathematical nicety or because in practice it results in some inequality." The Court rejected the "strict scrutiny" equal protection approach of Shapiro v. Thompson, 394 U.S. 618 (1969). See supra, § 11. It found no fundamental rights or suspect criteria in the case. Thus it did not matter that the legislation was poorly tailored to the means asserted:

> "For here we deal with state regulation in the social and economic field, not affecting

freedoms guaranteed by the Bill of Rights, and claimed to violate the Fourteenth Amendment only because the regulation results in some disparity in grants of welfare payments to the largest AFDC families. For this court to approve the invalidation of state economic or social regulation as 'over-.eaching' would be far too reminiscent of an era when the court thought the Fourteenth Amendment gave it power to strike down state laws 'because they may be unwise, improvident, or out of harmony with a particular school of thought'." 397 U.S. at 484.

In the views of the dissenting Justices, the asserted state rationales were insufficient and unpersuasive. Only a handful of AFDC families contain people able to work; thus the work incentive argument carried little weight. Further, the maximum grant limitation was grossly "underinclusive", because it did not encourage to work those who were able to do so but were living with small families. Justice Marshall argued further that the case should not be tested solely by a "strict scrutiny" approach requiring the presence of suspect criteria or fundamental rights. Rather, the Court should give weight to the fact that the case involved "the literally vital interests of a powerless minority" and required a state to show good cause for maximum grant legislation. This view in effect argued for a "middle range" of equal protection analysis, see supra §§ 11, 22–24, but failed to win a majority.

The decision in *Dandridge* ended the debate concerning the constitutionality of maximum grant limitations. The only remaining challenge rests upon 42 U.S.C. § 602(a)(23), discussed in the preceding section, in which Congress prohibited states from reducing their AFDC maximum grants below 1969 levels. Although states may apply lesser percentages to benefits generally, they cannot reduce maximums previously paid. This continues to be a subject of litigation. See Utah Welfare Rights Organization v. Lindsay, 315 F.Supp. 294 (D.Utah 1970) and Yearby v. Parham, 415 F.Supp. 1236 (N.D.Ga.1976). But maximum grant limitations remain constitutionally permissible.

§ 31. Discrimination: Intercategorical and Geographic

A traditional pattern of funding has involved discrimination between categories of assistance. Historically, a higher percentage of need has been paid to the aged, blind and disabled than to those receiving AFDC or General Assistance. The plaintiffs in Jefferson v. Hackney, 406 U.S. 535 (1972), challenged the pattern of discrimination which existed in Texas, favoring the "adult" categories of assistance by paying a higher percentage of need for the aged, blind and disabled than

[*370*]

for the dependent children. Texas had been paying only 50% of need in AFDC. That was raised to 75%, but it was still substantially lower than the amounts paid in the adult categories. The Supreme Court upheld the right of the state to engage in such discrimination.

It noted that the right to set levels of benefits was left with the states under the Social Security Act. Moreover, the pattern of discrimination involved in Jefferson v. Hackney had been present throughout the history of the Act and existed in the majority of states. It therefore had the acquiesence, if not approval, of HEW and Congress.

Moreover, the Court held that such discrimination was not wholly lacking in rationality. The Court held that a state might well believe that the aged, blind and disabled had lesser—if any—potential for augmenting their public assistance through employment. Their potential for independence was limited. In contrast, an AFDC unit might be viewed as having greater ability to generate income or reduce individual needs through "economies of scale." Both the caretaker relative and some of the children might be able to seek employment. Since some or all of such income might be disregarded in computing eligibility, it would be permissible for the state to pay a lesser percentage of need to AFDC recipients than to recipients of assistance in the adult categories.

Although this was at best only minimally rational, the Court held that discrimination between categories did not have to meet a higher standard of rationality. Traditional equal protection concepts left great latitude to the states. The Court therefore upheld the discrimination in Jefferson v. Hackney. It rejected an argument that a more demanding standard of equal protection analysis should be invoked because the discrimination against AFDC recipients fell peculiarly upon minority persons. It was true, statistically, that AFDC recipients disproportionately were members of minorities, and that this was far more true of AFDC recipients than of recipients of the adult categories of assistance. Nevertheless, the Court found no *explicit* evidence of racial discrimination. Moreover, it found evidence that Texas had increased the amounts of AFDC benefits more rapidly than adult benefits. Although the *impact* of the discrimination was along racial and ethnic lines, there was little hard or objective evidence to establish that this had been the legislative intent.

In Whitfield v. Oliver, 399 F.Supp. 348 (D.Ala. 1975), a different result was reached with respect to Alabama. There, the court found that the wide disparity between AFDC benefits and those paid through the Aid to the Aged program was racially motivated. Recipients of Aid to the Aged received 100% of need; recipients of AFDC received 55%. For more than 20 years AFDC had been a predominately black program. Alabama had been paying less than a third of the national average to AFDC recipients and was paying the second lowest figure among the states as of 1971. It was the only state paying lower AFDC benefits *per family* than Old Age benefits *per individual*.

Racially discriminatory purpose, the factor that was missing in *Jefferson,* was found through several means. First, there was a close parallel between the increasing minority composition of AFDC and the decreasing percentages paid. Secondly, state officials had been aware of this changing racial composition. Thirdly, state officials were candid in saying that legislators had been critical of AFDC on racial grounds and that, for this reason, AFDC had been neglected. Finally, the court emphasized the unbroken history of racial discrimination by the Alabama welfare department and the failure of any representative of that department to provide a rational explanation for continued discrimination against AFDC recipients.

Absent racial or other invidious motivation, intercategorical discrimination—like maximum grants—will escape constitutional challenge. This is true within the federally-funded programs involved in Jefferson v. Hackney; it is also true when comparing them with the state-funded programs of General Assistance. The only remain-

ing basis of challenge may arise where there is
not only a differential *between* programs but
where a person is discriminated against *because*
of another program.   Thus in Lee v. Smith, 43
N.Y.2d 453 (1977), 46 U.S.L.W. 2348 (1/78), the
New York Court of Appeals held that New York
could not deny Home Relief to needy, aged individuals simply because they received S.S.I.   But
it should be noted that programmatic exclusions
have been upheld in other contexts.   See Philbrook v. Glodgett, 421 U.S. 707 (1975), discussed
supra, §§ 20, 28.

One final area of discrimination involves geographical variations.   It is commonplace for
there to be extreme variations in benefits in the
AFDC program from state to state.   Typically,
Southern States such as Alabama, Mississippi,
Louisiana, and Arkansas pay far less in benefits
than Northern, industrial states such as Massachusetts, New Jersey, New York and Illinois.   On
a national scale, this simply reflects the historic
pattern which obtained under the Elizabethan
Poor Laws.   Benefits were set in localities and
varied according to the generosity and resources
of each community.   This remains true not only
on an interstate basis but also within state programs of General Assistance.

AFDC benefits vary widely from state to state
in amount and coverage.   HEW reported in 1975
that a total amount nationwide had been distributed to AFDC recipients which averaged $216 per

family in monthly benefits. The lowest states were in the South: Alabama ($96), Georgia ($102), Mississippi ($50), South Carolina ($88). In these states, AFDC was well below poverty levels. The highest average benefits were generally paid in industrialized states: Alaska ($264), California ($234), Connecticut ($271), the District of Columbia ($246), Hawaii ($306), Illinois ($292), Iowa ($281), Massachusetts ($353), Michigan ($264), New Jersey ($272), New York ($333), Pennsylvania ($261) and Wisconsin ($268). See the 1975 Annual Statistical Supplement, Social Security Bulletin.

These disparities raise, at least on the surface, equal protection questions. Presumably, the federal government could not fund and administer a program which would pay varying amounts according to the state in which a person lives. Similarly, a state could not establish a program in which benefits varied from locality to locality. Yet, in effect this is what has happened. State to state variations have been tolerated under the rubric of "cooperative federalism" because the structure of categorical assistance under the Social Security Act leaves determination of benefits to the states. Variations within a state have been tolerated because of the tradition of the Elizabethan Poor Laws. Yet such discrimination, interstate and intrastate, is largely irrational when viewed from the recipient's perspective.

These issues have largely evaded constitutional resolution. Interstate variations in federal programs have simply not been challenged. Local variations have also been tolerated. The latter are however coming under increasing scrutiny as states take over previously local programs, giving strength to equal protection arguments for state-wide uniform benefits. This rests, by analogy, upon the need for uniformity in welfare programs, such as AFDC, in which states administer federal funds. In Rothstein v. Wyman, 336 F. Supp. 328 (S.D.N.Y.1970), the plaintiffs challenged the payment of higher AFDC benefits in New York City than in adjacent counties. The court noted that three separate provisions of the Social Security Act require uniformity. First, each federally-funded state welfare program must be in effect throughout the entire state. Secondly, there must be state-wide financial participation. Thirdly, the Social Security Act requires that a single state agency be responsible for federally-funded programs. These requirements of the Act are implemented by HEW regulations requiring uniform and equitable treatment of people similarly situated. See supra, §§ 2, 4.

In *Rothstein,* the court rejected the State's rationale for paying higher benefits in New York City than in neighboring locales. It found that the legislature, although permitting discrimination, had not found a factual basis to justify it. In fact, the Bureau of Labor Statistics of the Department of Labor and the Commissioner of Welfare drew no distinctions in determining the cost of essential items of living between New York City and the immediate environs. The court therefore rejected the State's argument that there was a procedure by which suburban counties could apply for parity in payments, a procedure which the court found improperly and without reason placed the burden on the suburban counties when there was no reason for doing so. The discrimination was therefore contrary to the Social Security Act and void.

Rothstein invalidated discrimination in benefits involving a federally-funded program, but it did not deal with discrimination within a state where the funds were locally generated. Local variations in benefits are traditionally tolerated, although increasingly suspect as localities come to depend upon state funds for previously local programs. See supra, §§ 1, 7. A different form of discrimination is involved where *benefits* are uniform throughout a state, but the *funding* falls unequally on communities because of differences in numbers of welfare recipients in various communities. A prominent example is New York City. Challenges to this discrimination have not been successful. See supra, § 7.

In State of Wisconsin ex rel. Seehawer v. Schmidt, 363 F.Supp. 635 (E.D.Wis.1973), the court rejected a challenge to Wisconsin's system of funding public assistance. Under that system,

Wisconsin counties were partially reimbursed for the nonfederal portion of categorical assistance payments. But the scheme of reimbursement was in "inverse relationship" to the value of taxable property, with the result that richer counties received as little as 45% whereas the poorer counties received as much as 80% in reimbursement. The formula did not reflect the number of welfare recipients in each county. Consequently, a county with a great number of welfare recipients and a high total property value would pay out relatively more and recover relatively less than a county with fewer recipients and a lower total property value.

Nevertheless, the court held that the scheme did not violate the Constitution. It relied upon San Antonio Independent School District v. Rodriguez for the proposition that equal protection would not be denied where the class of citizens was "unified only by the common factor of residence in districts that happen to have more taxable wealth than other districts." The discrimination was against the districts, not the people residing there. The Court commented that:

> "Perhaps the programs could be designed to be more mathematically precise and to cast a more balanced burden on the counties. Presumably that would be possible by adopting a formula reflecting annual averages or actual numbers of welfare recipients residing within

each county. Arguably the problem presented here could be obviated by the state's assuming the entire cost. However, it is clear that this court is not the proper body to make such determinations." 363 F.Supp. at 637.

In San Antonio School District v. Rodriguez, 411 U.S. 1 (1973), the Supreme Court had upheld the state funding laws of Texas although they provided for unequal funding of school districts throughout the state. The plaintiffs argued that this led, inevitably, to unequal education. Individual school districts varied in the amount of taxable resources to them and in the amount of taxes raised to supplement the state funding. When all sources of funding—federal, state, and local—were combined, the Alamo Heights District expended $595 per pupil as compared with $356 per pupil in the Edgewood Independent School District. The Court held that this system of discriminatory financing withstood constitutional challenge since it did not involve a fundamental right or a suspect criterion such as race and was therefor tested only by the minimal requirements of traditional equal protection analysis. So viewed, the Texas funding system was a rational way of distributing limited funds to assure minimum quality education consistent with local control.

Writing for the majority, Justice Powell argued that discriminatory funding of school districts did not constitute a form of "wealth discrimination." The discrimination was among districts, not against individuals, based upon the wealth of the districts, not the individuals. Further, the deprivation was *relative*: there was no absolute denial of the benefit involved. Indeed, the state maintained that the education provided through state funding available to every district was minimally adequate. Finally, Justice Powell observed that even if the discrimination were against districts based upon the poverty of the people living in them or upon the absence of taxable property therein:

> "The system of alleged discrimination and the class it defines have none of the traditional indicia of suspectness: the class is not saddled with such disabilities, or subjected to such a history of purposeful unequal treatment, or relegated to such a position of political powerlessness as to command extraordinary protection from the majoritarian political process." 411 U.S. at 28.

In conclusion, it is obvious that courts will rarely invalidate broad-gauge discrimination in welfare. Such discrimination exists in programs, geography and funding. Yet courts are reluctant to discourage the incremental growth of welfare at varying places and levels of government, viewing that growth as healthy and the resulting discrimination as benign. Too, a finding of invalidity would lead to a confrontation forcing legislative appropriations or a termination of existing programs.   Rather, courts have limited their activity primarily to discrimination between individuals *within* legislatively defined units, such as that among AFDC recipients or Medicaid recipients, when the individuals argue that narrow line-drawing (e. g., based on sex or illegitimacy) is irrational even in light of legislative objectives.

VI. PROCEDURES

§ 32. Application and Prompt Action

Application processes for public assistance vary from program to program and place to place. They should be simple. A potential applicant should be able to call or appear at an office, inquire about eligibility, obtain an application and receive consideration within a relatively short period of time. In fact, all of this process may take a good deal of time, perhaps weeks or months, and may be complicated by the scarcity of personnel and resources in welfare programs as well as the complexity of the rules governing them. A further dimension may be the hostility of the people administering programs toward people who are intended as beneficiaries. Whatever the cause, the application process is oftentimes a harrowing experience. See supra, §§ 5, 15–16.

Federally-funded programs under the Social Security Act require that aid be provided with reasonable promptness to all eligible individuals. In the AFDC program, this appears at 42 U.S.C. § 602(a)(10). This provision has often been used to require a state to impose only those eligibility requirements which are mandated by the Social Security Act. See Townsend v. Swank, supra, § 3. It is also significant in mandating *prompt* action. This has been interpreted by HEW as meaning that an AFDC application must be approved or denied within 45 days. Similar requirements exist with respect to SSI and other federal programs, such as Medicaid and Food Stamps.

A state must provide for application by all eligible AFDC persons, who may be assisted by a person of their choosing, including a non-lawyer. 45 CFR 206.10. A Social Security number is required and an applicant must be assisted to obtain one. The state must fully advise people about the terms of eligibility and benefits and of the need to report changes in circumstances.

In some programs Congress has mandated that states undertake active and vigorous efforts to ensure participation. This is true with respect to Food Stamps, where a state is required under 7 U.S.C. § 2020(e)(1) to inform and ensure the participation of eligible households. In Tyson v. Norton, 390 F.Supp. 545 (D.Conn.1975), this was held to mean that a state must allocate sufficient personnel and resources to assure that the target population would learn about the availability of Food Stamps. EPSDT, a program connected with Medicaid, requires early periodic screening diagnosis and treatment. On one level, this is a preventive medicine program designed to reduce the demands upon Medicaid. On another level, however, EPSDT is a means of extending medical services to the broadest possible population and requires significant outreach. See supra, §§ 16–18.

Delays in the application process and the difficulty in relieving them through judicial intervention are illustrated by the course of litigation in Class v. Norton, 376 F.Supp. 496 (D.Conn.1974). There, in 1972, the district court had ordered the Connecticut Commissioner of Welfare to comply with federal regulations and act upon AFDC applications within thirty days. If no action was taken, the Commissioner was to presume eligibility. The Commissioner was further ordered to supply bi-monthly reports. Nevertheless, two years later the court found that AFDC applications had not been acted upon within thirty days in 1,300 instances during the preceding twelve month period. Some 20% of all applications took longer than thirty days in processing. The State argued that these delays were due to a lack of personnel. The court rejected the argument and mandated specific personnel to be assigned, within fifteen days, to initiate new procedures relieving the delay and backlog.

Similarily, in Perez v. Lavine, 422 F.Supp. 1259 (S.D.N.Y.1977), a federal district court ordered New York City's welfare department to provide an application form during a person's first or second visit to an income maintenance center for the purpose of applying for assistance. The court further ordered that application forms be provided at alternative locations throughout the community. The court then took the extraordinary step of listing such locations and requiring the Commissioner of New York's Department of Social Services to publicize the availability of application forms through such organizations. The court required a complete set of instructions in English and Spanish, with signs posted notifying people of their rights in both English and Spanish. In Perez v. Lavine the court also required an initial application interview within five working days and that necessary staff be transferred from other sections to *meet* the five working day requirement.

Courts have also mandated that action must be taken within a reasonable time, not to exceed 90 days, in applications to HEW for OASDI benefits. In Caswell v. Califano, 435 F.Supp. 127 (D.Me. 1977) the court noted that disability cases following a request for hearing before an administrative law judge posed a backlog "national in scope." As of May 1976, the average waiting time between request for hearing and scheduled date of hearing was 11.5 months for the New England region. The court held that such delays violated 42 U.S.C. § 405(b), requiring that HEW afford to an applicant "reasonable notice and opportunity for a hearing" and the Administrative Procedure Act, 5 U.S.C. §§ 555(b) and 706(1), providing that an agency must proceed to conclude a matter presented to it "within a reasonable time." The court commented, further, that "defendant's claim of inadequate resources does not justify violation of a federal statute." 435

F.Supp. at 135. In a similar case, White v. Mathews, 559 F.2d 852 (2d Cir. 1977) the Court went further and ordered interim payments to claimants who endured delays longer than the schedule allowed.

The application process frequently involves the physical presence of an applicant. On one hand, such presence is highly desirable to enable a caseworker to ask detailed questions and to be responsive to an applicant's need. It is also useful for determining credibility where factual inaccuracies may exist. On the other hand, physical presence may impose a substantial burden on an applicant. It may mean having to arrange child care or to dislocate schedules or to incur substantial travel expenses and responsibilities. This is particularly significant in rural areas where public transportation may be unavailable but it may also be a problem in urban areas as well. As a consequence, some programs such as Food Stamps do not require physical appearances at the application for benefits or the renewal of eligibility.

In Steinburg v. Fusari, 364 F.Supp. 922 (D. Conn.1973), the United States District Court held that Connecticut's unemployment compensation statute, by requiring seated interview procedures, denied due process. The Connecticut unemployment compensation statute required claimants to report to the local unemployment office bi-weekly to demonstrate continued eligibility by completing forms indicating availability for work and reasonable efforts to obtain employment. If questions arose during the routine bi-weekly re-certification a further "seated interview" with a fact-finding examiner for a more thorough inquiry was required.

Plaintiffs maintained this procedure violated 42 U.S.C. § 503(a)(1), requiring that payments be made "when due." At trial it appeared that some 19 to 26% of denials of benefits were reversed after significant delay; nearly 90% of the appeals of denials required more than one hundred days to resolve. The average delay was one hundred and twenty six days. The Court held that the failure to provide a full and ample hearing prior to terminating benefits denied due process of laws.

However, in Andrews v. Norton, 385 F.Supp. 672 (D.Conn.1974), AFDC recipients failed in their challenge to "face to face interviews" on re-determinations of eligibility at ninety day intervals. Because of the limited number of district offices in Connecticut, some welfare recipients were required to travel considerable distances at greater expense and inconvenience than others. Day care expenses were also involved. The court held that although these expenses were heavier for some applicants than for others, equal protection of the laws was not denied. Territorial uniformity was not a constitutional requisite.

The delay in processing an application—particularly one requiring a personal interview—may be inevitable, and perhaps justified by administrative necessity. See Barrett v. Roberts, 551 F. 2d 662 (5th Cir. 1977). Such delay should be distinguished from durational residency requirements or formal waiting periods to establish eligibility. These latter are generally void. See supra, §§ 12, 21. Cf., Weinberger v. Salfi, 422 U.S. 749 (1975). The delay for administrative processing is of quite a different order, but is justified only to the extent necessary to pass upon an application. And even then administrative delay cannot justify violating due process or statutory guarantees of "prompt action." That guarantee was one of the most significant innovations of the Social Security Act, creating entitlement to public assistance.

§ 33. Termination and Hearing

Procedural protections were among the revolutionary innovations of the Social Security Act in creating the federally funded welfare programs of the 1930's. The Social Security Act provided that a person was entitled to "reasonable promptness" on an application. 42 U.S.C. § 602(a)(10). This meant that even a person who had not yet been deemed eligible was entitled to a decision from responsible authorities. Once deemed eligible, a recipient was entitled to a "fair hearing" after benefits were terminated. These provisions concerning prompt action and fair hearings were required by the Social Security Act to be incorporated in state plans as a condition of receiving federal funds. The Social Security Act further required that state plans be in effect throughout a state and be administered by a single state agency. The procedural protections thus created were extended to all. See supra, §§ 2–4.

However, there was no provision for a hearing prior to termination of benefits. Any "fair hearing" would come only after benefits were terminated and the intervening delay would often consume several months. During that time, the welfare beneficiary would receive nothing. Since recipients rarely have assets or other income sufficient to support them, the denial of benefits without a *prior* hearing could work a significant, indeed grievous, hardship.

As discussed supra, § 13, this problem came before the Supreme Court in Goldberg v. Kelly, 397 U.S. 254 (1970). In that case, recipients of welfare sued the State of New York, challenging its failure to afford a hearing exploring the reasons for terminating benefits. The Court rejected various reasons offered by New York, such as the expense of hearings and the need to deal quickly with fraud. It found that the compelling needs of welfare recipients far outweighed, in due process terms, the need of the State to justify erroneous termination by fiscal imperatives.

During the pendency of *Goldberg* the State of New York amended its regulations to require that notice must be given to a recipient of the reasons for a proposed termination at least seven days prior to its effective date. Further, upon request a recipient could have the proposed termination reviewed by a local welfare official. As a part of the review, the recipient could submit a written statement demonstrating why the grant should not be discontinued. The regulation also provided that assistance would not be discontinued prior to decision. Thus the issue in Goldberg v. Kelly narrowed, from raising the question of whether a hearing must be afforded to raising instead the question of whether the hearing proposed by the new regulations was sufficient.

In Goldberg v. Kelly, the Court commented concerning welfare and poverty that a hearing prior to termination of benefits would advance "important governmental interests". It said:

> "From its founding the Nation's basic commitment has been to foster the dignity and well-being of all persons within its borders. We have come to recognize that forces not within the control of the poor contribute to their poverty. This perception, against the background of our traditions, has significantly influenced the development of the contemporary public assistance system. Welfare, by meeting the basic demands of subsistence,

can help bring within the reach of the poor the same opportunities that are available to others to participate meaningfully in the life of the community. At the same time, welfare guards against the societal malaise that may flow from a widespread sense of unjustified frustration and insecurity. Public assistance, then, is not mere charity but a means to 'promote the general welfare and secure the blessings of liberty to ourselves and our posterity'. The same governmental interests that counsel the provision of welfare counsel as well its uninterrupted provision to those eligible to receive it; pre-termination evidentiary hearings are indispensable to that end." 397 U.S. at 264–265.

The Court in *Goldberg* held that a recipient must be afforded a hearing before welfare benefits may be terminated, but that the hearing need not take the form of judicial or quasi-judicial trial. A complete record and comprehensive opinion would not be necessary and only minimum procedural safeguards were required. The seven days notice required by the New York provisions was held to be sufficient, as was the form of notice. However, the Court held that a recipient must be afforded the right to appear personally, with or without counsel, and an opportunity must be granted to confront and cross-examine adverse witnesses, as well as to present favorable witnesses.

Because of language difficulties, the Court held that a recipient could not be limited to written submissions; live testimony must be allowed in a pre-termination hearing. The decisionmaker's conclusion about a recipient's eligibility must rest solely on legal rules and the evidence adduced at the hearing. To assure this, the decision-maker must state the reasons for the decision and indicate the supporting evidence. An impartial decision-maker was essential; a welfare official might qualify, but not if he or she had participated in making the determination under review.

A major question after the decision in Goldberg v. Kelly was whether it would apply to social insurance programs as well as public assistance. The former, such as OASDI, have many of the "welfare" characteristics of AFDC. But typically they are not limited to the "needy," instead functioning like "earned" pensions. Although this distinction has lost much of its significance, as noted supra, § 19, it could mean that the grievous need emphasized in *Goldberg* might be found lacking with social insurance and, hence, due process might not mandate a hearing prior to termination of benefits.

This distinction underlay the Supreme Court's decision in Richardson v. Perales, 402 U.S. 389 (1971). The narrow question there was whether hearsay could provide the basis for termination of disability benefits, despite the emphasis in Goldberg v. Kelly on confronting and cross-examining witnesses. The Court held that hearsay was permissible. In part it did so on the basis that the recipient in *Perales* could have subpoenaed the missing witnesses. The decision also rested upon the nature of the testimony. The missing witnesses were physicians who had examined the claimant and determined that he suffered significant medical disability. The Court distinguished Goldberg v. Kelly, "where credibility and veracity" were at issue by saying that:

> "The *Perales* proceeding is not the same. We are not concerned with termination of disability benefits once granted. Neither are we concerned with a change in status without notice. Notice was given to claimant Perales. The physician's reports were on file and available for inspection by the claimant and his counsel. And the authors of those reports were known and subject to subpoena and to the very cross-examination that the claimant asserts he has not enjoyed. Further, the specter of questionable credibility and veracity is not present; there is professional disagreement with the medical conclusions, to be sure, but there is no attack here upon the doctor's credibility or veracity. *Kelly* affords little comfort to the claimant." 402 U.S. at 407.

The decision in Richardson v. Perales addressed the question of whether Goldberg v. Kelly would be applied beyond the public assistance field, to social insurance plans, but it did not answer the question except inferentially. It assumed that a hearing might be required but that the hearing actually afforded was adequate. Because a hearing was possible and confrontation through subpoena was available, the issue in *Perales* narrowed to the simple question of whether the failure of the claimant's attorney to subpoena opposing witnesses precluded the claimant from challenging a decision made on hearsay in the absence of those witnesses. Thus *Perales*, at most, involved questions concerning burdens of proof. The applicability of Goldberg v. Kelly beyond the welfare field was not resolved in that case.

However, the issue was squarely posed in Mathews v. Eldridge, 424 U.S. 319 (1976). In *Eldridge*, the plaintiff had been denied disability benefit payments under OASDI. He claimed that he should have been given a hearing similar to that mandated in Goldberg v. Kelly prior to termination of benefits. Since OASDI is a form of social insurance, this would have represented an extension of Goldberg v. Kelly beyond the public assistance or pure "welfare" context. Also, since the claimant had been eligible for benefits and had been receiving them, the case did not pose the problem involved in Richardson v. Perales, of whether Goldberg v. Kelly applied to initial applications for benefits. Rather, the question in *Eld-*

ridge was a narrow one: Whether due process required a hearing prior to termination of social insurance benefits. The answer was negative.

In Mathews v. Eldridge, the court reviewed its earlier decisions under the Due Process Clause and concluded that due process, unlike some legal rules, "is not a technical conception with a fixed content unrelated to time, place and circumstances", citing Cafeteria and Restaurant Workers v. McElroy, 367 U.S. 886, 895 (1961). This meant, in the Court's view, that resolution of the issue whether administrative procedures were constitutionally sufficient required "analysis of the governmental and private interests that are affected." The Court then said:

> "More precisely, our prior decisions indicate that identification of the specific dictates of due process generally requires consideration of three distinct factors: First, the private interest that will be affected by the official action; second, the risk of an erroneous deprivation of such interests through the procedures used, and the probable value, if any, of additional or substitute procedural safeguards; and finally the government's interest, including the function involved and the fiscal and administrative burdens that the additional or substitute procedural requirement would entail." 424 U.S. at 334–335.

The Court in *Eldridge* sought to distinguish Goldberg v. Kelly on several grounds. It noted that *Goldberg* emphasized that welfare assistance is given to "persons on the very margin of subsistence." The Court then observed with respect to social insurance:

> "Eligibility for disability benefits, in contrast, is not based upon financial need. Indeed, it is wholly unrelated to the worker's income or support from many other sources, such as earnings of other family members, workmen's compensation awards, tort claims awards, savings, private insurance, public or private pensions, veteran's benefits, food stamps, public assistance, or the many other important programs both public and private, which contain provisions for disability payments affecting a substantial portion of the work force . . ." 424 U.S. at 341.

The Court therefore concluded that the potential deprivation in *Eldridge* is "generally likely to be less than in *Goldberg*" although it conceded that there was little likelihood that a terminated recipient would be able to find even temporary employment. This conclusion of the Court hardly comports with the realities experienced by those relying upon OASDI for disability or retirement benefits.

The realities facing the terminated disability recipient were reflected dramatically in the footnotes of the majority opinion in *Eldridge*. The mean income of the family unit of a disabled worker in 1965 was $3,803, while the median in-

come was $2,836. The mean liquid assets totalled
$4,862, but the median was $940. (Footnote 26).
A disability recipient who was denied OASDI
would be ineligible for disability assistance under
the federal program of public assistance, SSI. It
is true, as the Court observed, 424 U.S. 327, at
note 27, that there are state and local welfare
programs which "may" supplement the worker's
income. It is also true that Food Stamps might
be available. However, at best these would be
minimal forms of assistance, indistinguishable
from those available to the welfare recipients in
Goldberg.

Thus the Court's distinction in *Eldridge* between the need of the welfare recipient in *Goldberg* and the need of the social insurance recipient was illusory. Both welfare and social insurance recipients are likely to be living at the edge
of subsistence. The simple statistic, which the
Court itself cited, that over 25% of disabled
workers who receive OASDI are also receiving
public assistance, supports this. Similar figures
apply to the aged and the blind.

The Court in *Eldridge*, after distinguishing
Goldberg on the ground that welfare recipients
are more "needy" than social insurance recipients, turned to a second consideration: The fairness and reliability of the existing pretermination
procedures and the probable value, if any, of additional procedural safeguards. The Court noted
that the relevant statutory standard required a

person to be unable to engage in any "substantial gainful activity by reason of any medically determinable physical or mental impairment . . ." 42 U.S.C. § 423(d)(1)(A). The Court deemed this medical standard to be "more sharply focused and easily documented" than in the typical welfare case. In the Court's view, a welfare case might include a wider variety of information, with issues of witness credibility and veracity becoming critical to the decision making process. The Court therefore concluded that the potential value of an evidentiary hearing is substantially less in the disability social insurance context than in the welfare context involved in *Goldberg.*

However, the statutory standard governing disability cases—contrary to the Supreme Court's view—can hardly be deemed simple or clear. Disability may involve subjective causes and subjective evaluations of incapacity. These relate to availability of work and the demands posed upon specific individuals, as well as their capacity to meet those demands. Even a cursory review of the caselaw in the district courts bears ample testimony to the complexity and subjectivity of the standards and testimony in disability cases. Certainly they rival the AFDC cases for which Goldberg v. Kelly required an evidentiary hearing prior to termination.

Perhaps most astonishing in Mathews v. Eldridge was the Court's treatment of what it called "the public interest." By this, the Court meant "the incremental cost resulting from the increased number of hearings and the expense of providing benefits to ineligible recipients pending decision." The Court did not attempt to calculate this with any precision. It simply observed:

> "We only need say that experience with the constitutionalizing of government procedures suggests that the ultimate additional cost in terms of money and administrative burden would not be insubstantial." 424 U.S. at 347.

These comments are in dramatic contrast to the comments of the Court in Goldberg v. Kelly, where the Court rejected governmental claims that hearings prior to termination would impose prohibitive administrative costs and loss of benefits which could not be recovered. In *Goldberg,* the Court had concluded that there were ways of minimizing these losses and, in any event, bearing them was in the public interest. If indeed the issues in *Eldridge* were as clear and simple as the Court maintained, and if the procedures already afforded were as ample and adequate as the court argues, then simply adding an evidentiary dimension would have posed far less of a burden than in the welfare context of *Goldberg*. It is perhaps on this score that the Court's attempt to distinguish Goldberg v. Kelly is least successful. Disability cases administered by federal agencies are vastly more susceptible to well managed evidentiary hearings than are the AFDC cases heard by state agencies.

It seems unlikely that Mathews v. Eldridge will have much impact beyond the highly structured, technical context of OASDI disability cases. Following that decision, the State of New York amended its Home Relief statute to deny a pre-termination hearing where benefits were denied to a recipient who "voluntarily terminated his employment or reduced his earning capacity for the purpose of qualifying" for Home Relief or where such person "without cause, refused to register with or report to" the New York Employment Service or accept appropriate employment. This was invalidated in Hurley v. Toia, 432 F. Supp. 1170 (S.D.N.Y.1977). The court noted that *Eldridge* had emphasized three factors: the private interest affected, the risk of error and the government's interest. The court in *Hurley* held that the first and third factors favored the recipients, since Home Relief—unlike the disability program involved in *Eldridge*—was based upon the financial need of the recipients. As to the second factor, the risk of error, the Court also found in favor of the claimants since that risk of error was substantial. The standards involved were "not a narrowly focused issue, capable of resolution by resort to limited, unbiased sources of information, but an issue that can only be determined after all the facts and circumstances of each individual case have been examined." 432 F.Supp. at 1176–1177.

There may well be some legislation which arguably escapes *Kelly* and *Eldridge* on the ground that no factual issues are posed; hence, no hearing is necessary. Perhaps this may be true of legislation abolishing an entire program or reducing benefits categorically. But even there, factual issues concerning application may warrant a hearing. More often, legislation, like that in Hurley v. Toia, involves a superficial objectivity which upon analysis requires hearings to determine applicability in individual cases.

In Cardinale v. Mathews, 399 F.Supp. 1163 (D. D.C.1975), suit was brought to challenge HEW regulations under SSI which did not afford a hearing in cases where amendments to federal law or an increase in benefits payable under federal law required "automatic suspension, reduction, or termination of benefits"; or clerical or mechanical error had been made and was being corrected; or the facts warranting suspension, reduction or termination were supplied by the recipient and "the conclusions to be drawn from such facts are not subject to conflicting interpretations." 20 CFR 416.1336(a). The rationale of these exclusions was that Goldberg v. Kelly did not require a hearing in such cases. HEW argued that there could be no dispute concerning credibility or veracity in the excluded instances, since the facts were all conceded and what was involved was simply a matter of policy or procedure.

The court rejected the arguments of HEW. As to the denial of hearings where "automatic" adjustments were required in SSI benefits, the court said of the Secretary:

> ". . . he fails to recognize, or at least minimizes, the possibility that specific amendments to federal law may not apply to the person against whom defendant directs his adjustment. For example, the defendant might erroneously reduce SSI benefits of one who is not even receiving Social Security benefits." 399 F.Supp. at 1171.

The court noted that, while there may be no right of due process for a recipient to participate in rule-making, a hearing would be necessary in *applying* rules to a recipient.

The court made similar observations concerning the denial of hearings in cases where "clerical errors" were being corrected. It said:

> "Defendant, having admitted by his own regulation that a clerical or mechanical error may occur, appears to maintain that his corrections are infallible. Because if defendant admits that his corrections may themselves be erroneous, there remains the possibility of factual mistakes which, as Goldberg v. Kelly teaches, it is the role of procedural due process protections to prevent." 399 F. Supp. at 1172–1173.

The court also rejected HEW's argument that no hearing was necessary where a reduction or termination was based on facts supplied by the recipient. Errors there, too, are possible either in misunderstanding the recipient or misinterpreting the information supplied by the recipient.

The regulations involved in Cardinale v. Mathews involved a basic distinction between fact-finding, for which hearings might be necessary, and implementation of policy, for which no hearings might be necessary. In Russo v. Kirby, 453 F.2d 548 (2nd Cir. 1971), the Court of Appeals held that there "was no occasion for a hearing" where the sole basis for challenging terminations was that the state law was unconstitutional. Similarly, in Schneider v. Whaley, 541 F.2d 916 (2nd Cir. 1976), the Court held that assistance (funding of a day care center) could be reduced without a hearing where the "sole issue involved is one of policy or change in state or federal law".

However, in Viverito v. Smith, 421 F.Supp. 1305 (S.D.N.Y.1976), the court invalidated a New York statutory provision which permitted denying benefits prior to a hearing where the sole issue is "one of state policy . . . and neither one of fact or judgment, nor whether the state's policies . . . were correctly applied to the facts of the particular case." In *Viverito,* the State had published a new schedule of shelter allowances. As a result, it reduced the grants of a number of AFDC recipients.

The court held that hearings were required pursuant to Goldberg v. Kelly. Although the shelter allowances had in fact been reduced, the impact in any particular case might well be a subject of dispute. One of the plaintiffs in *Viverito* maintained that application of the shelter reduction would create an "emergency" situation. Other plaintiffs maintained estoppel or hardship defenses. In holding that hearings were required pursuant to Goldberg v. Kelly, the court said:

> "Since none of the plaintiffs here seek to challenge the validity of the new maximum shelter allowances itself, but rather claim that the new ceilings were for one reason or another incorrectly applied to their individual case, § 358.8 itself would seem to require a hearing prior to termination or reduction of benefits. Although the state purports to be acting under that regulation, their method of doing so is not well calculated to deny pretermination hearings only to persons raising questions of policy alone. The state has apparently decided that all challenges to the reduced shelter allowances, regardless of the individual allegations, raise issues of policy alone . . ." (citations omitted) 421 F. Supp. at 1310.

The court further noted that the state's approach apparently violated the federal regulation concerning "aid continuing," which provided that a denial of "aid continuing" on the grounds that the recipient raises issues of policy alone may be made only "at the hearing." 45 CFR 205.10(a) (6)(i)(A).

The decisions in *Cardinale* and *Viverito* suggest that it will rarely be true that a hearing can be denied as involving only "policy" and not "facts" unless there is *first* a hearing to determine that the claimant so views the matter. The Court in *Viverito* itself suggested that the fact/policy distinction was inherently unworkable as a means of *a priori* limiting Goldberg v. Kelly by administrative fiat. Accord: Yee-Litt v. Richardson, 353 F.Supp. 996 (N.D.Calif.1973), aff'd 412 U.S. 924 (1973). Thus the potential limitation on the scope of *Goldberg* would seem illusory. Most litigation has instead focused on whether *Goldberg,* which involved total denial of benefits, relates as well to delays or reductions in benefits.

Reductions in benefits have generally been held to require *Goldberg* hearings unless they applied to all welfare beneficiaries, as with an across-the-board percentage reduction. But delays have sometimes been permissible where they amounted to only a few days or weeks for legitimate administrative purposes. See Barrett v. Roberts, 551 F.2d 662 (5th Cir. 1977) (8 to 20 days for semi-annual recertification). See supra, § 32. Delays of two to six months have been held unreasona-

ble. See Cornelius v. Minter, 395 F.Supp. 616
(D.Mass.1974). And of course any delay in initial certification or decision for eligibility may
run afoul of the Due Process Clause and the provisions of the Social Security Act requiring
prompt action on applications. 42 U.S.C. §
602(a)(10).

§ 34. Support Payments and Fraud

The most significant asset available in many
welfare cases is support from the absent parent.
Since the mid-1960's Congress has required
AFDC recipients to cooperate in seeking such
support. The program early became known as
NOLEO, for notice to law enforcement officials.
More recently, the emphasis on support has generated extensive amendments in part IV–D of the
Social Security Act. These provisions are in response to the extensive litigation surrounding the
earlier NOLEO program.

A number of states had early provided that
public assistance would be terminated if the
mother refused to cooperate, even to initiating a
paternity or nonsupport suit. Such requirements
were universally held to be void as constituting
an additional standard of eligibility. See supra, §
3. In Doe v. Rampton, 497 F.2d 1032 (10th Cir.
1974), the state argued that terminating assistance for noncooperation was not an additional
condition of eligibility but rather a means of

gathering information "so that actual need and therefore eligibility may be determined." The court simply noted that "it is clear that the state conditions continued aid upon a mother's compliance with the sections. This is contrary to the teachings of Townsend v. Swank."

In Shirley v. Lavine, 365 F.Supp. 818 (N.D.N. Y.1973), aff'd 420 U.S. 730 (1975), the State of New York had adopted a regulation which terminated assistance only to the caretaker relative for refusal to cooperate in bringing a paternity suit against the putative father. The State argued that this was not a penalty imposed upon the child. The court rejected this, saying that Congress had recognized the "interdependency of provisions for and to the child and its caretaker mother." It quoted from a Congressional report for the proposition that:

> "Since the person caring for the child must have food, clothing, and other essentials, amounts allotted to the children must be used in part for this purpose if no other provision is made to meet her needs." 365 F. Supp. at 822.

The court noted that HEW had promulgated a regulation essentially authorizing what the state had done. It found that the regulation itself ran counter to the Social Security Act.

In 1975, Congress added Part D to Title IV of the Social Security Act, which requires, as a condition of eligibility, that each applicant cooperate with the state to establish paternity and obtain support payments. 42 U.S.C. § 602(a)(26)(B). This legislation clearly established the right of the state to insist upon cooperation, subject to an exclusion where there is "good cause" for a mother to insist upon non-cooperation. Failure to cooperate means that any aid for the child is provided in the form of "protective payment". 42 U.S.C. § 606(b)(2).

Title IV–D of the Social Security Act provides for the creation of federal and state administrative procedures for "locating absent parents, establishing paternity and obtaining child support." 42 U.S.C. § 651. A separate administrative unit is established within HEW and mandated for each state for sharing of information and pursuit of delinquent support obligations. Specific provision is made to establish a Parent Locator System. States must proceed to establish paternity and secure support payments unless doing so "is against the best interests of the child." 42 U.S.C. § 654(4)(A). Amounts collected remain with the state as reimbursement until the family becomes ineligible for assistance. 42 U.S.C. § 657.

The Social Security Act requires states to provide for "prompt notice" to the state child support agency of assistance to any child who has been deserted or abandoned by a parent. 42 U.S.C. § 602(a)(11). Each applicant must assign rights to support and cooperate in efforts to establish paternity and support, 42 U.S.C. § 602(a)(26), unless good cause is shown. Although the non-cooperating relative may lose benefits, the Act does provide that "nothing in this subsection shall be construed to make an otherwise eligible child ineligible for protective payments because of the failure of such parent to so cooperate." 42 U.S.C. § 606(f).

The state plan must provide that as a condition of eligibility each applicant for AFDC will assign to the state any rights to support from any other person. 45 CFR 232.11. If a relative fails to comply, a dependent child shall receive benefits, but they shall be paid to another person for the child's benefit, 45 CFR 232.11(a)(3) and 234.60, as protective payments. Further, each applicant is required to cooperate in establishing the paternity of a child born out of wedlock and in obtaining support. "Cooperate" includes giving information, appearing in court and testifying. Failure to cooperate renders the applicant ineligible, although the child remains eligible for protective payments.

HEW has issued regulations under Part IV–D of the Social Security Act requiring states to pursue support payments for AFDC recipients. 45 CFR 301. A separate administrative unit must be established, to be called the IV–D agency. It establishes paternity and support for any child receiving AFDC as to whom an assignment of rights, required for eligibility under AFDC, was executed. It collects the payments and retains them for past payments; the family remains eligible for AFDC unless the support is adequate to replace current AFDC. The IV–D agency may also assist others in collecting support. The amount owed must be established by court order, other legal process or agreement, subject to adjustment for present needs and abilities of the parent and child. Administrative hearings are provided for this complex process and may review agency findings as to paternity and amounts due. The adequacy of these proceedings raises substantial due process questions.

The 1975 child support and establishment of paternity amendments to Title IV of the Social Security Act created a "good cause" exception for non-compliance with the requirement that AFDC recipients assist in establishing paternity and locating absent spouses to provide support for their children. In Coe v. Mathews, 426 F.Supp. 774 (D.D.C.1976) the National Welfare Rights Organization, the State of Alaska and five AFDC recipients sued for mandamus to compel HEW to issue standards implementing the good cause exception under 42 U.S.C. §§ 602(a)(26)(B) and 654. The exception for good cause was to be created by state law under standards prescribed by the Secretary, taking "into consideration the best interests of the child." The plaintiffs in *Coe* challenged HEW's proposed regulations, which limited good cause to those situations involving incest, forcible rape or adoption where, "in the opinion of the IV–D agency, it would not be in the best interests of the child" to undertake the establishment of paternity. 45 CFR 303.5(b). The status of these regulations and the outcome of this suit are presently unclear.

Compulsory cooperation in identifying a non-supporting spouse involves important concerns. An AFDC mother may well fear retaliation, physical or otherwise, if the identity or whereabouts of the child's father are disclosed. Psychological injury may also be posed for the child. Beyond concerns for privacy, there are also constitutional concerns for freedom of association and potential self-incrimination. Thus, the "good cause" exception in § 606(a)(26) raises troublesome issues of interpretation. Court decisions, however, tend to support the validity of compelling cooperation as a means of enabling the state to pursue assets of a non-supporting parent to defray welfare costs.

In Doe v. Norton, 365 F.Supp. 65 (D.Conn.1973) the challenged Connecticut statute provided that if a mother of an illegitimate child refused to disclose the name of the putative father under oath to the welfare commissioner or to a selectman of the town the mother could be cited to appear before a judge and compelled to disclose the father's name and to institute an action to establish paternity. If the mother failed to cooperate, she could be held in contempt of court. The court held that this provision did not conflict with the Social Security Act, and in fact furthered the interest of the AFDC provisions in determining the paternity of needy children. The court noted in particular that the Connecticut provision would not deny either the mother or the child the benefits of food, shelter, or clothing in accordance with their needs although it might impair, for a period of time, the ability of the recalcitrant mother to spend time with her child. The court therefore held that the provision did not constitute an eligibility requirement additional to those provided for in the Social Security Act.

In Doe v. Norton, the court rejected a claim that requiring disclosure of the putative father's name, on penalty of criminal contempt, violated the mother's constitutional right to privacy. The court referred to Griswold v. Connecticut, 381 U. S. 479 (1965) and Roe v. Wade, 410 U.S. 113 (1973) for the proposition that the right of personal privacy extends only to personal rights that can be deemed "fundamental" or "implicit in the concept of ordered liberty." Compelling testimony is a long established governmental practice in a number of settings and the invasion did not involve unreasonable use of force in violation of the Fourth Amendment. Further the objective was reasonable: "To enforce a familial monetary obligation, not to interfere with personal privacy." 365 F.Supp. at 77. The interference was even less than that permitted by the Supreme Court decision in Wyman v. James, 400 U.S. 309 (1971), upholding home visits. Finally, the court concluded that any risks of self-incrimination had been resolved by the statute, which provided for immunity from prosecution. See also, Burdick v. Miech, 385 F.Supp. 927 (E.D.Wis.1974).

Compelling cooperation in pursuing non-supporting parents relates to a basic concern in welfare programs, that recipients may withhold assets or potential assets. This is akin to eligibility requirements concerning employability and it is one of the reasons justifying home visits to verify eligibility. See Wyman v. James, 400 U.S. 309 (1971). These concerns have led to an expansion in the information sought during the application process and in the uses of such information to verify eligibility. This search for fraud has been facilitated by the wide-spread availability of computers, posing serious problems concerning privacy of individuals.

Each applicant for AFDC must supply a social security number. 42 U.S.C. § 602(a)(25). A state is required by the Social Security Act to guard the privacy of information submitted by applicants, 42 U.S.C. § 602(a)(9), restricting disclosure to purposes directly connected with the administration of assistance, including any criminal or civil investigation or proceeding. Information disclosed in an application or otherwise is limited to purposes relating to eligibility, assistance and services. 45 CFR 205.40. But it may also, according to HEW regulations, be used for criminal or civil proceedings "in connection with the administration of any such plans or programs" or other federal need-related programs. Disclosure of names to legislative committees is prohibited, as is publishing lists.

Privacy in the application process of one who seeks welfare is a concern which competes with the need to prevent fraud. Federal regulations require that states establish methods and criteria for identifying situations where fraud may exist and for referring those situations for investigation and prosecution. 45 CFR 235.110(a). The rule does not forbid agency investigations concerning those whose applications have been approved and who are receiving assistance. See United States v. McDaniels, 370 F.Supp. 293 (E. D.La.1973). The HEW regulations require the state plan to develop procedures and designate officials for investigation of fraud by recipients and for referral of cases where "there is valid reason to suspect that fraud has been practiced". 45 CFR 235.110(a)(2). In the referral process, the state agency may disclose portions of the recipient's file but may not disclose portions which are unrelated to the fraud charges and which are otherwise confidential. 45 U.S.C. § 602(a)(9).

The information required of welfare applicants provides an effective tool for ascertaining fraud. The difficult issues relate primarily to *dealing* with fraud: terminating benefits to an AFDC child would seem impermissible, statutorily and constitutionally. The two techniques which are most effective, however, are diverting payments for the child to someone other than the fraudulent caretaker or undertaking recoupment from that caretaker. These are the subjects of the next sections of this text. It should be noted, however, that termination of benefits in programs other than AFDC—Food Stamps, for example—is permissible, since it does not directly affect benefits intended for someone other than the person committing the fraud.

§ 35. Vendor and Protective Payments

Welfare benefits are usually thought of as being grants of money. In fact, cash grant benefits are relatively recent developments. The Elizabethan Poor Laws involved benefits of an in-kind nature: food, shelter, and employment. The state and locallyfunded programs of General Assistance which preceded the Social Security Act in the 1930's were similarly conceived, and today General Assistance programs still rely heavily upon vendor payments for food and shelter. Currently, federallyfunded programs of assistance are oftentimes in-kind: for example, this is true of federal housing programs, education, Food Stamps, Medicaid and legal services.

The Social Security Act represented a departure from the reliance upon in-kind payments.

42 U.S.C. § 606(b) defines AFDC as being payments in cash directly to the beneficiaries This was also true of the other categorical programs created by the Social Security Act and remains true of them, although they are now subsumed under SSI and administered federally. This emphasis upon the money payment principle was revolutionary and a matter of considerable controversy during the Congressional debates about the Social Security Act. See supra, § 1–2. The advocates of the principle maintained that direct money payments were consistent with dignity and independence and were necessary to assure the personal development of welfare recipients. Only recently have vendor and protective payments come into more common usage in AFDC.

The Social Security Act provides that a state agency may make protective payments on behalf of a child where aid is not being "used in the best interests of the child." 42 U.S.C. § 605. The state may seek appointment and substitution of a guardian or other civil or criminal remedies. AFDC is defined as "money payments" to a child or caretaker relative or on their behalf,

> "to another individual who . . . is interested in or concerned with the welfare of such child or relative, or are made on behalf of such child or relative directly to a person furnishing food, living accomodations, or other goods, services or items . . ." 42 U.S.C. § 606(b).

The state may make protective or vendor payments only where the relative is unable to manage funds and must attempt to provide services to enhance the relative's management capabilities.

However, protective payments may be made to others for the beneficiaries in other instances. 45 CFR 234.11. In AFDC cases, these include situations where payments have not been used to benefit children or where an applicant has refused work under WIN or has refused to cooperate in seeking support for the child, in which case payments may be made to caretakers or vendors of services. 45 CFR 234.60. HEW regulations require careful procedures before such action, including court appointment of a guardian if protective payments are continued for longer than two years. Protective payments may not exceed 10% of the AFDC caseload in any given month, excluding the WIN and support cases. Protective payments may also be made for adults who are unable to manage their funds. 45 CFR 234.70.

Protective payments are one form of incursion on the money payment principle; vendor payments are another. To the extent that the vendor, for example a landlord, can by-pass the recipient and contract directly with the welfare department, the recipient becomes dependent upon both the welfare department and the vendor. In this sense, vendor payments have the potential for rendering a recipient doubly powerless or dependent. Protective payments have a similar impact, inducing desired behavior or punishing non-conforming behavior, and thereby curbing the independence or freedom of choice of welfare recipients.

The United States Supreme Court has passed upon these developments in only one case, Engelman v. Amos, 404 U.S. 23 (1971). In that case, the district court had enjoined the State of New Jersey from making vendor payments under its state welfare statutes to persons who provided services to welfare recipients. The district court had found that the state regulation conflicted with the Social Security Act, 42 U.S.C. § 606(b). The Supreme Court reversed that portion of the district court's judgment on the ground that "there is nothing in the federal statute that prohibits a state from making vendor payments so long as they are made from state funds without federal matching." 404 U.S. at 24. The Court noted that the Social Security Act neither provides reimbursement to the state for vendor payments nor prohibits them. The Court thus did not reach the question of whether such payments infringed either constitutional or statutory interests of recipients, although it seems likely that vendor and protective payments are permissible.

In Roberts v. Harder, 320 F.Supp. 1313 (D. Conn.1970), the plaintiff challenged a Connecticut practice under which welfare benefits were withheld and paid directly to a landlord. The plaintiff had not received her welfare check and filed a complaint. The landlord had complained to the welfare department about non-payment and therefore received rent payments directly. The failure to pay was not the plaintiff's fault; nor was a hearing provided to the plaintiff before the vendor payments were ordered.

The court held that there was not a protectable interest in the right to receive money payments. The content of due process and the right to a hearing under due process, the court held, turn upon the nature of the underlying laws. In *Roberts,* the court's view was that the recipient had not lost benefits, since they were being paid directly to the landlord who was, in fact, providing shelter to the recipient. Rather, the only interest which was lost was that in receiving cash grants. The money payment principle, the court held, was not sufficient to warrant protection under the Due Process Clause. Money payments, at most, would have given the plaintiff economic bargaining power with the landlord, which, in the court's view, was not constitutionally significant.

Similarly, protective payments have been upheld against constitutional challenge. Payment to representatives is mandated in 42 U.S.C. § 1382(a)(2)(A) with respect to any aged, blind or disabled person receiving SSI where the person eligible is "medically determined to be a drug addict or an alcoholic unless such individual is undergoing any treatment that may be appropriate."

In Hodges v. Weinberger, 429 F.Supp. 756 (D. Md.1977) this provision was challenged on the ground that:

> "[P]ayment to a person other than themselves would increase the danger of delay, non-receipt, or misuse of their respective SSI payments; that their independent management of their SSI payments is therapeutic to them; and that, if given the opportunity, they could establish these contentions by evidence . . ." 429 F.Supp. at 758.

The plaintiffs further argued that mandatory appointment of a representative payee denied equal protection of the laws and constituted an unconstitutional irrebuttable presumption of incompetence.

The court rejected these arguments, holding that Congress could properly decide to impose an eligibility requirement in the expectation that it would lead alcoholics and addicts to seek treatment. In the court's view, this was a legitimate legislative goal and the means chosen were appropriately tailored. In addition, Congress may well have been concerned about the possibility of abuse and chosen a means to avoid it.

Protective and vendor payments are thus constitutionally permissible and are common in General Assistance and in-kind programs. The increasing use of such payments with AFDC is a result of efforts to control fraud and mismanagement by caretaker relatives. Another response to those problems has been the increasing use of recoupment.

§ 36. Recoupment and Reimbursement

Most welfare programs contemplate that assistance is to be provided only if other assets and income are insufficient. This is not true, for example, of social insurance. But programs such as General Assistance or AFDC have long incorporated state common law and statutory provisions which make relatives responsible for each other and which make those receiving public assistance liable for repayment when they become self-supporting. Further, a state may seek to recoup prior payments from present payments if the earlier assistance was, for any reason, improper. Recoupment and reimbursement are two closely related concepts. However, recoupment seeks repayment while a person is still receiving assistance; reimbursement reaches the individual after he or she has ceased to be dependent upon welfare. Thus, recoupment of benefits comes at a time when an individual is least able to repay. It therefore poses severe economic problems and dangers for welfare beneficiaries.

A state may provide, under HEW regulations, for recoupment of AFDC overpayments only from assets or income beyond present assistance, 45 CFR 233.20(a)(12), unless the recipient willfully withheld information. In such cases, current assistance may be reduced. Recoupment is limited to overpayments during the preceding twelve months. Recoupment may include disregarded income but must be designed to minimize undue hardship. These limitations apply to AFDC. Recoupment in other programs may not be subject to such limitations, and the rules governing each program—General Assistance, SSI or social insurance, such as OASDI—must be consulted separately.

Recoupment is mandated in Social Security disability cases arising under OASDI, except "there shall be no . . . recovery by the United States from any person who is without fault if such . . . recovery would defeat the purpose of this Title or would be against equity and good conscience." 42 U.S.C. § 404(b). In determining whether a person is without "fault," the HEW regulations mandate consideration of all pertinent circumstances, including age, intelligence, education, and physical and mental condition. Fault may be found if the applicant made an incorrect statement or failed to furnish material information or knowingly accepted an overpayment. 20 CFR 404.507. Defeating the "purposes" of the Act would occur, under 20 CFR 404.508, where the person from whom recovery is sought "needs substantially all of his current income (including Social Security monthly benefits) to meet current ordinary and necessary living expenses." And the reference to "equity and good conscience" is interpreted at 20 CFR 404.-509 to include the situation in which an individual "by reason of the incorrect payment, relinquished a valuable right . . . or changed his position for the worse." All of these factors must be considered in an evidentiary hearing and are subject to judicial review.

In Cucuzzella v. Weinberger, 395 F.Supp. 1288 (D.Del.1975), the court reversed an order of recoupment where the recipients' understanding of the meaning of the statutory term "disability" was unclear and the evidence that the family could afford repayment was insufficient. As to the "equity and good conscience" provision, the court commented:

> ". . . the change of position may be quite minor, as long as it involves an expenditure which would not have been made but for incorrect benefit payment. And, money being fungible, if the benefits received are merged with common funds, but other money is spent in a way in which it would not have been but for the receipt of the benefits, the reliance standard of the regulations will be satisfied. Thus, if Joanne's attendance at college was made possible only by the benefits which had been received for Lee, the criteria of § 404.509 may well have been met." 395 F.Supp. at 1298.

The disability standard interpreted in *Cucuzzel-la* is perhaps the most elaborately developed standard limiting the right of recoupment. It prohibits recoupment if the overpayment disadvantaged the recipient or was the product of legitimate error, even though there may be funds available for recoupment. Most recoupment statutes are far less tolerant and the impact on present grants can therefore be quite serious. That impact can best be sustained where the present grant is in excess of basic needs, but this is rarely true. Courts have therefore sought to keep grants above subsistence levels by liberal interpretations of recoupment statutes.

In Hagans v. Wyman, 399 F.Supp. 421 (E.D.N. Y.1975), the State of New York provided that an advance allowance could be made for a person who was being evicted for nonpayment of rent and who had previously received a grant. However, such an allowance would be provided only where the recipient "requested" that his grant be reduced in equal amounts over the following six months to repay the amount of the advance allowance. The court rejected the argument that this was "voluntary":

> ".   .   .   the real voluntariness of any recipient's consent is questionable. It is true that a consent given under this regulation would probably be a knowing consent, that is, the person giving it would know the con-

sequences of consenting it. There is a difference, however, between a knowing consent and a voluntary consent; the latter implies something more than mere knowledge of the consequences. Here, the circumstances surrounding the giving of the consent make the consent involuntary. The recipient is ostensibly given a choice, but it is a choice between consenting to the recoupment and being evicted. This is nothing more than a Hobson's choice. The recipient is forced by his situation to agree to the recoupment." 399 F.Supp. at 423.

The court further criticized the agreement to permit recoupment on the basis that:

"[AFDC] is intended to support and maintain family life and encourage the raising of dependent children in their own homes. The recoupment provision violates this purpose by reducing in a given month the living allowance available to a grant recipient. It in effect punishes the dependent children for the mismanagement of funds by their parents who are actually little more than disbursing agents under this program." 399 F. Supp. at 423.

The court also found that the recoupment provisions violated HEW regulations. 45 CFR 233.-20(a)(12) prohibited recoupment unless there was income "currently available" exclusive of the current assistance payment." Otherwise, a state could recoup only where overpayment was due to the recipients willful withholding or mis-statement of income. The court therefore granted a permanent injunction against the state statute saying that:

> "The recoupment procedure is being used to teach proper management of funds; its result is to punish dependent children for allocation errors made by those who are responsible for raising them. The recoupment provision, as it exists now, continues to contravene the intention and the language of the AFDC program as stated in the Social Security Act, 42 U.S.C. § 601 . . ." 399 F. Supp. at 425.

In *Hagans*, the recoupment did not relate to misconduct or error by the recipient; nor did it relate to error by the welfare department. Rather, recoupment was being sought as a precondition to meeting the current and legitimate needs of recipients. In contrast, in Gardenia v. Norton, 425 F.Supp. 922 (D.Conn.1976), the State of Connecticut sought to recoup benefits by terminating or reducing AFDC grants to supervising relatives who had been convicted of welfare fraud.

These provisions were upheld. The court noted that when states had relied upon presumptions imputing income to reduce grants, courts have found such presumptions to violate the Social Security Act. But the present controversy involved "the converse proposition: does a state violate the Act when it reduces AFDC grants without finding or even presuming that income is available to a child?" 425 F.Supp. at 926. The court held that, while a state might not be permitted to impose new eligibility standards or reduce the standard of need, it could determine to pay an amount less than the level of need. The court did hold that recoupment could not impose "hardship" upon the AFDC children despite the misconduct of the parents and that recoupment must be waived if an eligible child needs the full AFDC assistance payment.

In Gardenia v. Norton, recoupment from current benefits would have been allowed only where the recipients had been *convicted* of welfare fraud. In Jacquet v. Bonin, 425 F.Supp. 863 (E. D.La.1975), plaintiffs challenged the HEW regulation which would have permitted recoupment where the recipients had "willfully" withheld information but had been convicted of nothing. See 45 CFR 233.20(a)(12). The court upheld the regulation. It found to be essential "that a state agency receive accurate information regarding each recipient's income so that it may distribute its limited resources in a fair manner." 425 F. Supp. at 865. Recoupment eliminated any incentive for inaccurate reporting. The court observed that there was no other reasonable remedy, since suing the recipients and recovering civil judgments would likely be expensive and unreward-ing.

While recoupment of benefits may be proper for fraud or willful misconduct, and while it may be permissible where the state has made advances or overpayments, in Cooper v. Laupheimer, 316 F.Supp. 264 (E.D.Pa.1970), the court invalidated a Pennsylvania practice of recouping from cur-rent grants to recover extra AFDC payments which had been made to replace a lost, stolen, or delayed check. Duplicate payments would result with such emergency checks when the recipient subsequently found or received the regular check and failed to return it. The court noted that the recipient might act from innocence or without fraudulent intent. Also, in such cases, the origi-nal check may have been stolen and forged by the thief.

Recoupment from present grants may reduce them in a way that conflicts with basic policies. For example, reduction of a grant may make it impossible to continue working. AFDC grants are enhanced by an earned income disregard; re-coupment may effectively deny this. Neverthe-less, the Court of Appeals in Swasey v. Whalen, 562 F.2d 831 (1st Cir. 1977) upheld a New Hampshire regulation permitting recoupment of up to one-half of the amount disregarded, leaving no benefits for the recipient. The court reasoned that the recipient was still left with one-half of the disregard and so still had funds available for living purposes, consistent with the HEW regulations, 45 CFR 233.20(a)(12). Although there might be a conflict in policy, the state recoupment was not barred specifically by the Social Security Act.

Recoupment of benefits paid, as well as the seeking of reimbursement of such benefits, is permissible absent specific statutory prohibitions. There are such prohibitions in various programs. For example, Medicaid requires that a state plan for medical assistance must provide:

> "That no lien may be imposed against the property of any individual on account of medical assistance paid or to be paid on his behalf under the plan (except pursuant to the judgment of a court on account of benefits incorrectly paid on behalf of such individual) . . . ." 42 U.S.C. § 1396(a)(18).

In 42 CFR 449.70, the Medicaid prohibition is interpreted to include, as "property," "not only the homestead but all other personal and real property in which the recipient has a legal interest," and a money payment under another program may not be reduced as a method of recovery for vendor payments incorrectly paid under Title XIX of the Act. In Wilczynski v. Harder, 323 F. Supp. 509 (D.Ct.Conn.1971), the court held that this prohibited state efforts to recoup monies expended pursuant to the plan.

In Philpott v. Essex County Welfare Board, 409 U.S. 413 (1973) the United States Supreme Court reversed a New Jersey Supreme Court judgment which had upheld the right of the State of New Jersey to attach a bank account containing OASDI benefits in order to satisfy payment to the state for state welfare benefits previously paid. New Jersey required a recipient to agree, as a condition of eligibility, to reimburse the county welfare board for all payments. The Supreme Court held that the attempt by the state to reach the federal funds was barred by 42 U.S.C. § 407, which provided that none of the monies paid or payable for disability purposes would be "subject to execution, levy, attachment, garnishment or other legal process." The State argued that if the amount of Social Security benefits had been received monthly, rather than as a lump sum retroactive payment, the state benefits could have been reduced. Nevertheless, the Supreme Court held that the state was barred, saying "we see no reason why a state, performing its statutory duty to take care of the needy, should be in preferred position as compared with any other creditor." 409 U.S. at 416.

As a third example of prohibitions on recoupment, in Davis v. Smith, 431 F.Supp. 1206 (S.D. N.Y.1977), the court invalidated the New York practice affording advances for utility emergencies on AFDC payments, from which the advance would be later recouped, rather than granting

Emergency Assistance. The court held that this violated 42 U.S.C. § 606(e), funding Emergency Assistance without regard to the source of the emergency. The court distinguished Hagans v. Berger, 536 F.2d 525 (2d Cir. 1976) where the Court of Appeals had held that Emergency Assistance could be denied for rent advances to AFDC recipients facing eviction on the ground that the state need not provide Emergency Assistance to the "anticipated demands created as the result of everyday life." The court in *Davis* distinguished this by noting that the plaintiffs before it had all diligently paid utility bills and could not have anticipated, because of gross billing errors, that they would suddenly be required to pay large amounts of money for the same period of service.

Recoupment is most troublesome because it seeks payment while a person is still needy. Another practice is to seek reimbursement after the person is no longer needy. Frequently this will be pursuant to assignments of assets made at the time of application with execution being deferred, as with an apartment or home in which the applicant is living. See Charleston v. Wohlgemuth, 332 F.Supp. 1175 (E.D.Pa.1975); Snell v. Wyman, 281 F.Supp. 853 (S.D.N.Y.1968). Such provisions usually relate to a wide variety of assets and later reimbursement may reach beyond them if the total of assistance warrants.

Reimbursement may also be sought from parents or children under relative responsibility laws. A clear example of this is provided in the Title IV–D provisions concerning non-supporting parents, supra, § 34. In addition, adult children may be required to support parents receiving welfare. In Swoap v. Superior Court, 516 P.2d 840 (Cal.1973), plaintiffs had been ordered to pay $70 per month for their mothers. The court upheld the statutes, noting their origins in the Elizabethan Poor Laws and rejecting the claim that they denied equal protection of the laws on the ground that as children they had received benefits which the State could reasonably expect them to repay. As with recoupment, however, the duty to repay is limited by the necessity that there be sufficient funds available.

Recoupment and reimbursement implement legitimate state interests in conserving limited welfare funds by assuring that only those who are truly eligible receive benefits. But enforcing these interests is problematic. All too often overpayments are the product of confusion or misinformation, rather than culpability or fraud on the part of the recipient. And even where fault may be attributed to the recipient, forcing repayment may simply be at the expense of a person whose poverty leaves no margin for repayment or whose dependents should not bear the brunt of errors by a caretaker relative.

§ 37. Judicial Review and Litigation

This entire text has developed the basic premise of entitlement: that welfare recipients now have interests which are created by government and may be asserted against government. If administrative agencies ignore their statutory and constitutional obligations, ultimate redress may be sought in the courts. This is not true with charity; it is true with modern concepts of welfare. Welfare is no longer a privilege, but a legally enforceable entitlement. See supra, § 8. The ultimate method for enforcement is through suits in the courts. Although such suits may be brought in state courts, increasingly during the last decade they have been brought in federal forums. This section will develop a brief explanation of why and how this is done. See also, supra, §§ 2, 5 and 15.

Assuming a meritorious claim, as with the denial of a right to a hearing, federal jurisdiction can usually be found. State welfare defendants can be sued under 28 U.S.C. § 1331, if $10,000 is at stake, or § 1343, if a constitutional claim is at issue. Federal defendants, such as HEW, may also be sued under 28 U.S.C. § 1331 or for mandamus under 28 U.S.C. § 1361. It may be necessary, with federal defendants, to exhaust administrative remedies first, as with denial of OASDI or SSI benefits under 42 U.S.C. § 405(g), but ultimately review may be sought in a federal court.

In the late 1970's it seems clear that *jurisdiction* is no longer a problem for a welfare litigant in federal court. The important question is whether there is a substantive basis for the suit, for example, a denial of benefits without a hearing. The litigant must look to different statutes, depending upon whether the denial was by state or federal officials.

Several statutes passed by Congress during the 1860's and 1870's were designed to provide federal forums for civil rights claims, primarily against state officials. The most important of these statutes, 42 U.S.C. § 1983, reaches any denial of federal rights under color of state law. The other statutes do not require "state action" but are limited to discrimination claims. Together, these statutes, 42 U.S.C. §§ 1981–1988, reach a broad range of interests important to the poor, including welfare, housing, consumer, school and prison issues.

The caselaw under these statutes emphasizes that they represent a profound change in policy for the federal courts. The Reconstruction Era Congress intended, by these statutes and their companion Constitutional Amendments, to impose a federal judiciary upon the States. See, e. g., Monroe v. Pape, 365 U.S. 167 (1961) and Jones v. Alfred H. Mayer Co., 392 U.S. 409 (1968). This intent represented a radical break with the past and has opened the federal courts to forms of litigation which had traditionally been relegated to state forums.

Since *Monroe*, § 1983 has had widespread application, creating a body of constitutional tort law. Although § 1983 was born of a Reconstruction concern for racial justice, it is not so limited by its terms. Indeed, it has been used for a wide variety of constitutional claims, ranging from voting cases to prisoners' litigation. Of immediate importance, § 1983 has provided the basis for much poverty litigation, such as that concerning welfare and housing claims.

Several cases have also held that violations of federal *statutes* are actionable under § 1983, which refers to the "Constitution *and laws*" of the United States. In Blue v. Craig, 505 F.2d 830 (4th Cir. 1974), the Court held that plaintiffs could sue under § 1983 for violations of federal welfare statutes requiring transportation for Medicaid applicants. Similarly, in Gomez v. Florida Employment, 417 F.2d 569 (5th Cir. 1969), a § 1983 claim was sustained where the offending conduct violated a federal farm labor statute. In both instances, suits were possible against *state* officials for violating *federal* statutes.

The availability of § 1983 for statutory claims is important for two reasons. First, it may enable a suit where the federal statute does not *expressly* create a remedy. Cases such as *Blue* and *Gomez* are also important whenever $10,000 is not at stake, as in much welfare litigation, and general federal question jurisdiction, 28 U.S.C. § 1331, is thus unavailable. *Blue* and *Gomez* would mean that jurisdiction nevertheless can be based on § 1983 and 28 U.S.C. § 1343 (civil rights jurisdiction), which does not have a requirement that $10,000 be in controversy.

Section 1983 actions are commonly brought against state officers in their *official* capacities. This was true of the myriad of cases cited throughout the earlier Sections of this text. By naming the state officers, the litigation avoids the bar of the Eleventh Amendment, precluding suits against states in federal courts. Relief, in a technical sense, runs against the officer, not the state. By this fiction, the state can be forced to comply with federal constitutional or statutory requirements. See supra, §§ 4–5. The Eleventh Amendment remains a problem only with recovering *past* wrongful denials of benefits: as to those, suit is best brought in state courts or, where possible, against federal agencies, since the Eleventh Amendment does not bar suits in state courts or federal suits against federal defendants. See Edelman v. Jordan, 415 U.S. 651 (1974) and supra, §§ 2 and 5.

Federal defendants may be sued for failing to perform duties in a wide range of statutes concerning welfare, medical services, Food Stamps, housing and education programs, to mention only a few. And such suits may reach beyond civil rights claims to purely statutory aspects of entitlement. For example, denial of welfare benefits without a hearing may generate a constitutional claim. But if a hearing was conducted, the recipient's claim may simply be that certain aspects of the hearing—or the denial itself—did not comply with statutory or regulatory requirements. Such non-constitutional claims are often brought against federal defendants by welfare recipients.

Until recently, the chief impediment to such suits has been showing that $10,000 was involved, to meet jurisdictional requirements under 28 U. S.C. § 1331. The Administrative Procedure Act, 5 U.S.C. § 701 et seq., and the Mandamus Act, 28 U.S.C. § 1361, were used as jurisdictional devices to avoid this. However, § 1331 was amended in 1976 to eliminate any amount requirement as to federal defendants; hence, there is no impediment to such suits now. See 45 U.S.L.W. 165 (1976).

Oftentimes, a non-constitutional claim will be authorized or governed by the statute establishing the program involved. This is true, for example, concerning survivors benefit claims under Title II of the Social Security Act, governed by 42 U.S.C. § 405. See Weinberger v. Salfi, 422 U. S. 749 (1975). But federal programs frequently provide benefits without specifically creating a right to judicial review of action or inaction. In such cases, a litigant must proceed either under the Administrative Procedure Act or by persuading the court to imply a remedy from the basic statute.

The A.P.A. creates a right of review of any agency action, 5 U.S.C. § 702, on behalf of anyone "suffering legal wrong . . . or adversely affected or aggrieved by agency action within the meaning of a relevant statute." The chief exclusion is for action "committed to agency discretion by law," 5 U.S.C. § 701. This exception is narrowly read by the courts; indeed, there is a presumption of reviewability. See Barlow v. Collins, 397 U.S. 159 (1970); Abbott Laboratories v. Gardner, 387 U.S. 136 (1967). Thus in NWRO v. Finch, 429 F.2d 725 (D.C.Cir. 1970), the Court sustained the right of welfare recipients to sue, challenging HEW's refusal to allow them to intervene in a conformity hearing, despite HEW's claim that the issues were solely within its discretion.

The agency "action" subject to review is broadly defined in 5 U.S.C. § 551(13) as including the "whole or a part of" a "rule, order, license, sanction, relief, or the equivalent or denial thereof, or *failure to act*" (emphasis supplied). This sweeping definition is further broadened in § 551 by equally broad definitions of each of these constituent elements of "action." Thus, the chief limitation on review under § 702 lies not in its scope, but the *standard* for courts in conducting review.

The standard for judicial review is found in 5 U.S.C. § 706(2), authorizing review of the "whole record," with a court empowered to set aside "action, findings and conclusions found to be (A) "arbitrary, capricious, an abuse of discretion or otherwise not in accordance with law." A court is also authorized to act if the agency action is contrary to the Constitution, statutes or substantially unsupported by facts. In Citizens to Preserve Overton Park v. Volpe, 401 U.S. 402 (1971), the Supreme Court held that even where a judicial review of the facts underlying an administrative decision is not specifically mandated, still the "arbitrary, capricious" language of the A.P.A. compels authority and procedures and—to that extent—a limited inquiry into the underlying facts and record.

The Administrative Procedure Act separately requires an agency to follow certain procedures for adoption of federal agency regulations. 5 U.S.C. § 553. These may create a distinct, *substantive* cause of action for non-compliance. In Lewis v. Weinberger, 415 F.Supp. 652 (D.N.Mex. 1976), the court held that HEW policies denying medical care to off-reservation Indians were invalid, because there had been no advance publication in the Federal Register, no opportunity to receive comments and no statement of the rules' basis or purpose. These steps were required, the court found, because the policy statement made a significant change in policy. It was a statement of *general* policy (5 U.S.C. § 552(a)(1)(D)) and did not affect only "internal or housekeeping operations," nor was it merely an interpretive statement or one concerning only policy. Hence, it was void. Cf., Morton v. Ruiz, 415 U.S. 199 (1974).

Suits under the A.P.A. must involve redress of a legally cognizable injury, by reference to a statute or constitutional right. This requires looking to underlying federal statutes, such as those creating SSI, OASDI, AFDC, Medicaid or Food Stamps. This is often necessary, too, where the suit proceeds outside the A.P.A., for example where a state welfare department—not covered by the A.P.A.—is sued. Often such statutes do not explicitly confer a right to sue. Nevertheless, courts frequently "imply" a remedy on behalf of those intended to benefit. See Bivens v. Six Federal Agents, 403 U.S. 388 (1971). In Norwalk CORE v. Norwalk Redevelopment, 395 F.2d 920 (2d Cir. 1968), the Court upheld a suit against the Redevelopment Agency for failure to relocate people displaced by urban renewal. It did so despite the absence of a specific right to sue, on the basis that the residents were injured, were intended to benefit from the legislation requiring relocation, were functioning as "private attorneys general" and were effecting Congressional policy in a way that administrative processes might compromise. Similar reasoning upheld a suit by farm workers in Gomez v. Florida Employment

Service, 417 F.2d 569 (5th Cir. 1970) against state and federal agencies who brought the workers to Florida but did not enforce regulations guaranteeing decent working conditions.

The most significant Supreme Court decision on implication of remedies is Cort v. Ash, 422 U. S. 66 (1975). There, plaintiff stockholders asserted a private cause of action against corporate directors under a criminal statute prohibiting political contributions in presidential elections. The Court denied relief. It noted that four factors are necessary to imply a private cause of action where Congress failed to create one specifically: that the plaintiff be a member of a class intended to benefit specially, that Congress indicate an intent to create a remedy, that such a remedy be consistent with the overall plan and, finally, that the remedy not be "one traditionally relegated to state law." The plaintiffs failed on each point.

Welfare litigants, however, will usually be able to make a stronger case for implication of remedies. As in *Gomez* or *Norwalk CORE,* they will not be invoking criminal statutes, but will be seeking to assure benefits conferred upon them under civil statutes designed to benefit them as a special class. Further, their suits are frequently necessary only because of administrative inaction. Injunctive relief—not addressed in *Cort*—can only be designed to effectuate Congressional purposes. In the end, implication of remedies may be difficult chiefly where the poverty litigants are seeking damages. Cf., Edelman v. Jordan, 415 U.S. 651 (1974).

The doctrine of implication of remedies is of obvious importance to the poor, who are often dependent upon administrative agencies and complex statutes to assure benefits. In many respects, analysis under the doctrine is akin to that with standing: a court must find the plaintiffs have been injured and were within the zone of interests Congress intended to protect. See Barlow v. Collins, 397 U.S. 159 (1970). Thus, caselaw concerning standing—a "procedural" matter—bears directly on the "substantive" question of whether a poverty litigant has a claim. See supra, § 15.

Other procedural matters, in addition to standing, arise in welfare litigation. Class actions are frequently initiated under F.R.C.P. § 23(b)(2) to broaden the scope of relief and to avoid mootness. Exhaustion of remedies may be necessary with federal and state *administrative* agencies, to assure a "final" and reviewable action, although exhaustion of state *judicial* remedies is not required. Monroe v. Pape, supra. Federal courts may abstain from acting if a state statute is unclear, although in most welfare litigation this is not a problem because interpretation is needed not of state statutes but of federal statutory or constitutional principles. These—and other—

concerns may arise in federal welfare suits. But such suits are widely and commonly brought in federal courts, with the primary question really being when a welfare recipient should *choose* a federal rather than a state forum.

A comparison of state and federal courts is necessary before bringing any action. But generally, the federal courts will have more favorable procedures concerning temporary relief, class actions and discovery. In addition, docket flow and preliminary hearings are more expeditious. This is as true of appellate courts as of the district courts.

Personnel may also be more favorable in federal court. Judges are insulated from political pressures and local controversies. In many jurisdictions, the process of appointment leads to more rigorous screening of federal judges. These considerations are equally true of federal clerks. Federal juries are generally drawn from wider districts than in a state court, assuring some insulation from parochial influences. In the background, of equal importance, are the supporting services in federal courts. Judicial clerks, libraries, availability of experts are all generally superior to state resources. More ample funding, quite simply, generates more time and scholarship for adequate consideration of difficult or novel cases.

It is also true that federal personnel are more familiar with resolving the federal questions often raised in welfare litigation. Federal judges are experienced in dealing routinely with federal statutes and state or federal agencies. Interpreting Congressional intent is not a novel undertaking for them.

This, of necessity, means that federal courts are more disposed to consider complex welfare litigation. It also means that a welfare client's attorney can learn in advance how a judge has ruled in the past. This is particularly true where an appeal is anticipated, since federal Courts of Appeals will frequently have published opinions bearing on an issue or case, providing guidance to counsel to an extent missing in state courts. And federal statutes provide a broad range of pecuniary and injunctive relief. Usually, these are superior to state remedies, particularly with injunctive or class relief. Federal process can run district, state or nationwide.

In conclusion, the choice of forum is important. But the important point is that there *is* a choice and welfare relief may be sought in federal courts. This is a product not only of litigational developments during the past decade but also of changes in basic substantive concepts concerning welfare. If welfare is not quite a "right," it is clearly no longer a "privilege" but a protected interest. The development of entitlement, traced through the preceding Sections of this text, finds its ultimate reality in this concluding Section: judicial enforceability through litigation.

INDEX

INDEX
References are to Pages

[446]

[447]

INDEX
References are to Pages

INDEX

References are to Pages

FEDERAL/STATE RELATIONS—Continued

Conformity hearing, 42
Cooperative federalism, 7–9
Funding, state and local, 24, 42
General assistance funding, 75, 80
Preemption, 63
    Supremacy distinguished, 60
Residency requirements, 10–11
State challenges to federal power, 7–8
State option, 28
Supremacy of federal statutes, 25
Tenth Amendment, 64

FOOD STAMPS

Amendments 1977, p. 173
Benefits, 169
Bonus value, 168
Financial eligibility, 150
Governmental assistance as income, 322
Household, 170
In-kind program, as, 158

FRAUD

    See also Recoupment
Condition of eligibility, 37
Recoupment, 37, 422
Survivors benefits, 122
Termination of assistance, 414
Transfer of assets, 314

GENERAL ASSISTANCE

Administration, 70
Benefits, 72
Due process, 72–73
Relation to federal programs, 67, 70
Tenth Amendment, 65
Written standards, 72–73

HEARINGS

See Due Process

HOME VISITS
Constitutionality, 37, 96

ILLEGITIMACY
  See also Morality
Eligibility for social insurance, 263
Eligibility for welfare, 260

INCOME
Availability, 326
Deemed or imputed, 329
Disregards,
    Earned Income, 308, 324
    SSI, 225
Food stamps as, 322
Governmental benefits, counted as, 107, 171, 225, 321
Household members, 329
Imputed or presumed, 129
Set offs, 320
Spenddown, 326
Work expenses, 332
Workmen's compensation as, 319

IN-KIND PROGRAMS
Conflicts in goals, 156
Financial eligibility, 151
Quality control, 160
Under-usage, 157

LITIGATION AND JUDICIAL REVIEW
Abstention, 442
Administrative Procedure Act, 438
Choice of forum, 443
Civil rights jurisdiction, 49
Civil rights statutes, 434
Damages, 436
Eleventh Amendment, 50, 436
Exhaustion of remedies, 54, 55, 227, 433
Federal statutes, 435
Implication of remedies, 165, 440
Injunctions, 51, 53, 58
In-kind programs, 163

[451]

INDEX
References are to Pages

INDEX